# CREATION AND COVENANT

# CREATION
# AND
# COVENANT

## THE SIGNIFICANCE OF
## SEXUAL DIFFERENCE IN THE
## MORAL THEOLOGY OF MARRIAGE

### CHRISTOPHER CHENAULT ROBERTS

T & T CLARK INTERNATIONAL
*A Continuum imprint*
NEW YORK • LONDON

2007

T & T Clark International, 80 Maiden Lane, New York, NY 10038

T & T Clark International, The Tower Building, 11 York Road, London SE1 7NX

T & T Clark International is a Continuum imprint.

www.continuumbooks.com

Copyright © 2007 by Christopher Chenault Roberts

Printed in the United States of America

Library of Congress Cataloging-in-Publication Data

Roberts, Christopher Chenault.
  Creation and covenant : the significance of sexual difference in the moral theology of marriage / Christopher Chenault Roberts.
    p. cm.
  Includes bibliographical references and index.


  ISBN-13: 978-0-567-02746-7 (paperback)
  ISBN-10: 0-567-02746-5 (paperback)

  1. Sex differences—Religious aspects—Christianity. 2. Marriage—Religious aspects—Christianity. I. Title.

BT708.R53 2007
241'.63—dc22
                                        2006039614

# CONTENTS

# ACKNOWLEDGMENTS

This book would still be a PhD thesis sitting on the shelves in the library at the University of London if it were not for Phyllis Tickle, formerly of *Publishers Weekly*, and Henry Carrigan, formerly of T&T Clark. I thank both of them for reading the manuscript and discussing it with me. I have never asked whether they agree with me or not on substance, but I deeply appreciate their confidence in this project and their unwavering support for the contribution I am attempting to make to the conversation in today's churches. I am also grateful to Henry's colleagues at Continuum, Jeff McCord (for editing) and Abigail Cox (for marketing); I especially appreciate their forbearance when my inexperience with publishing tried their patience.

Also helpful in the transition from thesis to book were Mark Doorley and Mary Quilter, both in the Ethics Program at Villanova University. I thank both of them for their encouragement and for their practical help as I printed and prepared the manuscript.

It is impossible for me to imagine this book without my supervisor, a wide cohort of friends and colleagues, my parents, and my wife. Naming their contributions is one way in which I hope to thank them.

Michael Banner was a superb PhD supervisor at King's College, University of London. Sometimes other postgraduates at King's envied those of us privileged to study with him. He invested a lot of time in me, insisted on clear arguments, and sent me down fruitful paths. I admire him and hope to keep learning from him in the future. Whatever conceptual breakthroughs occurred in this research could not have happened without him.

Nigel Biggar first suggested five or six years ago that I write a PhD thesis probing the relationship between autonomy and theological anthropology, and he has remained in friendly conversation ever since. Oliver O'Donovan helped me formulate one of my earliest questions about sexual difference over dinner at a meeting of the Society for the Study of Christian Ethics. Professors Biggar and O'Donovan were my tutors for my master's degree in Christian ethics. I don't know what they might think of this book, but I hope they see in it that I have learned from their methods, patience, goodwill, and ecumenical disposition.

Besides implicitly critiquing anthropologies of unnuanced autonomy, another implicit theme in this book has been a critique of Gnosticism. On that point I should note that very early in my research, before I had officially matriculated as a PhD student, Ken Myers suggested that whatever topic I chose to pursue I somehow pay attention to Gnosticism. He realized that various gnostic temptations and tendencies are problems in many of today's churches and that these issues require serious attention. Although there are many intermediate steps between that conversation and this book, I have basically taken his advice.

Sustaining me during all those intermediate steps were the other research students at King's, who created a wonderful environment of friendship and collegiality. In particular, I thank Najeeb Awad, Demetios Bathrellos, Rufus Burton, Andrew Cameron, Almut Caspary, Ovidiu Creanga, Paul Cumin, Sandra Fach, Eric Flett, Lincoln Harvey, Babu Immanuel, Kelly Kapic, Douglas Knight, Nicola Knight, Wai Luen Kwok, Vladimir Lelmesh, Teck Peng Lim, Mihail Neamtu, Agneta Sutton, and Justin Thacker for reading chapters and outlines, for being in reading groups and swapping bibliographies, for teaching me about new aspects of theology, for providing opportunities to grow intellectually and professionally, and/or for just generally sweating it out together with prayers, meals, good humor, and conversation. (Mark Poulson, while not a student at King's, was an essential part of this fellowship as well.) For all these things to an even higher degree, I especially thank Luke Bretherton, Brian Brock, and Anna Poulson.

Without Goodenough College, a residential college in Bloomsbury, being a postgraduate student in London would have been much harder and a lot less fun. This place allowed many of my King's colleagues and their families to be neighbors as well. Worshiping, praying, and eating with Stephanie Brock, Andrea Burton, Melanie Cumin, Derek Brower, JoAnn Flett, Usha Immanuel, Annie and Moray Thomas, Juan and Bronwyn Garces, and all the folks at the Anglican and Roman Catholic chaplaincies were an intrinsic part of my postgraduate experience. Thank you all.

Moira Langston was an essential friend and an administrative supporter; her Christian character helped bridge many different worlds. Rusty Reno, Douglas Farrow, David Ford, Steve Holmes, Murray Rae, Denys Turner, Timothy Radcliffe, and Mark Thiessen Nation all read sections, or responded to thesis outlines, and made helpful and encouraging comments. Brian Horne was especially gracious with regard to several issues related to the chapter on Bernard. Oliver Davies stepped in at the last minute as an encouraging secondary supervisor, and Christopher Hamilton was excellent as an internal examiner.

Linda Woodhead and Alan Torrance were the external examiners for my thesis, and they were superb. They gave me several pieces of advice about how to improve this manuscript; while I agreed with almost all of their suggestions, in the end, for various reasons, I was not able to act on most of them. My wife and I had a baby, we moved across the Atlantic, I started a new job teaching at Villanova University—it was either publish the thesis as it was, or postpone it indefinitely. I apologize to Dr. Woodhead and Dr. Torrance for that, and I hope that any future writing I am able to do will bear the marks of their helpful criticism.

Tim Wainwright and Casimir Adjoe provided indispensable spiritual support. They helped integrate what was happening in this book with what was happening in the rest of life. They helped me to be a theologian who prays.

Sadly, two people I would like to thank died before this book was finished. One is Colin Gunton, who discussed the structure of the project with me at a very early stage. He is also largely responsible for attracting the people and setting the tone that made studying at King's so wonderful. The other person who died is Daniel Twomey, who belongs with Tim and Casimir as an essential personal support. He would disagree with me about homosexuality, but his wisdom, kindness, and insight taught me a great deal.

I would probably have never done a PhD unless Bill Moyers and Bob Abernethy had repeatedly urged me to do it; Stanley Johnson is in the background there too, having helped me find my voice. My parents, John and Marylynn Roberts, have been unwaveringly supportive, always available for help with discernment and offering to do whatever chore might make things easier. My father was my first teacher in theology, and his ways are an indelible influence upon me. I think of my parents, and I think of Psalm 16:6 and Philippians 1:3–5.

I scarcely know what to say to Hannah Roberts, my wife, in regard to thanking her for her role in this project. Both of her parents died during the years I was at work on this project; these have not been easy years. During the same period, we also welcomed the birth of our daughter Martha; she is both joy and challenge. I have been studying the theology of marriage, and Hannah has been with me in this research every step of the way, both academically and experientially. Whatever I have learned about how God calls, blesses, commands, loves, and judges men and women in this sphere of life, Hannah has shared with me, or, more often than not, been the person to teach me, or, too often, the person to suffer when I've fallen short. Hannah, Philippians 1:6 can be for us.

Finally, there are others. A further "cloud of witnesses," implicit and sometimes explicit dialogue partners who shape the way I write, especially (but not only) various liberal friends, gay friends, and agnostic friends, who might not appreciate a metaphor evoking the communion of saints. But I thank them for being open with me and for letting me be me in response; I ask for their forgiveness when I have been too academic and argumentative at the wrong time. I am all too aware of many of these moments. I hope they feel like we are friends, and that they too expect that our life together still has a lot of conversation left in it yet.

# ABBREVIATIONS

*AC* = *Alexandrian Christianity: Selected Translations of Clement and Origen with Introductions and Notes.* Edited by Henry Chadwick and John Ernest Leonard Oulton. London: SCM Press, 1954.

*ANF* = *The Ante-Nicene Fathers.* Edited by A. Roberts and J. Donaldson. 1885–1887. 10 vols. Repr. Peabody, MA: Hendrickson, 1995.

*NPNF2* = *A Select Library of the Christian Church: Nicene and Post-Nicene Fathers, Second Series.* Edited by P. Schaff and H. Wace. 1890–1900. 14 vols. Peabody, MA: Hendrickson, 1995.

*NRSV* = New Revised Standard Version of the Bible

*SCC* = *Sermones super Cantica Canticorum*

*SCG* = *Summa contra Gentiles*

*ST* = *Summa Theologiae*

Regarding works by Augustine: Translators differ about the titles of Augustine's works. *De Genesi contra Manichaeos*, for instance, is often either *Commentary on Genesis against the Manichaeans* or *On Genesis: A Refutation of the Manichees*. To avoid confusion, I use full Latin titles on first reference (as listed in the SBL handbook) and Latin abbreviations afterward. The abbreviations are the standard scholarly ones as listed in *The SBL Handbook of Style: For Ancient Near Eastern, Biblical, and Early Christian Studies.* Edited by Patrick H. Alexander, John F. Kutsko, James D. Ernest, Shirley A. Decker-Lucke, and David L. Petersen. Peabody, MA: Hendrickson, 1999.

Regarding works by Luther, since I cite a single, standard English series of Luther's works, I use the English titles from that series.

# INTRODUCTION

Is sexual difference theologically significant? Specifically, when speaking about the ethics of marriage, does sexual difference matter? When the Christian tradition has claimed that the two parties in a marriage should be sexually differentiated—that is, a male and a female—what is at stake? What makes sexual difference morally significant? This book addresses these questions by studying the history of the moral theology of marriage in primarily Western Christianity.

In recent years, several branches of Christianity have been debating the question of same-sex marriage, and this debate lies in the background to this book. Nevertheless, the questions of this book are more basic than this debate. One can ask about the significance of sexual difference without having questions of homosexuality in mind. Therefore, in most chapters, this book will ignore the debate, allowing historical sources to speak on their own terms and pursuing sexual difference as a topic in its own right. Yet the debate about same-sex marriage helps explain why this book is timely and important, and I will discuss this debate in chapter 8 and in the conclusion. Therefore a few introductory observations about this debate are appropriate.

The ongoing debates about homosexual marriage can be framed and understood in a variety of ways. One way is to understand them as debates about whether churches can or should sanction marriage without sexual difference. In other words, the contemporary debates at least implicitly ask whether the difference between male and female matters for marriage, and if so, how and why. Are there theological reasons

1

that oblige the churches to the traditional understanding of marriage, in which the sexual difference of husband and wife is a *sine qua non*? Or is marriage a more flexible covenant, which any two people can keep and for which sexual difference is indifferent? Such questions can lead to further questions, including: Why has the tradition believed that sexual difference was a necessary component for a marriage to exist and actually be a marriage? Are there sound and persuasive theological reasons for these beliefs, or are they merely deeply held but unfounded assumptions, theoretically open to modification? Might the logic of Christian marriage imply that existence as male or female is in some way a vocation, a summons to a particular way of life that builds upon sexual difference, a call to which we are in some way accountable, or is sexual difference something Christians can treat relatively indifferently, freeing us for more important matters?

Surprisingly few Christians seem to ask these questions explicitly in the current debates. Instead, for instance, some conservative Christians think that certain passages from Leviticus or Romans end the discussion. These passages can be cited and deployed legalistically against those who would propose something like gay or sexually indifferent marriage. But these scriptures, while condemning homosexuality, do not straightforwardly answer this book's questions about sexual difference. Mere opposition to same-sex marriage is not the same thing as a positive theological and evangelical account of sexual difference, no matter how great the weight of Scripture or tradition may be. Similarly, some conservatives also appeal to the role of procreation for marriage. But in such instances, one still needs to give a reason why marriage must be procreative. Why should marriage have any necessary relationship to biological procreativity and thus to sexual difference? Why would one claim that the potential fecundity of sexual difference is morally significant? To insist on sexual difference in marriage will cause many people discomfort, for their initial desires at least appear not to be sexually differentiated. Thus explicit reasons need to be offered: Why should these people accept a limitation on their desires? What is significant about sexual difference that makes it a constraint worth enduring, even when it is not easy? Those who would make conservative appeals to traditional moral law must address these questions, lest their law appear arbitrary and detached from the gospel. Any account of the significance of sexual difference must be profound enough to speak to the deepest levels of human personhood, explaining why it matters so much. What significance must sexual difference have if it is to lead to a definition of marriage that will cause some people to embark on a long and difficult ascetical struggle?

Meanwhile, many liberal Christians tend to emphasize acceptance, autonomy, and pastoral experience in their explanation of why same-sex marriages should be embraced by the church. Yet this language is a retreat from the categories of theological anthropology and from Christianity's historic confessions about marriage and celibacy. For instance, in the Anglican communion, the Eames Commission recently asked the U.S. Episcopal Church to explain its liberal views on homosexuality. Afterward, a member of the commission noted that "given the chance to make their case, Episcopal Church leaders argued on secular, human rights and social justice grounds."[1] Rhetorically and conceptually, such language is bound to fail to persuade those who realize, on the basis of worshiping the Christian God, the need to seek a theological logic for their claims. By definition, the language of liberalism fails to engage on common terms with the communion of saints and the lordship of Christ. Arguments about sexuality that dispense with theological logic and that are premised on human autonomy and experience are incongruous in debates within the churches, even when glossed with appeals to justice or love, for such liberal arguments suggest that we can know ourselves sufficiently apart from revelation and doctrine, as if there were parts of life removed from God's grace, address, vocation, command, judgment, or teleology.

This book is an attempt to move beyond both left and right, and toward a higher standard of theological conversation. Even when we will be studying famous theologians, in this book it would seem that we are bound to examine familiar material in an unfamiliar way, since all too few people have taken the trouble to subject this classic material to these pressing questions.

Furthermore, while the conclusions of this book should inform the debate about homosexuality, this book also asks questions that are more general and deeper than that debate has tended to encourage. In an essay commenting on the St. Andrew's Day Statement,[2] which itself was an attempt to put the ecclesiastical conversation about homosexuality on a less partisan and more transparently theological basis, Oliver O'Donovan noted that "the task of the theologian is not simply to engage in the debate on the side that appears to have the greater right; it is to safeguard the Gospel integrity of the debate, by clarifying what the questions are that must be at issue."[3] This book is in sympathy with that description of the theological task. In asking questions about the significance of sexual difference, and in searching among historic theologians on marriage for answers, the theologian's foremost task is not to retrieve ammunition for today's combatants. Instead, this research investigates whether certain monumental theologians in the history of theology of marriage have anything to say that might reveal a meaning or significance, or an insignificance, for sexual difference. Only then, when one has looked at the tradition in its own right and from a more disinterested perspective, can one return to the present debates. Only then can this book hope to offer resources and better questions for the present.

There are other reasons for sustained and patient engagement with the tradition and, at least at the outset, not reading it through the lenses of today's anxiety. We could frustrate ourselves were we to dig too insistently for answers to questions that might not have been asked by previous generations; we are anachronistic if we fault them for failing to respond to our own era's challenges. The possibility that earlier generations might not have asked and answered our questions in ways that satisfy us means that, in principle, we have to be prepared for this research to have "negative results." There may not be straightforward answers to our questions. We will want to guard against overtheorizing and drawing conclusions that are too grand for the original material to bear. We therefore must try to stay close to the primary sources and be prepared to meet arguments that have perhaps an awkward relationship to the questions we are ultimately asking. After all, in earlier eras, apparently no one was contesting the question of sexual difference as is happening today; in theology, it often requires a debate before a doctrine is clarified and defined.

However, if we were to find only partial answers to our questions, or if we were to learn that our material is not sufficient for answering our questions, then such results would still be useful. Such results might imply that today's confusion arises at least partially because Christianity has only recently had occasion to develop explicit and systematic answers to our questions, in which case we will have some sympathy for why the church is not unanimous today. We will then understand a little more clearly that, to the extent that the tradition does have answers, the church today might be assimilating what has only recently been heard and understood. The extent of the originality of today's theological predicament will then be clearer. Equally, of course, neither should we discount the possibility that the tradition has well-developed and precise arguments about today's questions which we should hear readily and directly. Perhaps the tradition has already encountered our questions, answered them well, and the church needs to repent of its amnesia.

It is not only partisans in today's homosexuality debates who should be interested in this research. Anyone interested in a complete Christian theology of marriage should want to know about the significance of sexual difference. If we can become more articulate about the relationship between various theological doctrines, moral practices concerning sexuality, and sexual difference, then it stands to reason that the church's profession and witness will be more coherent.

Moreover, feminists of all varieties, in and out of the church, have reasons for being interested in questions of sexual difference. As Linda Woodhead recently concluded, "What is needed, it seems, is fresh and creative reflection on the mystery of human sexual difference which is as responsibly related to the Christian tradition as it is to contemporary concerns."[4] Feminist theory helps raise the question of what it means to be sexed, and a history of why classic theologies of marriage have thought that sexual differences matter (or not) has a role in that discussion.

Once one has asked theologically about sexual difference, there are many possible ways of proceeding. Biblical scholars have exegeted key passages in Genesis, the Pauline corpus, and elsewhere in order to gather material for today's debates about sex and gender.[5] One could also approach the significance of sexual difference through the question of who is eligible for ordination to holy orders,[6] or by examining the issue of inclusive language in theological discourse.[7] In a painstaking project, Prudence Allen has completed two volumes in a projected multivolume quasi-encyclopedic attempt to compare and contrast dozens of individual philosophical and theological anthropologies of sexual difference, from the pre-Socratic philosophers to the present.[8] Featuring prominently in Allen's project and elsewhere are technical discussions of Aristotelian or Thomistic metaphysics and biology, and what they imply for sexual difference.[9] Allen and other substantial historical studies have also scrutinized some of the classic theological anthropologies of the past for evidence of proposed hierarchy, complementarity, or equivalence between the sexes.[10] Other scholars who attempt to account for sexual difference by means of more systematic (as opposed to historical) theological anthropology include Hans Urs von Balthasar[11] and, more recently, Gavin D'Costa.[12] Some theologians have also proposed original christological approaches to sexual difference, asking, for instance, about the implications of the ascension: What might it mean that Jesus' embodied (and hence male) particularity is affirmed at precisely that moment when such a corpus would seem to have the least earthly utility, and what might that indicate about the eschatological significance of the bodies and sexual differences for those who follow him in the resurrection?[13] One could also study a particular theologian known for being significant with respect to issues of anthropology and embodiment, such as Irenaeus,[14] or one might study church policies and councils, such as the Council of Gangra in the fourth century, where matters of marriage and asceticism were debated with particular thoroughness.[15] Contemporary philosopher Luce Irigaray has famously framed questions of sexual difference with respect to feminism and the history of Western philosophy, employing a post-Christian quasi–Roman Catholic rhetoric in the process.[16] Irigaray's work contends that the history of Western discourse about sex is compromised because its interlocutors are forced to use grammar and modes of rationality that inevitably articulate the world from a male point of view and hence inevitably obscure the true difference between the sexes.

Faced with such an overwhelming and complex field of potential inquiry—and there are certainly many other approaches that could be proposed—this book must, on its own, be insufficient to its ambitions. One book cannot finally separate the overlapping strands of this complex subject, and yet any final answers to our questions must engage on all of these fronts. Thus one book cannot do everything that needs to be done.

However, I offer this defense for the approach of this book: I have chosen to study the significance of sexual difference in the moral theology about marriage. This classic literature on marriage is a worthy topic in its own right among the many possible inquiries into sexual difference, and, although it might not be finally sufficient, it is at least a necessary element in any comprehensive deliberation on the topic. Moreover, since it is to some extent the present discussion about the possibility of gay and lesbian marriages that prompts our questions about sexual difference, it is logical to begin seeking answers by reviewing prior traditions of moral theology about marriage. Do these traditions offer explicit or implicit arguments about sexual difference? Before deconstructing their authors' perspectival influences, or before quarreling with their biblical hermeneutics, or before proposing exotic solutions to the various problems the tradition appears to have bequeathed, it would seem prudent to make sure we have identified and understood the arguments that the tradition actually makes or presupposes, and to do so on terms that are not alien or anachronistic to that tradition.

It is also worth acknowledging that often in theological history, discussions of marriage have occurred in relation to discussions of celibacy. For that reason, from time to time and fairly often, our argument must be generous in what it understands to be the moral theology about marriage. The significance of sexual difference with respect to celibacy will need to be considered, since marriage and celibacy were often discussed as interlocking and mutually reinforcing vocations.

By focusing on sexual difference, this book is not emphasizing what some might term "gender difference." The distinction between "sex" and "gender" is arguable and subtle, but commonly scholars use "gender" to refer to the "psycho-social-cultural characteristics" that can exist or be constructed in light of the biological differences between male and female.[17] If one accepts the distinction, concepts such as "masculinity" or "femininity" refer to gender, but "male" and "female" refer to sex. It might be helpful, then, to say that to the extent the sex-gender distinction is possible and sustainable, this book will prioritize sex. What sexual difference means and why it matters is the subject of this book, and that generates a closely associated but nevertheless distinct agenda from the questions of gender studies. The significance of gender in marriage is a valid and overlapping research project, but it is subtly different. For instance, asking whether it is appropriate to define certain roles in marriage as masculine or feminine is not the same as asking why it might matter that there are two sexes at all. Asking how one sex might or might not have dominated and defined the place of the other sex is not the same as asking whether the phenomenon of two sexes should have significance. My point is simply to say that in this book I will usually, but not always, concentrate on whether and how the biological difference between male and female has or has not mattered in moral theology about marriage. I will usually, but not always, focus on sex and not gender. One can easily imagine a project on similar questions that reverses this priority, but that is not my present intention.

This book is organized chronologically. The first chapter surveys five patristic theologians and shows that the early Christian tradition was somewhat inchoate about the significance of sexual difference. In their theologies of marriage and celibacy, these five theologians only rarely addressed questions of sexual difference. To learn what they believed, one often has to make inferences, or scrutinize comments that were made as mere asides or rhetorical flourishes. However, to the extent one can discern their beliefs, they seem to contradict one another, with incompatible views about the status of sexual difference.

However, as we will see in chapter 2, these disagreements resolve into a more coherent position with Augustine. Augustine, as is evident from both explicit and implicit arguments, believed that sexual difference is an ontologically significant feature of humanity in every era of theological history, from creation to eschaton. For Augustine, sexual difference derives its significance in the first instance by enabling procreative marriage, which is necessary for populating the heavenly city and thus fulfilling God's purposes in history. But the significance of sexual difference appears to go beyond marriage and procreation for Augustine. His argument, often rooted in anti-Manichaen polemics, commits him to the goodness of embodied, material life, and that leads him to suggest that sexual difference will be adapted to some new use in heaven, in the eschatological era when marriage is obsolete.

The next three chapters—on Bernard of Clairvaux, Thomas Aquinas, and the Reformers Martin Luther and John Calvin—show continuity with Augustine. Bernard's sermons on the Song of Songs are premised on Augustine's framework, as Bernard relies on the basic goodness of sexual difference in marriage as privileged material for allegories of God's love. Aquinas recapitulates Augustine to an extent, but his assimilation of Aristotelian biology leads him to relate sexual difference, procreation, and celibacy in ways that depart from Augustine. This departure is perhaps trivial initially, but it will matter in the modern period, and it needs to be noted at its source. The Reformers, while apparently emphasizing marriage at the expense of celibacy, argue that sexual difference is a fundamental aspect of being human, regardless of whether one is married or not. For Luther especially, to be a man or a woman is to be confronted with the question whether and when one will marry; Luther's way of describing this question, as a basic precondition for obedient life under God, has the effect of connecting sexual difference to the life of the church.

By the end of these first five chapters, it seems that while the classic theologies of marriage in Western theology have not offered lengthy, explicit, and sustained treatments of sexual difference, they have nevertheless raised the issue from time to time, suggesting a certain consensus. This consensus believes that sexual difference ought to be treated as morally significant. From Augustine to the Reformation, there was a consensus that God created human beings in sexual differentiation, that Christian social life will affirm this difference through marriage and the regulation of erotic life, and that sexual difference will be redeemed in the eschaton.

The rest of the book—three more chapters and a conclusion—studies several theologians in the twentieth and twenty-first centuries. Two chapters focus on Karl Barth and John Paul II, respectively, whose arguments about sexual difference seek to deepen and clarify the traditional premise that sexual difference has moral significance. The last chapter reviews three contemporary theologians—Graham Ward, Eugene Rogers, and David Matzko McCarthy—who argue in various ways that sexual difference is morally insignificant. Finally, in the conclusion, I review and consolidate the arguments from each chapter of the book.

We will see that the revisionist theologians of today—like their counterparts at the beginning of the Christian era—do not subscribe to the traditional view of the significance of sexual difference. However, there is at least one difference between the early and the contemporary hetero-geneity of belief. Today it is possible to juxtapose arguments for the insignificance of sexual difference with traditional, post-Augustinian claims for its significance. This juxtaposition enables us to ask whether the contemporary revisionists adequately respond to these arguments, to see why questions about sexual difference are important, and to pose fresh questions. I shall conclude that the revisionists have not adequately understood or responded to the post-Augustinian consensus that links sexual difference to the purposefulness of God's creation. In other words, the standard of argument must be higher before the revisionist case can claim to have succeeded; the revisionists must engage points they have left hitherto untouched. The pre-Augustinian theologians could not be held accountable to what subsequent tradition believed and argued, but the contemporary revisionists can be. The contemporary revision-ists claim to be responding to the likes of Barth and John Paul II, and yet, especially on those points where Barth and John Paul II bring the post-Augustinian consensus to light, the revisionists appear to misread or misunderstand their twentieth-century interlocutors.

The lacunae in the revisionist case are not necessarily culpable faults, for the kinds of questions this book will put to the tradition are rarely asked. The tradition itself has perhaps not been as explicit as it might have been about its beliefs and arguments, not least because these argu-ments were not previously contested. The number of times I must speak of "inference" or "presupposition" in the early chapters will be testimony to this phenomenon. The originality of the first seven chapters consists partially in bringing to light what might have been obscure in whatever the tradition might have thought or implied about sexual difference, as well as achieving clarity about what the tradition does not say. We might want therefore to moderate our frustration with contemporary theologians who do not engage ideas that have not been as accessible as we might want them to be.

What I claim, nevertheless, is that once the historical recovery has been made, the inadequacies of the revisionist case are newly visible. To make this claim is not to damn the authors or their motives, or to make final pastoral responses for a church in pain or disarray, or to say everything that needs to be said about the theological significance of sexual difference. It is simply to say that the tradition has better arguments and richer ideas than the revisionists have perhaps real-ized, and that recovering these resources enables us to speak coher-ently and faithfully today and thus to set the theological context for subsequent discusions.

# Notes

1. William Sachs, "Anglican Disunion: The Global Response to a Gay Bishop," *Christian Century*, November 16, 2004, 8.

2. See Michael Banner et al., "St. Andrew's Day Statement: An Examination of the Theological Principles Affecting the Homosexuality Debate," in *The Way Forward? Christian Voices on Homosexuality and the Church* (ed. Timothy Bradshaw; London: Hodder & Stoughton, 1997), 5–11.

3. Oliver O'Donovan, "Homosexuality in the Church: Can There Be a Fruitful Theological Debate?" in *The Way Forward?* 22.

4. Linda Woodhead, "Woman/Femininity," in *The Oxford Companion to Christian Thought* (ed. Adrian Hastings et al.; Oxford: Oxford University Press, 2000), 757.

5. Recent examples include Francis Watson, *Agape, Eros, Gender: Towards a Pauline Sexual Ethic* (Cambridge: Cambridge University Press, 2000); and Douglas A. Campbell, ed., *Gospel and Gender: A Trinitarian Engagement with Being Male and Female in Christ* (Edinburgh: T&T Clark, 2003).

6. See, e.g., A. M. Allchin et al., *A Fearful Symmetry? The Complementarity of Men and Women in Ministry* (London: SPCK, 1992). Also see the Hans Urs von Balthasar references in note 11, below.

7. See, e.g., Miroslav Volf, *After Our Likeness: The Church as the Image of the Trinity* (Grand Rapids: Eerdmans, 1998), 170; and Alan Torrance, "'Call No Man Father!' The Trinity, Patriarchy and God-Talk," in *Gospel and Gender: A Trinitarian Engagement with Being Male and Female in Christ* (ed. Douglas A. Campbell; Edinburgh: T&T Clark, 2003), 179–97.

8. Prudence Allen, *The Concept of Woman: The Aristotelian Revolution, 750 B.C.–A.D. 1250*, 2nd ed. (Grand Rapids: Eerdmans, 1997); and *The Concept of Woman*, vol. 2, *The Early Humanist Reformation, 1250–1500* (Grand Rapids: Eerdmans, 2002).

9. See Michael Nolan, "What Aquinas Never Said about Women," *First Things*, no. 87 (1998) for a position challenging Allen.

10. Other examples include Kari Elisabeth Boerresen, *Subordination and Equivalence: The Nature and Role of Women in Augustine and Thomas Aquinas* (trans. Charles H. Talbot; Washington, DC: University Press of America, 1981); and Paul K. Jewett, *Man as Male and Female: A Study in Sexual Relationships from a Theological Point of View* (Grand Rapids: Eerdmans, 1975).

11. See, for example, Hans Urs von Balthasar, *The Dramatis Personae: Man in God* (vol. 2 of *Theo-Drama: Theological Dramatic Theory*; trans. Graham Harrison; San Francisco: Ignatius, 1990), 365–82. See also Balthasar, "Women Priests?" in *New Elucidations* (trans. Mary Theresilde Skerry; San Francisco: Ignatius, 1986),

187–98. For a discussion profoundly influenced by von Balthasar, see David L. Schindler, "Catholic Theology, Gender, and the Future of Western Civilization," in *Heart of the World, Center of the Church* (Grand Rapids: Eerdmans, 1996), 237–74. Agneta Sutton compares von Balthasar's theology of sexual difference to Barth's and John Paul II's in "The Complementarity of the Two Sexes: Karl Barth, Hans Urs von Balthasar, and John Paul II," *New Blackfriars* 87, no. 1010 (2006): 418–33.

12. Gavin D'Costa, *Sexing the Trinity: Gender, Culture, and the Divine* (London: SCM Press, 2000).

13. Steve Holmes and Sandra Fach have raised versions of this question with me in seminars and informal conversation. Fach suggests that Douglas Farrow, *Ascension and Ecclesia: On the Significance of the Doctrine of Ascension for Ecclesiology and Christian Cosmology* (Edinburgh: T&T Clark, 1999), 13n47, might be opening possibilities along these lines.

14. John Behr, *Asceticism and Anthropology in Irenaeus and Clement* (Oxford: Oxford University Press, 2000), 220, argues that Irenaeus had an anthropology of "the fullness of our created, fleshly, sexual being."

15. The Council of Gangra documents may be found in *NPNF2*, vol. 14.

16. Among Irigaray's many works are *An Ethics of Sexual Difference* (trans. Carolyn Burke and Gillian C. Gill; London: Athlone, 1993), and *Marine Lover of Friedrich Nietzsche* (trans. Gillian C. Gill; New York: Columbia University Press, 1991).

17. Allen, *Concept of Woman*, 2:15–16.

# Chapter 1
# FIVE EARLY THEOLOGIANS

In this chapter we will study Tatian, Tertullian, Clement of Alexandria, Gregory of Nyssa, and Jerome. Besides these five theologians, there are, of course, other early patristic theologians who wrote about marriage, celibacy, and sexual difference. But these five theologians arguably had more influence on subsequent tradition than their other contemporaries, and, in any case, five theologians is a sufficient sample for establishing that in the earliest stages of the church's theological reflection there was no consensus about the theological significance of sexual difference. Is sexual difference a biological epiphenomenon, something that should be transcended en route to an angelic-like existence, or is sexual difference "integral to God's vision for His creation, and as such . . . an enduring feature of ourselves"?[1] Often the theologians of this era have little or nothing to say in response to this question. In other instances, they do have something to say, but, as we shall see, the diversity of their beliefs indicates a collective inchoateness in early Christianity about sexual difference.

## Tatian

Tatian has virtually nothing to say about the theological significance of sexual difference in the sources that still exist today, although a few inferences can be made.

Although he was excommunicated in Rome in 172, Tatian continued to be respected in the Christian East. Part of Tatian's ambiguous legacy means that he is sometimes suspected of having held gnostic attitudes toward God, creation, the human body, and asceticism. Indeed, judging from the brief quotations surviving in Tatian's foes, it would appear that he was either an actual gnostic such as Valentinus or a supposed gnostic such as Marcion.[2] Sometimes his foes cited the fact that Tatian's followers, known as Encratites, insisted on sexual continence (and dietary restraints) for all the baptized at all times; to these critics, Encratic asceticism suggested that Tatian must have been teaching unorthodox attitudes toward sex and the body.

However, as Henry Chadwick notes, "there is all too little evidence of the details of the heretical doctrines he came to hold."[3] We can even say that when we examine Tatian through his only treatise to survive in its entirety, *Oratio ad Graecos*, a picture emerges that reveals nongnostic foundations for his extreme asceticism. Listening to this text, it would appear that Tatian's thought is more complex than simple denunciations of his alleged Gnosticism would allow. Nevertheless, even when we listen carefully and draw out a more rounded portrait of Tatian's asceticism, we still learn little about sexual difference.

In *Oratio*, Tatian professes that "the construction of the world is excellent"[4] and that there is but one God, the sole creator of all that is, and who, as Spirit, is utterly distinct from all created matter.[5] In saying these things, he makes no appeal to any intermediary aeons or demiurges, and says much else that disavows characteristic gnostic explanations. The oration offers an anthropology and a doctrine of creation in which the constitution of a human being is both flesh and soul, a combination like a temple in which God can dwell.[6] For Tatian it is possible to "descend" through the flesh to the level of wild beasts (excelling them in "articulate language only"), but the fault lies not in the intrinsic nature of flesh but in free will influenced by passions.[7] What we long for, Tatian maintains, is not an escape from creation, which would be standard gnostic longing, but a restoration of its pristine state.[8] Eschatologically, Tatian confesses a "resurrection of bodies after the consummation of all things."[9] But nowhere in this basic but orthodox doctrine of the created body do we find an extended treatment of sexual difference.

Tatian also counsels Christians to "despise all worldly things," including and perhaps especially sexual intercourse.[10] But this counsel is probably best regarded as a rhetorical exhortation to love God above all other things, or to shape the human will so that it is "superior to the passions,"[11] which would distinguish it from the conventional gnostic disdain for creation itself. For example, Tatian declares that Aphrodite "finds joy in the bonds of marriage,"[12] and so we should avoid marriage because we want to love the true God and avoid giving succor to Aphrodite.[13] That is not the attitude of a gnostic denigrating a material phenomenon, such as the sexual body, simply because it is material. Indeed, Tatian insists God has created nothing bad.[14] Instead, a repeated theme in the *Oratio* is that Tatian believes that demons (often in the guise of pagan gods, like Aphrodite) use material objects to encourage our baser appetites and make us slaves to passionate feelings, and so we should reject matter in order to master our feelings and repudiate these demons/pagan gods.[15] Worldly things inevitably stimulate our passions.[16] Of course, this is subtly but significantly different from rejecting matter because matter is, as matter, despicable. In sum, Tatian is more than a little suspicious about materiality's capacity to encourage idolatry, but it is a suspicion that, he seems to claim, is born of zeal for the true God rather than antimateriality. One avoids fleshly unions because unions that inevitably rival the Holy Spirit, unions in which passions for lesser goods are enjoyed, are intolerable.[17] Tatian's priority, then, is to seek practices that rigorously shape and reflect spiritual loyalties; in this pursuit, he does not address our questions about sexual difference.

In addition to the *Oratio*, one can also study Tatian's *Diatesseron* for clues to his theology. In the *Diatesseron*, Tatian worked as editor, redacting the gospel texts into a single narrative that was copied, reedited, and circulated in the Greek and Syrian East for several centuries after his death. Looking at the *Diatesseron* manuscripts, we are forced to work on an especially inferential and tentative basis. Here Tatian is clearly not the author in a straightforward sense, but perhaps he can be heard to speak through his editorial choices. Arthur Vööbus describes Tatian's technique: "Here a gloss, there a little change in word order, or an addition, sufficed to make it unmistakably plain that [for Tatian] the Gospel of Salvation demands a radical renunciation of the whole human life, and that the price of eternal life is virginity."[18] As an example, Vööbus cites Tatian's version of Luke's birth narrative, which is written to avoid referring to Joseph as Mary's husband.[19] Similarly, in several *Diatesseron* manuscripts (but not all), Matthew 1:19 and 24 are redacted to suggest that Joseph was not Mary's husband.[20] Other scholars note that the *Diatessaron* omits references to Jesus' genealogies because Tatian does not like to associate Christ with biological generation.[21] Or, in a further example, the *Diatessaron* account of Jesus' teaching on divorce found in Matthew 19 and Mark 10 is attributed to Adam rather than God, as if God himself would not comment on such lowly matters.[22] A gloss on Luke 2:36 makes it seem as if the prophetess Anna lived with her husband as a virgin.[23] Multiple explanations for all of these editorial choices are of course possible, but the pattern is to diminish the prominence of marriage and sexually differentiated interactions in the Bible. As presented by Tatian, the

Scriptures do not seem interested in exploring the significance of sexual difference, except to imply that it is best ignored.

## Tertullian

In the late second and early third centuries, the Carthaginian Tertullian produced a series of treatises and polemics on marriage and celibacy. These works make occasional statements and include implications that give modest evidence for beliefs about sexual difference.

In these works, one of the most explicit and consistent themes is the argument that monogamous marriage should be allowed, but with reservations. Tertullian reasons that in Eden, God devised "the union of man and woman . . . for the replenishment of the earth, and the furnishing of the world," and therefore marriage today is "permitted, yet singly."[24] In other words, God created sexual difference for the purpose of uniting for procreation, and thus marriage is permitted, but only once per person. Remarriage after the death of a spouse, for instance, would not be permitted by Tertullian; he believes that the first marriage establishes a rule which allows monogamy for succeeding generations, but only monogamy of this particular and rigorous type.

Tertullian does not try to ignore or redact away a divine teleology for sexual difference or a divine blessing upon the first marriage, as Tatian does. To emphasize God's preference for monogamy, Tertullian argues that God could have created a more polygamous relation between the sexes, but he did not: "There were more ribs in Adam, and hands that knew no weariness in God; but not more wives in the eye of God."[25] Furthermore, citing Ephesians 5, Tertullian believes Christ and the church set a monogamous standard for marriage, for he declares, "We are bound to recognise a duplication and additional enforcement for us of the law of unity of marriage, not only in accordance with the foundation of our race, but in accordance with the sacrament of Christ."[26] As Adam had literally one spouse, as Christ had figuratively one spouse, so may Christians have only one spouse.

One might expect Tertullian to warmly commend marriage to all Christians, since he has located its origins among God's prelapsarian creation and gone so far as to echo Paul's reference to marriage as a "great sacrament of Christ and the Church."[27] However, Tertullian also believes that Christ's celibacy sharply relativizes the precedent of Ephesians 5. To those desiring perfection, Tertullian believes that Christ "stands before you, if you are willing (to copy Him), as a voluntary celibate in the flesh. If, however, you are unequal (to that perfection), He stands before you a monogamist in spirit, having one Church as His spouse, according to the figure of Adam and Eve."[28] In other words, to those who are weak, Tertullian reckons that Christ permits monogamy according to Ephesians 5 and the Edenic example, but to those who desire God's highest perfection, Christ's own singleness stands as the preferable example.

Thus, although Tertullian has called monogamous marriage a sacrament, this marriage is not so much a good in itself, producing spiritual or other fruits desirable in their own right; rather, such marriage is an economic measure for those gripped by sexual desires, a merciful gift from the Paraclete for "the heat of the flesh to foam itself down."[29] Other arguments on behalf of marriage—such as the pleasure of children or the opportunity to create a household to care for ourselves when we age— Tertullian treats skeptically: "Further reasons for marriage which men allege for themselves arise from anxiety for posterity, and the bitter, bitter pleasure of children. To us this is idle."[30] Thus, while Scripture leads Tertullian to accept marriage as permitted, he is likely to regard a person's interest in marrying as evidence of that person's weakness. Tertullian argues that what God indulges should not be confused with what God wills or desires—"albeit some things seem to savour of 'the will of God,' seeing that they are *allowed* by Him, it does not forthwith follow that everything which is *permitted* proceeds out of mere and absolute will of him who permits"[31]—and that marriage is among what is indulged, not willed, by God. In its essence, he claims that marriage is not so different from fornication: "It is laws which seem to make the difference between marriage and fornication; through diversity of illicitness, not through the nature of the thing itself."[32] Thus, even if marriage was created by God and in a sense modeled by Christ and the church, marriage actually has a second-class spiritual status, to be sought only when desire and appetite make voluntary celibacy impossible.

Given his wariness toward marriage, it is perhaps not surprising that to the extent Tertullian considers sexual difference directly, he believes it will have relatively little ultimate significance. In Tertullian's interpretation of Matthew 22:30 and Mark 12:25, eschatological men and women will not only resemble angels in that they will not marry and procreate, but they will also share angelic sexlessness; at least, that is what one highly ambiguous quotation appears to suggest: "You realize, of course, that the same angelic nature is promised to you, women, the selfsame sex is promised to you as to men, and the selfsame dignity of being a judge."[33] The passage seems to suggest that the two sexes are destined to be dissolved into an asexual angelic nature, in which the characteristics that distinguish the sexes now, such as the "dignity of being a judge," will be obsolete. It may be that it is specifically femininity that is liable for obsolescence. Whether or not that is so, we can say that Tertullian is not exploring any meaning that might arise from the eschatological interaction of sexual difference; he is alluding only to its absence or supersession.

Before drawing conclusions, however, we should also note Tertullian's prescriptions for virginity. Tertullian does not counsel male and female to guard their chastity in the same way, and, following this logic, we see that, to the extent that it exists in the present fallen era, sexual difference must be accommodated as an obstacle or stubborn necessity. He tells virgin women to wear the veil to surround themselves with a "stockade of bashfulness" and to "rear a rampart for your sex,"[34] lest they either tempt others or become themselves enamored of too much attention. But men have their own responsibilities in this regard, for to unveil and gaze on a virgin is to violate her: "You have denuded a maiden in regard of her head, and forthwith she wholly ceases to be a virgin to herself; she has undergone a change!"[35] Men and women are joined together in a mutually implicating system of chastity, with sexually differentiated duties: "To blush if he sees a virgin is as much a mark of a chaste man, as of a chaste virgin if seen by a man."[36] Tertullian urges the Christian widower, who might wish to marry again on account of loneliness or the desire to produce heirs, to turn to the church for companions and to remember that he is already, by virtue of being a Christian, disinherited from the world and, unlike pagan men, in need of no heirs.[37] Christian women, married and virginal alike, are urged to wear the veil for the sake of the men in their community: "If a mother, for your sons' sakes; if a sister, for your brethren's sakes; if a daughter, for your fathers' sakes."[38] Thus there is a reciprocal, interdependent pattern for sexually differentiated continence in these strictures. To guard their spiritual purity, the two sexes need to live differently. Tertullian makes Christian virginity a practice that includes efforts on behalf of the chastity of one's fellows. By virtue of having a sex in a sexually differentiated world, certain obligations are incumbent, and appropriate behavior for a male or female virgin takes its shape in relation to the other sex.

In sum, Tertullian's presupposition is that everyone will be more or less vulnerable to sexual desire, and the only choice is to socialize that desire into the sexually differentiated roles of husband or wife, male virgin or female virgin. He has argued for a created order in which God made sexual difference for the sake of reproduction and that allows but does not encourage marriage. Having been reinterpreted by Christ, Tertullian believes marriage is not to be sought as something God actively wills, but as something merely conceded to those unable to endure celibacy. Celibacy itself is indeed fragile, for it requires sexually differentiated social roles in order to be maintained. Sexual difference therefore plays a role of some significance in Tertullian's thought—not as a subject that attracted his sustained attention in its own right, but as a condition that we have seen in the background to his description of pre-eschatological life. Sexual difference in Tertullian is significant until that day, in heaven, when desire is no longer a threat and sexual difference either ceases to exist or becomes irrelevant. It is, in short, a troublesome but temporary feature of humanity.

## Clement of Alexandria

Clement of Alexandria, who lived almost contemporaneously with Tertullian, believed there is both sameness and difference between men and women:

For the individual whose life is framed as ours is, may philosophise without Learning, whether barbarian, whether Greek, whether slave—whether an old man, or a boy, or a woman. For self-control is common to all human beings who have made a choice of it. . . . Accordingly woman is to practice self-restraint and righteousness, and every other virtue, as well as man, both bond and free; since it is a fit consequence that the same nature possesses one and the same virtue. We do not say that woman's nature is the same as man's, as she is woman. For undoubtedly it stands to reason that some difference should exist between each of them, in virtue of which one is male and the other female. Pregnancy and parturition, accordingly, we say belong to woman, as she is woman, and not as she is a human being. But if there were no difference between man and woman, both would do and suffer the same things. As then there is sameness, as far as respects the soul, she will attain to the same virtue; but as there is difference as respects the peculiar construction of the body, she is destined for child-bearing and housekeeping. "For I would have you know," says the apostle, "that the head of every man is Christ; and the head of the woman is the man: for the man is not of the woman, but the woman of the man. For neither is the woman without the man, nor the man without the woman, in the Lord" [1 Cor 11:3, 8, 11]. For as we say that the man ought to be continent, and superior to pleasures; so also we reckon that the woman should be continent and practised in fighting against pleasures.[39]

In other words, men and women possess the same moral nature and belong together "in the Lord," but there are bodily differences between them that call for living in sexually differentiated roles and that make man "the head." Men and women are called to the same interior struggle for self-control and mastery over appetite, but their bodily differences indicate that women are "destined for child-bearing and housekeeping." As Clement explains elsewhere, "The virtue of man and woman is the same. For if the God of both is one, the master of both is also one; one church, one temperance, one modesty; their food is common, marriage an equal yoke; respiration, sight, hearing, knowledge, hope, obedience, love all alike."[40] It is, in Clement's theory, only in matters arising from reproduction or bodily difference that sexual difference has ethical significance.

Clement's theory rests on two premises: first, that the duality of sex has protological justification in the God-given capacity of the two sexes for procreation; second, that it is asexual qualities such as self-control which are essential for cultivating virtue. Justifying his protological premise, Clement explains that Adam and Eve had their union "by nature" and not on account of sin.[41] Clement denounces "docetics" who do not believe that God made the male and female parts to fit together in intercourse for reproduction, as if the genital and reproductive aspect of ourselves was the product of something other than God's will.[42] He denounces the view, which he attributes to Cassian, that the "coats of skin" in Genesis 3:21 are human bodies, as if we had bodies only in light of the fall, or as if our embodiment and capacity for sexual procreation were at odds with our heavenly destiny.[43] Instead, in Clement, the claim is that "birth is holy. . . . Without the body how could the divine plan for us in the Church achieve its end?" An embodied life with all its consequences—sexual activity, children, a household—is a life in "co-operation with the work of creation."[44] Adam and Eve could have had proper, godly intercourse in the garden of Eden—Clement believes that their sexual sin was to have sexual relations too soon, before they were mature and while under the influence of Satan's deceit.[45] It was the timing or overeager manner of the protological couple's sexual intercourse, and not the intercourse itself, that was problematic; thus, in certain circumstances, sexual intercourse can continue to be permissible after the fall, and the divine plan for sexual reproduction as a feature of creation continues until "the restoration of the elect."[46]

Of course, couples who have intercourse today must learn the suitable timing or manner for coitus, lest they repeat the mistake of Adam and Eve. The question of timing raises the issue of Clement's second premise, about asexual self-control over passionate impulses. If sexual difference is natural until "the restoration of the elect," then, as with other things that are natural, it cannot and should not be eschewed but ought to be regulated:

> For, in a word, whatever things are natural to men we must not eradicate from them, but rather impose on them limits and suitable times. For man is not to laugh on all occasions because he is a laughing animal, any more than the horse neighs on all occasions because he is a neighing animal. But as rational beings, we are to regulate ourselves suitably, harmoniously relaxing the austerity and over-tension of our serious pursuits, not inharmoniously breaking them up altogether.[47]

Clement describes a figure whom he calls the "true Gnostic," who illustrates the suitable use of what is natural. This figure's virtuous qualities are not limited to men: "In this perfection it is possible for man and woman equally to share."[48] This "true Gnostic" is an ideal Christian, a serene, sage-like figure who participates in creation yet does so with detachment born from ordering his life toward knowledge of God. Clement is convinced that it is impossible to know God if we are in bondage to worldly pleasures (he quotes Luke 16:13, that no man can serve two masters),[49] and so detachment from pleasure and passion is what he believes Christians must seek: "To attain the knowledge of God is impossible for those who are still under control of their passions."[50] "Our great contest of arms is not waged against flesh and blood, but against the spiritual powers of passionate affections working in the flesh."[51] In the case of the protological teleology of the two sexes for sexual intercourse, that means affirming that it is good, but limiting it to procreation with detachment, or without passion. The true gnostic

> will value highest not living, but living well. He will therefore prefer neither children, nor marriage, nor parents, to love for God, and righteousness in life. To such an one, his wife, after conception, is as a sister, and is judged as if of the same father; then only recollecting her husband, when she looks on the children; as being destined to become a sister in reality after putting off the flesh, which separates and limits the knowledge of those who are spiritual by the peculiar characteristics of the sexes. For souls, themselves by themselves, are equal. Souls are neither male nor female, when they no longer marry nor are given in marriage. And is not woman translated into man, when she is become equally unfeminine, and manly, and perfect?[52]

There are several important ideas in this passage. First, once procreation has been accomplished, husbands and wives are to resist any ongoing desire for one another; they are to regard one another as siblings lacking the differentiating features of the flesh and to see one another as equals, as fellow men. Procreation having been accomplished, husbands and wives have come to the end of what sexual difference can mean to them theologically. To use sexual difference with detachment means to use it in light of its protological naturalness but also in light of its eschatological obsolescence.

This eschatological vision, this call to act in light of the time "when they no longer marry," includes an eschatological homogenization of the sexes not into something sexless but so that woman is "translated into man . . . manly and perfect." The erasure of the sexes appears to be by means of the transformation of femaleness into one masculinized humanity. Elsewhere Clement is ambivalent on this point, saying that as it is only in marriage or reproductive matters that "the female is distinguished from the male" and so in heaven, where there is no marriage (citing Luke 20:34), "the rewards of this social and holy life, which is based on conjugal union, are laid up, not for male and female, but for man, the sexual desire which divides humanity being removed. Common therefore, too, to men and women, is the name of man."[53] In this latter case, Clement intends the word "man" to refer to the generically human and not necessarily the masculine. He means that the rewards of social life, which are pursued through sexually differentiated roles, are reaped not by sexually differentiated humans in heaven but by creatures who exist beyond desire and sexual difference, but not necessarily in some masculinized ideal. Thus it is unclear whether Clement believes the eschatological erasure of sexual difference leads to a masculinization of the two sexes or toward generic sexlessness. In either case, the point holds that sexual difference is not part of humanity's future. Whenever humans live in sexually differentiated roles, they do so on the basis of protology rather than eschatology.

These sexually differentiated roles are highly prescribed in Clement. He says that men should not wear their ring "on the joint; for this is feminine" but should place it "on the little finger at its root." Boys and young men should exercise in the gymnasium, but women should take their exercise "in spinning, and weaving, and superintending the cooking if necessary."[54] Such examples proliferate, and the point appears to be that some visible difference should mark the two sexes, for Clement believes that when "men play the part of women, and women that of men . . . no passage is closed against libidinousness." Such circumstances "coerce . . . nature."[55] In other words, unless there are some ritualized differences (the content of those differences and how that content is derived being a separate question) between the sexes, then, in Clement's estimation, the sexual aspect of life is chaotic and thus open to "libidinousness," that is, to dynamics other than procreativity, and for Clement such passion is forbidden. Thus these exhortations toward sexually differentiated roles are appealing to moral purposes. "To yield in subjection to the passions is the lowest form of slavery, just as to conquer them is the only true freedom."[56] Both man and woman are to claim freedom and ascend to God by mastering the "wild elements" in the self, by controlling the "impulses of ignorance" and putting a new divine "stamp" on the mind.[57] The prescribed sexual roles are a type of self-mastery in support of this program, acknowledging what is for Clement the correct moral significance of sexual difference. We can surmise that by providing limits, the behavioral codes check and contain the self's wild elements, and keep sexual difference from overtaking its created teleology.

Clement's vision of marriage, which as far as we know makes chiefly procreative use of sexual difference, can be seen more clearly in light of these gender roles, which recognize but also contain sexual difference. Once the business of procreation is accomplished and the spouses are at the stage of regarding one another as asexual siblings, the codes help make the point that male and female have nothing to gain from further encounter as male and female. For Clement, true gnostics do not "mount their females at the appointed season and immediately abandon them," as do the beasts,[58] yet this uniquely human postcoital coexistence does not make any appeal or draw any benefit from sexual difference. The way in which husband and wife continue to live together after procreation does not continue to draw further meaning from sexual difference. For instance, note the way in which Clement believes virtue accrues to a husband who continues to live with his wife and children:

True manhood is shown not in the choice of a celibate life; on the contrary the prize in the contest of men is won by him who has trained himself by the discharge of the duties of husband and father and by the supervision of a household, regardless of pleasure and pain—by him, I say, who in the midst of his solicitude for his family shows himself inseparable from the love of God and rises superior to every temptation which assails him through children and wife and servants and possessions.[59]

In this account, marriage and procreation give rise to a set of conditions that test the high standards of self-control one needs to become a true gnostic.

In these trying conditions, the individual is called to self-possession, and interaction between the sexes as two sexes is not explored:

> For the rest of humankind, marriage finds concord in the experience of pleasure, but the marriage of true lovers of wisdom leads to a concord derived from the Logos. It tells women to beautify their character rather than their appearance; it enjoins husbands not to treat their wives as sex-objects, making their goal the violation of their bodies, but directing their marriage to support throughout life and to self-control at the highest level.[60]

For the true gnostic, marriage has its origins in sexual difference, but once procreation is left aside, marriage is a project in which individuals try to maintain their poise despite the challenging circumstances of household life. God is "with those who responsibly marry and produce children," but once that is accomplished, God "is with the man who shows self-control in the light of the Logos." We should love creation "for the sake of God the maker of all things," but the life of true Gnosticism means "effortlessly embracing the state of self-control following the likeness of the Saviour."[61]

Clement's view of sexual difference, then, can be summarized by saying that it has some significance, but a significance that is strictly contained in the past. That past might be either, to speak in theological time, in the protological era, or, to speak in terms of a married couple's life together, in the early days of marriage, when the couple is trying to have children. But this significance is quickly superseded, either eschatologically as humanity resolves into sexlessness or masculinity, or in a marriage in which individuals seek to regard one another as souls that "are neither male nor female."

## Gregory of Nyssa

The Cappadocian Gregory of Nyssa, who lived several generations after Clement, in the mid- to late-fourth century, is famous for allegedly believing what has come to be called the "garments of skin" hypothesis, or the suggestion that Genesis 3:21 refers not to clothes but to the postlapsarian origins of the human body.[62] We have already in this chapter briefly encountered this hypothesis in Clement, who did not discuss it at length but who noted it and repudiated it.[63] In the twentieth century, this hypothesis has generated controversy, especially within Eastern Orthodoxy.[64] When this perspective is applied to Gregory, the contention is that Gregory believed that embodiment, and sexual difference itself and reproduction by means of coitus, are postlapsarian, remedial provisions from God. In this scenario, humanity's division into male and female "is a departure from the Prototype," or a departure from human ontology and thus an ultimately superficial feature occluding what we most deeply are.[65] The theory holds that God superimposed the division of sex on originally sexless human beings "to moderate the bitterness of humankind's punishment by death"[66] or "to enable human beings to continue to exist in exile from Paradise . . . and, through disgust produced by their experience . . . freely to desire to return to God."[67] Such summaries represent the traditional and, until recently, virtually unanimous view of the sexed body in Gregory.[68]

Gregory provides ample evidence for concluding that these were his beliefs. In his most important treatise on anthropology, *De hominis opificio*, Gregory distinguishes the "image of God" in humanity from our male and female sex; if God is sexless, that which is sexed in us is not of God's image.[69] Our creation "is in a sense twofold: one made like to God, one divided according to this distinction" of sexual difference. The "distinction of male and female . . . has no reference to the Divine Archetype."[70] These premises seem to suggest that human beings are not sexed at the most fundamental level. Moreover, when Gregory quotes Jesus to the effect that in the resurrection there is no marriage, Gregory goes on to say that "the resurrection promises us nothing else than the restoration of the fallen to their ancient state," at least in terms of returning us to a state of grace, such as the angels enjoy.[71] Therefore he speculates that in a paradise without sin, reproduction would have occurred not on the basis of sexual marriage but along asexual angelic lines, in contrast to the present mode of marriage and sexual generation, which was created only on account of our temporary and fallen inclination to transient and bestial ways.[72] Our present mode of creation by sexual difference was given to us by God not because it was the best way for us to live, but because it was the best way for us to live given the conditions after our sin, which God anticipated:

But as He perceived in our created nature the bias towards evil, and the fact that after its voluntary fall from equality with angels it would acquire a fellowship with the lower nature, He mingled, for this reason, with His own image, an element of the irrational (for the distinction of male and female does not exist in the Divine and blessed nature);—transferring, I say, to man the special attribute of the irrational formation, He bestowed increase upon our race not according to the lofty character of our creation; for it was not when He made that which was in His image that He bestowed on man the power of increasing and multiplying; but when He divided it by sexual distinctions, then He said "Increase and multiply, and replenish the earth."[73]

Thus we can see how it is plausible for most readers of Gregory to conclude that sexual difference has a lower status in Gregory's protology, for it appears that, like clothes or "garments of skin," it would not have existed without sin.

In keeping with this anthropological foundation, Gregory's most famous ascetical treatise, *De virginitate*, can be read as a program for what marriage and virginity look like if sexual difference is a suspiciously ambivalent anthropological feature. In this treatise, Gregory fears that the erotic potential of marriage could have dire consequences and lead to repetition of the fall's turning from God, and he urges extreme caution "lest under cover of the excuse of lawful indulgence, passion should gain an entrance into the citadel of the soul." Like Clement, Gregory maintains a sense that marriage is a testing ground, and, again like Clement, suggests that the morally less-than-heroic might want to take refuge in virginity: "He who is so weak a character that he cannot make a manful stand against nature's impulse had better keep himself very far away from such temptations, rather than descend into a combat which is above his strength."[74]

Moreover, Gregory appears to have a skeptical regard for the body itself. Gregory refers to our "earthly envelopment" that must be shed to return to the beauty of the pure soul. Apparently, marriage and embodied sexual life are compensation for the fall, or "compensation for having to die."[75] But as compensation, this bodily life is still bound by the terms of the fallen economy; it is poignant when Gregory acknowledges a husband's delight in having a wife as a companion, and in gazing upon the "beloved face" of his wife, because while Gregory obviously appreciates those happy moments, he cannot overlook marriage's associations with death.[76] Any succor in marriage is only a kind of procrastination before the inevitability of death.[77] Marriage may start well and feel compensatory, but it eventually leads to calamities such as widowhood, orphanhood, and grief over lost children. Marriage is intimately connected with tragedy for Gregory and is the route into a "mob of moral diseases" that Gregory specifies as fame, wealth, public honors, power, and luxury.[78] Gregory grew up and was a pastor amid the patrician social system in Cappadocia, which was built on "the ancient, civic urge to pile up wealth, to gather kinsmen, and to beget descendants."[79] Marriage and the household system bind all these powerful urges together. Thus when Gregory counsels virginity, he is not only recommending a refuge for the morally weak, but he is counseling Christians to renounce the whole civic system of prestige and pride, as well as transcending the trap of embodiment, and coming as close as possible to the sexless life of the pure soul. Hence virginity has so much to commend itself for Gregory: "We should wean ourselves from this life in the flesh, which has an inevitable follower, death; and . . . we should search for a manner of life which does not bring death in its train. Now the life of Virginity is such a life."[80]

These various readings of Gregory are supported by Gregory's reception in Christian tradition. From Maximus the Confessor to Thomas Aquinas, formidable theologians have been confident in treating Gregory this way.[81] However, in the last decade or so, scholarship on Gregory of Nyssa has shown an openness to a revisionist reading that might lead to a different theological anthropology if it turns out to be true. M. D. Hart unfolds the structure of *De virginitate* to try and show that Gregory is writing on two levels: a plain sense which is indeed commending virginity, but also an ironic sense with a high theology of marriage and its significance for church life. Inspired by Hart, another contemporary Orthodox theologian, John Behr, has published a similarly revisionist reading of *De hominis opificio*.[82] This case argues that Gregory believes it is proper to the nature of human beings to be bodily and sexed; human beings were never meant by God to be purely intellectual, incorporeal beings. As Rowan Williams notes elsewhere, also discussing Gregory, the soul for Gregory is "essentially without gender" but "the ungenderedness of the soul is never the actual state of a real subject."[83] The sexless image of God in humans is their freedom to participate in the goodness and rationality of God,[84] and their vocation is to use this freedom to ascend to God through their materiality. But as material creatures, features such as sexual difference are appropriate even if they are not in God's image, because it is precisely these features that enable them to fulfill their human purpose.[85]

Nevertheless, this revisionist reading is not what Gregory bequeathed to most of his subsequent readers in the Christian tradition, and there are stubborn passages mitigating against the revisionists, such as Gregory's plain statements that humans would have had some other, nonsexual mode of living or vocation if they were not separated from God and fallen. In that light, it is hard to see how sexual difference can be anything but tainted and associated with what is tragic, even if it is providential and part of redemption. If one wanted to create intellectual space for the revisionists to mount their case, perhaps one may say that Gregory did not leave a clear record and that he did not confront the topic with an explicitness and directness that satisfy all the questions we might like to ask. Gregory himself can take a fairly humble tone when framing arguments about sexual difference, admitting a certain apophaticism, especially about the creation stories: "The cause, indeed, of this device, only those can know who were eye-witnesses of the truth and ministers of the Word; but we, imagining the truth, as far as we can, by means of conjectures and similitudes, do not set forth that which occurs to our mind authoritatively, but will place it in the form of a theoretical speculation before our kindly hearers."[86]

## Jerome

Jerome, who lived from about 342 to 420, is the last of our early Christian ascetics. His beliefs about sexual difference are particularly clear in two polemical treatises about marriage and virginity. The first was written earlier in his career, in 383, and extols Mary in order to rebuke a heretic named Helvidius. Jerome portrays Mary as a prototypical virginal figure who eschews sexual intercourse even while married and, in so doing, sets an example for all women.[87] Helvidius had evidently written that virginity and sexually procreative marriage are equal to one another in glory, and had added that Mary had not been a virgin postpartum. Jerome's patrons were scandalized, and, replying on their behalf, Jerome appeals to the precise meaning of certain words in Scripture: Does "to know" in Matthew 1:24–25 imply that Joseph ever had coitus with Mary? When the Gospels refer to Jesus' brothers, do they mean spiritual or biological relations?[88]

Jerome is also concerned that his proclamation of Mary's perpetual virginity should not be taken "to condemn marriage."[89] He believes that marriage is permitted by God, particularly among the Old Testament patriarchs who lived before the present era of eschatological imminence.[90] Nevertheless, since this treatise is also against Helvidius's attempt to give virginity and marriage equal status, Jerome concludes with several chapters of practical arguments against marriage: With the "prattling of infants," the pressure of household expenses, the constant effort to stay beautiful and attractive, Jerome is sure that no married woman could find time to pray and think of God.[91]

It is possible that Jerome is suggesting that the godly woman is not really a woman in a sense, for, whether married or not, a godly woman abstains from sexual intercourse and so ceases to live as a woman in relation to man: "Observe what the happiness of that state must be in which even the distinction of sex is lost. The virgin is no longer called a woman."[92] On the other hand, perhaps Jerome means that the virgin is still a woman but not in any important sense that social discourse needs to name, for the distinction of sex simply stops mattering when coitus is foregone and foresworn. It is hard to know precisely what Jerome means, since this sentence is Jerome's only passing thought about sexual difference in this treatise. It would seem to hint at an idealized, possibly eschatological, erasure of sexual difference, and it would seem to imply that it is the possibility of coitus which makes sexual difference socially significant. But it is very difficult to draw firm conclusions from such brief consideration.

The second treatise was written ten years later and continues to argue for the superiority of virginity over marriage, but at greater length and with more attention to sexual difference. This time the opponent, Jovinian, also argued that ascetic practice confers no hierarchy among the baptized. By virtue of common baptism, Jovinian believed that the married and the continent would be equal on judgment day; the abstainers receive no higher reward in heaven. Jerome's rebuttal, and the main thesis of this treatise, is that if one claims all the baptized are equal regardless of sexual practice, then one has slurred not only virgins but also married people, implicitly putting the married on par with digamists and "whore-mongers."[93] Thus, for the dignity of all concerned, a sense of a hierarchy among sexual behaviors should be maintained. In this argument, Jerome endorses Tertullian's distinction between virgins and the married: What God wishes (virginity) is not as good as what God pardons (marriage); what is merely excusable is not desirable.[94] In Jerome's mind, this position entitles him to claim a higher esteem for marriage than its opponents, such as Tatian. He only half-accurately describes Tatian—he says Tatian wants to "inculcate perpetual abstinence, to destroy and express . . . hatred and contempt for the works of the Creator"—and he describes his own views as reverence for creation but nuanced by a simple preference for "leanness to corpulence, abstinence to luxury, fasting to fullness."[95]

Also in this treatise, Jerome seems to believe that any sexual intercourse in marriage inherently corrupts. Pressing 1 Corinthians 7 to a further extreme, he argues, "If it is good not to touch a woman, it is bad to touch one." In relation to the body of Christ, he declares, "All sexual intercourse is unclean." He says that "if we are to pray always, it follows that we must never be in the bondage of wedlock." All marital relations are viewed with a similar attitude, for "the defilement of marriage" is not "washed away by the blood of martyrdom."[96] Jerome appears to link this stain upon marriage with the very nature of sexual difference itself: "As then he who touches fire is instantly burned, so by the mere touch the peculiar nature of man and woman is perceived, and the difference of sex is understood."[97] It would appear that Jerome cannot imagine a sexually differentiated relationship without sin, and that the mere fact of sexual difference is tainted. In this metaphor, knowledge of sexual difference is like being burned. Spiritually, he says, to be born again in Christ means assuming a way of life in which sexual difference no longer matters: "When the difference of sex is done away, and we are putting off the old man, and putting on the new, then we are being born into Christ a virgin, who was both born of a virgin, and is born again through virginity."[98]

However, and significantly, Jerome nevertheless (and perhaps inconsistently) defends sexual difference as the creation of the good God. He says that although God prefers virginity, the good Creator fashioned "our hinder parts . . . the lower portions of the abdomen," and hence the "difference of sex" exists by God's wish.[99] Jerome claims that even if we are living as virgins and not using our sexual organs for procreation, the difference of sex is still to be honored and cherished as the work of God. He wants to rebut those who would argue that the lifestyle of virginity, as commended by himself and his interpretation of the Apostle Paul, could be taken to imply that sexual differentiation had no purpose. Jerome imagines a critic who might say to Paul:

Why are you like other men, Paul? Why are you distinguished from the female sex by a beard, hair, and other peculiarities of person? How is it that you have not swelling bosoms, and are not broad at the hips, narrow at the chest? Your voice is rugged, your speech rough, your eyebrows more shaggy. To no purpose you have all these manly qualities, if you forego the embraces of women.[100]

Against this, Jerome objects that sexual difference is not pointless among the continent. He does not specify what that purpose is; he simply points to Christ as one who was sexually differentiated:

Our Lord and Saviour, Who though He was in the form of God, condescended to take the form of a servant, and became obedient to the Father even unto death, yea the death of the cross—what necessity was there for Him to be born with members which He was not going to use? He certainly was circumcised to manifest His sex.[101]

It appears that, although Christ did not assume male flesh in order to have intercourse with women, it is still important to Jerome that he was genuinely male. Jerome goes on to assert that similarly, the sexual differences of virgins, who live in ways that imitate Christ, are equally not pointless. He says that virgins are living a life now which foreshadows heaven, and the body we will have in heaven can be seen in Christ's resurrection body, which was a real male body and not something "contrary to nature."[102]

Hence, while Jerome's moral theory could find no significance for sexual difference that was not tainted by sin in practice, his Christology nevertheless implies that sexual difference is fundamental to being human. Because Jerome insists on the particularity and genuineness of Christ's humanity, and that this humanity includes his maleness, it follows that being a sex is important for others to be genuinely human. On the basis of Christ's precedent, Jerome, whether he is aware of it or not, is implicated in believing that there is significance to sexually differentiating features even when they have no obvious (procreative) utility. Perhaps indicating some awareness of these implications, elsewhere in this same treatise, again when considering how sexual difference might be transformed in the eschaton, Jerome does not take Matthew 22:30 (that in heaven we will no longer marry but have a sexuality like angels) to require a complete erasure of sexual differences, as Tertullian does. Instead, Jerome can see space for ambiguity:

> If likeness to the angels is promised us (and there is no difference of sex among the angels), we shall either be of no sex as are the angels, or . . . though we rise from the dead in our own sex, we shall not perform the functions of sex.[103]

In this passage, he is allowing for the possibility that someday sexual difference might disappear in human beings, but also that it might remain. His preference seems to be for the latter, for again, thinking christologically, he argues that Christ's resurrection body had the same substance as any natural body, "though of a higher glory."[104]

If it is difficult to tell what Jerome believed about sexual difference when writing against Jovinian, this ambiguity is dispelled by various letters written in the years afterward. In 399, he wrote, "When it is said that they neither marry nor are given in marriage but are as the angels in heaven, there is no taking away of a natural and real body."[105] In 400, he argued that in heaven we will rise with the same sexual differences we now know in flesh and bones, even as Christ did.[106] By 404 he felt clear that if the woman shall not rise again as a woman nor the man as a man, there will be no resurrection of the dead. For the body is made up of sex and members. But if there shall be no sex and no members what will become of the resurrection of the body, which cannot exist without sex and members? And if there shall be no resurrection of the body, there can be no resurrection of the dead.[107]

Thus we can see Jerome growing in confidence that though our genitals will not be used for marrying and having intercourse in the eschaton, they and our sexually differentiated identities will be maintained as a permanent feature of human identity. It would appear that Jerome's views changed since the dream he had in 383, when he wrote in passing against Helvidius about the happiness when "the distinction of sex is lost."

## Conclusion

In this chapter, five theologians have told us about—or, in some cases, their theories about other matters have implied—a mixture of contradictory and complementary things. For instance, we have heard that sexual difference is irrelevant to being human, except insofar as it contributes to distracting us with worldly allegiances, and it should be transcended and ignored in order to live the life of faith (Tatian). Or we have heard that sexual difference is an important part of being human, part of God's creation, but that it is now seriously threatening Christian integrity because it provokes sexual desires that need to be contained through marriage, or through the distinct gender roles of celibacy; in this account, these burdensome sexual differences will, however, someday be transcended and set aside (Tertullian). We also have heard that sexual difference exists to enable procreation and, in being used for this purpose, is the foundation for a way of life that honors creation but that this life should be strictly ordered to ensure that sexual difference does not have significance other than procreation, until the eschaton arrives, at which point sexual difference will be erased (Clement). We also have seen a theologian who was somewhat unclear, probably believing that sexual difference is not a permanent or fundamental feature of being human, but who arguably also believes that it is part of God's providential economy for the time being (Gregory of Nyssa). Finally we have seen how one theologian, who had a very limited account of how sexual difference might be edifying in marriage, nevertheless believed in the eschatological permanence of sexual difference and reversed a position he once seemed to hold (Jerome). On the basis of these five different accounts, we can conclude that there were a variety of beliefs and no single systematic account of sexual difference in early Christianity.

This variety of views, and the lack of a single confession on this subject, is significant for the rest of this book. Through this exercise, if nothing else, we have learned about the form that responsible claims about sexual difference will need to take. No one can read the early theologians and believe afterward that there is anything obvious about how sexual difference and Christianity go together. Sexual difference within Christianity is therefore a subject that needs to be articulated and examined, rather than simply taken for granted. Positions about sexual difference within Christianity will be contingent, based on judgments about matters such as protology, anthropology, Scripture, Christology, and eschatology. Even apparently similar practices among churchmen can mask different beliefs: for example, the practice of sexually differentiated marriage in Tertullian versus Clement. For Tertullian, marriage was a place to indulge and release sexual tensions. For Clement, marriage was a place where passions should be mastered and transcended. Perhaps these two positions are not necessarily incompatible, but it is possible to imagine someone who is sensitive to his or her own moral frailty who might have married under Tertullian lest he or she burn but who prefers to be celibate under Clement, lest he or she be exposed to even more snares. In sum, this chapter has helped our investigation into sexual difference because it has taught us not to make quick and superficial judgments about how belief and practice correspond, and it has taught us not to assume that the Christian story is so plain about sexual difference that no discussion is necessary.

The diversity in this chapter does not necessarily imply chaos. For instance, our five theologians appear to presuppose at least some significance for sexual difference; none of them treat it as a trivial or indifferent matter. Even Tatian's attempt to ignore it does not mean that it was meaningless for him. Tatian, as with the others, gives Christians the capacity, on the basis of theological propositions, not to assume the inevitability of inherited cultural predispositions about sexual difference, such as its relation to family life and reproduction. All five theologians have visions of an alternative Christian pattern for sexuality, in which sexual differences can be habituated in accountability to a profession of faith. All five theologians believe that this Christian pattern will transcend and condemn pagan practices based on household prestige or lustful self-interest. Furthermore, our five theologians are all wrestling with the same (or, recognizably similar, in the case of Tatian's *Diatessaron*) biblical story, trying to remain accountable to the dynamics of creation, fall, and redemption. So the diversity in this chapter occurs within broad but real outlines. These common features mean that the project of interpreting Christianity in order to learn the meaning of sexual difference is not a boundless, arbitrary enterprise. Common boundaries mean that, in principle, Christians should be able to measure diverse proposals for their relative coherence. When theologians give reasons for why they believe what they believe about sexual difference, we can judge the adequacy of those reasons against the criteria of theology.

Identifying relevant criteria, and tracing the path through which more consensus developed within the church about sexual difference, is part of the project of the rest of this book. The next chapter, a treatment of Augustine on sexual difference, explains arguments that are directed not only against certain pagans and heretics but that also intend to offer theological reasons for reconceptualizing sexual practices within the church. These arguments will present themselves as being truer than their rivals within Christianity and more faithful to the key claims of the Christian story. To the degree that these arguments cohere and succeed, they give a theological yardstick to subsequent generations for evaluating claims about sexual difference.

## Notes

1. John Behr, "A Note on the Ontology of Gender," *St. Vladimir's Theological Quarterly* 42, nos. 3–4 (1998): 364.

2. The main fragments are collected in Molly Whittaker, ed., *Tatian: Oratio Ad Graecos and Fragments* (Oxford: Clarendon, 1982), 78–83; and Tatian, "Address to the Greeks," in *ANF*, 82–83. Jerome reports that Tatian says Christ's flesh is imaginary. Irenaeus claims that Tatian appealed to "invisible Aeons" in his doctrine of creation. Clement of Alexandria and Origen say that Tatian interpreted "Let there be light" in Genesis as a prayer of the creator god to the higher God. Clement also apparently believed Tatian permitted but discouraged sexual intercourse among his followers (cf. Clement of Alexandria, "Stromateis III, on Marriage," in *AC*, 12.81), which goes against all the other evidence about Tatian.

3. Chadwick and Oulton, "General Introduction," in *AC*, 22-23. This argument is also a central thesis of Emily J. Hunt, *Christianity in the Second Century: The Case of Tatian* (London: Routledge, 2003).

4. Tatian, 73, §19. Page numbers refer to the specific translation used. "Tatian" means the translation in *ANC*. "Whittaker" means the translation edited by her. Section symbols, §, refer to the chapter numbers, which are standard in both translations.

5. Whittaker, 9–11, §4–5.

6. Tatian, 71, §15.

7. Ibid., 71, §15; 70, §11.

8. Ibid., 74, §20.

9. Ibid., 67, §6.

10. Ibid., 73, §19.

11. Ibid.

12. Whittaker, 15, §8.

13. Kathy L. Gaca, "Driving Aphrodite from the World: Tatian's Encratite Principles of Sexual Renunciation," *Journal of Theological Studies* 53, no. 1 (2002) elaborates on this point.

14. Tatian, 70, §11.

15. Ibid., 72, §16.

16. Ibid., 73, §19.

17. Peter Brown, *The Body and Society: Men, Women, and Sexual Renunciation in Early Christianity* (New York: Columbia University Press, 1988), 91–92.

18. Arthur Vööbus, *Celibacy: A Requirement for Admission to Baptism in the Early Syrian Church* (Stockholm: Papers of the Estonian Theological Society in Exile, 1951), 17.

19. Ibid., 18–19.

20. Hunt, *Christianity in the Second Century*, 146.

21. See R. Grant, "Tatian and the Bible," *Studia Patristica* 1 (1957): 303.

22. Vööbus, *Celibacy*, 18; and Hunt, *Christianity in the Second Century* 146–47.

23. Hunt, *Christianity in the Second Century*, 147.

24. Tertullian, "To His Wife," in *ANF*, 39, §2.

25. Tertullian, "An Exhortation to Chastity," in *ANF*, 53, §5.

26. Ibid.

27. Tertullian, "On Monogamy," in *ANF*, 62, §5.

28. Ibid.

29. Ibid., 60, §3.

30. Tertullian, "To His Wife," 41, §1.5.

31. Tertullian, "Exhortation to Chastity," 51, 53. Emphasis in translation.

32. Ibid., 55, §9.

33. Tertullian, *Disciplinary, Moral, and Ascetical Works* (trans. Rudolph Arbesmann, Emily Joseph Daly, and Edwin A. Quain; vol. 40 of *The Fathers of the Church: A New Translation*; Washington, DC: Catholic University of America Press, 1959), 120–21, §1.2.5.

34. Tertullian, "On the Veiling of Virgins," in *ANF*, 37, §16.

35. Ibid., 29, §3.

36. Ibid., 28, §2.

37. Tertullian, "Exhortation to Chastity," 56–57, §12.

38. Tertullian, "On the Veiling of Virgins," 37, §16.

39. Clement of Alexandria, "The Stromata, or Miscellanies, Book IV," in *ANF*, 420, §8.

40. Clement of Alexandria, "The Instructor (Paedagogus)," in *ANF*, 211, §1.4.

41. Clement of Alexandria, "Stromateis III, on Marriage," in *AC*, 88, §3.17.102.

42. Ibid., 83, §13.91.

43. Ibid., 85, §14.95.

44. Ibid., 89, §17.103; 70–71, §9.66–67.

45. Ibid., 89, §17.103.

46. Ibid., 69, §9.63.

47. Clement of Alexandria, "Instructor (Paedagogus)," 250, §2.5.

48. Clement of Alexandria, "Stromata, or Miscellanies, Book IV," 431, §19.

49. Clement of Alexandria, "Stromateis VII, on Spiritual Perfection," in *AC*, 138, §12.71.

50. Clement of Alexandria, "Stromateis III, on Marriage," 59, §5.43.

51. Clement of Alexandria, "Stromateis VII, on Spiritual Perfection," 104, §3.20.

52. Clement of Alexandria, "The Stromata, or Miscellanies, Book VI," in *ANF*, 503, §12.

53. Clement of Alexandria, "Instructor (Paedagogus)," 211, §1.4.

54. Ibid., 285, §3.11; 283, §3.10.

55. Ibid., 276, §3.3.

56. Clement of Alexandria, "Stromateis, Book Two," in *Stromateis: Books One to Three* (The Fathers of the Church: A New Translation; Washington, DC: Catholic University Press of America, 1991), 253, §144.3.

57. Clement of Alexandria, "Stromateis VII, on Spiritual Perfection," 102, §3.16.

58. Clement of Alexandria, "Stromateis, Book Two," 253, §144.1.

59. Clement of Alexandria, "Stromateis VII, on Spiritual Perfection," 137, §12.70.

60. Clement of Alexandria, "Stromateis, Book Two," 253, §143.1.

61. Clement of Alexandria, "Stromateis, Book Three," in *Stromateis: Books One to Three* (The Fathers of the Church: A New Translation; Washington, DC: Catholic University Press of America, 1991), 298, §10.68.1; 299, §10.69.1.

62. John Behr, "The Rational Animal: A Re-Reading of Gregory of Nyssa's 'De Hominis Opificio,'" *Journal of Early Christian Studies* 7, no. 2 (1999): 221n5, lists scholars who associate Gregory with the hypothesis.

63. See above, note 43.

64. See Behr, "Note on the Ontology of Gender," for a summary of this debate.

65. Gregory of Nyssa, "On the Making of Man [De hominis opificio]," in *NPNF*, 405, §16.7.

66. Michael Banner, *Christian Ethics and Contemporary Moral Problems* (Cambridge: Cambridge University Press, 1999), 22.

67. Behr, "Rational Animal," 221.

68. Other examples of this reading can be found in Brown, *Body and Society*, 294ff.; V. E. F. Harrison, "Gender, Generation, and Virginity in Cappadocian Theology," *Journal of Theological Studies* 47 (1996), 38-68; and Panayiotis Nellas, *Deification in Christ: Orthodox Perspectives on the Nature of the Human Person* (trans. Norman Russell; Crestwood, NY: St. Vladimir's Seminary Press, 1987).

69. Gregory of Nyssa, 405, §16.7 and 8, discussed in Behr, "Rational Animal," 234.

70. Gregory of Nyssa, 405, §16.8; 406, §16.14.

71. Ibid., 407, §17.2; 406, §17.1; see also §22.4 and 22.5.

72. Ibid., 407, §17.2, 17.5.

73. Ibid., 411–12, §22.4.

74. Gregory of Nyssa, "On Virginity," in *NPNF2*, 353, §8.

75. Ibid., 358, §12.

76. Ibid., 346, §3.

77. The theme of procrastination is used similarly by John Behr, "Shifting Sands: Foucault, Brown, and the Framework of Christian Asceticism," *Heythrop Journal* 34, no. 1 (1993): 16.

78. Gregory of Nyssa, "On Virginity," 359, §13; 350, §4.

79. Brown, *Body and Society*, 303.

80. Gregory of Nyssa, "On Virginity," 359, §13.

81. John Zizioulas is confident that Maximus followed Gregory in this way. See Zizioulas, *Being as Communion: Studies in Personhood and the Church* (New York: St. Vladimir's Seminary Press, 1985), 52n46. For Aquinas, see p. 108n1.

82. Behr, "Rational Animal."

83. Rowan Williams, "Macrina's Deathbed Revisited: Gregory of Nyssa on Mind and Passion," in *Christian Faith and Greek Philosophy in Late Antiquity* (ed. Lionel Wickham and Caroline Bammel; Leiden: E. J. Brill, 1993), 243–44. See also Sarah Coakley, *Power and Submissions: Spirituality, Philosophy, and Gender* (Oxford: Blackwell, 2002), 165.

84. Gregory of Nyssa, "On the Making of Man," 405, §16.10–11, discussed in Behr, "Rational Animal," 235.

85. Ibid., 405, §16.12, discussed in Behr, "Rational Animal," 237.

86. Ibid., 406, §16.15; see also Behr, "Rational Animal," 246.

87. See Averil Cameron, "Redrawing the Map: Early Christian Territory after Foucault," *Journal of Roman Studies* 76 (1986): 270ff.; and Cameron, "Virginity as Metaphor: Women and the Rhetoric of Early Christianity," in *History as Text:*

*The Writing of Ancient History* (ed. Averil Cameron; London: Duckworth, 1989), for discussion of how this kind of rhetoric about virginity functioned historically to control women.

88. Jerome, "On the Perpetual Virginity of the Blessed Virgin Mary against Helvidius," in *Jerome: Dogmatic and Polemical Works* (The Fathers of the Church; Washington, DC: Catholic University Press, 1965), 13, §3; 33–34, §15.

89. Ibid., 38, §19.

90. Jerome, "Against Helvidius," in *NPNF2*, 344, §22.

91. Jerome, "On the Perpetual Virginity," 40–41, §20.

92. Jerome, "Against Helvidius," 344, §22.

93. Jerome, "Against Jovinianus," *NPNF2*, 348, §1.4. "Digamists" are people who remarry after the death of their first spouse.

94. Ibid., 351, §1.8; 358, §1.14.

95. Ibid., 400, §2.16.

96. Ibid., 350, §1.7; 361, §1.20; 351, §1.7; 366, §1.26.

97. Ibid., 350, §1.7.

98. Ibid., 360, §1.16.

99. Ibid., 373, §1.36.

100. Ibid., 373–74, §1.36.

101. Ibid., 374, §1.36.

102. Ibid.

103. Ibid.

104. Ibid.

105. Jerome, Letter LXXV, in *NPNF2*, 155, §2.

106. Jerome, Letter LXXXIV, in *NPNF2*, 178, §5 and 6.

107. Jerome, Letter CVIII, in *NPNF2*, 208, §23.

# Chapter 2
# AUGUSTINE

In chapter 1 we examined the ascetical works of five early theologians in order to learn about early attitudes toward the meaning and significance of sexual difference. We saw that there was no unanimity on the subject. Sometimes we encountered specific discussions of sexual difference, but we also had to draw inferences from asides and even from silences. We saw widely differing beliefs about the status of sexual difference in the created order, the destiny of sexual difference in the eschaton, and the moral implications of sexual difference in the present day.

In this chapter we will also encounter a diversity of beliefs about sexual difference. However, this time that diversity is traced across the chronological development of a single theologian—Augustine. These texts have been chosen because they are either directly concerned with sexual difference, or because they develop closely related anthropological and moral issues. As the exegesis accumulates, we will begin to sense that what became Augustine's mature argument was not reached arbitrarily but as a result of considering, rejecting, and sometimes even assimilating alternative positions. Augustine's early beliefs about sexual difference are sometimes, when pressed, found to be resting on unclear and possibly contradictory premises. Almost always, at many stages in his career, sexual difference was discussed less as a topic in its own right and more as an aside or implication arising from other (usually polemical) concerns. But the later Augustine resolves many ambiguities and conflicting beliefs about sexual difference, although, even then, his position is still dynamic and open to further evolution.

## De Genesi contra Manichaeos

The first of Augustine's commentaries on Genesis, *De Genesi contra Manichaeos*, appears to have been written in 388 or 389.[1] Several times the text describes sexual difference in Genesis as having primarily allegorical and spiritual significance. This abstract treatment becomes confusing and even, at times, perhaps contradictory. But this apparent shortcoming is mitigated if we also consider that Augustine's views in this treatise about sexual difference are best described as views that can be imputed to him as merely implications of his polemical agenda, rather than views that are the result of a systematic treatment of the theme. As its title indicates, this commentary was written in response to the Manichees, who, among other things, disparaged Christian beliefs about God for being materialistic and anthropomorphic; for instance, verses such as Genesis 1:26 ("let us make humankind in our image") meant, according to the Manichaen view of Christianity, that God was as limited and changeable as one having a human body.[2] Thus part of Augustine's polemic is to show the Manichees that Scripture should not be read so crudely and that the God of the creation accounts is not so primitive. In other words, this treatise is designed to show the suitability of the creation stories for spiritual progress and forming an accurate impression of God over against Manichaen misunderstandings. This treatise does not attempt a complete theological anthropology based on creation, including a self-conscious and deliberated account of sexual difference. Thus when Augustine makes comments about sexual difference in this treatise, we should usually treat them as asides in the service of anti-Manichaen polemic. Consequently, while we can exegete this commentary and press its material in order to speculate about sexual difference, we should also be wary of concluding that we have here anything like an attempt at a full and complete account of the early Augustine's beliefs. It will be more accurate to claim that this text represents several strands of possible thought on the subject, strands we shall eventually see Augustine clarifying and codifying in subsequent writing.

In fact, Augustine explicitly denied that anything he said in this treatise on sexual difference could purport to be the final word on the subject. Specifically, he is open to a literal or concrete interpretation of the relevant passages in Genesis in some other instance—it just happens not to be his present approach:

Accordingly, even if the real, visible woman was made, historically speaking, from the body of the first man by the Lord God, it was surely not without reason that she was made like that—it must have been to suggest some hidden truth. . . . So whether all this was said in a figurative way, or whether it was even done in a figurative way, it was certainly not pointlessly that it was said or done like this. No, it is all assuredly pointing to mysteries and sacraments, whether in the way I with my slender capacities am attempting to explain it, or whether it is to be interpreted and understood in some other and better way, but still in accordance with sound faith.[3]

Exactly what hidden truth might be suggested by the creation of sexual difference? For this early Augustine, the allegory of sexual difference in Genesis reveals the relationship between an individual's rational understanding and his or her flesh. When Adam greets the newly created Eve as "bone out of my bones, and flesh from my flesh," Augustine hears it as a greeting "as a boss might say of a minion."[4] This "bone of my bones" indicates a hierarchal relationship between masculine and feminine, a relationship between that which decides and that which obeys, and so sexual difference is an illustration of a relationship that Augustine believes to be operative in any individual (of whichever sex), an internal dynamic between that which rationally wills and that which actually performs visible actions. In other words, this parable of the hierarchy between the sexes, although superficially about two characters named Adam and Eve, is not so much a real relationship between persons as an apt illustration of what happens within a single person:

In this way what can be seen more clearly in two human beings, that is, in male and female, may be considered in a single person; that the interior mind, like the manly reason, should have as its subject the soul's appetite or desire, through which we put the limbs and parts of the body to work, and by a just law should keep its help within bounds—just as a man ought to govern his wife.[5]

Augustine claims a woman is "hidden inside each one of us," and this aspect of ourselves must submit "to the reason as to its husband." In fact, both sexes exist within each of us, both that "which has the right to govern" as well as "that lower element which has to be governed," and "it was to provide an example of this that the woman was made."[6]

For Augustine, this example is worthy of understanding and emulating because its fruits are pleasing to God: "Woman came to be made . . . as a help for the man, so that by a spiritual coupling she might bring forth spiritual offspring, that is, the good works of divine praise; while he directs, she complies; he is directed by wisdom, she by the man."[7] There is a spiritual fecundity, issuing in divine praise, in Eden's ordering of the two sexes, whenever a person's interior life is rightly ordered. The subordinate female position in this interiorized sexual hierarchy is not bad or less good, for it enables the allegory's and the individual's spiritual fertility to exist. Both sides of the male-female difference are good when in their proper order as created by God. Augustine regards the hierarchy in Genesis as the same sort of hierarchy he believes is suggested by 1 Corinthians 11:7–12, with God, man, and woman taking glory from each other in a descending hierarchy of headship.[8] To disparage one element in the relational sequence is to disparage the whole.

But does this figurative and introspective reading of sexual difference apply to the dynamics between enfleshed and visible maleness and femaleness in actual men and women? There is a vagueness or presumption on this point, owing to the anti-Manichaen polemical agenda and also perhaps to latent patriarchal assumptions. One can imagine that in the late classical context, a hierarchy between the sexes was a commonsense experience, and so it would be easy for Augustine to presume it and exegete in light of it. But whether that is the case or not, practical social life between actual male and female persons does not appear to be a concern in *Gen. Man.* As we have seen, Augustine is not opposed to treating the Genesis story in a more literal way—a way that might lead to a more concrete perspective on sexual difference—and he professes to admire those who might be able to exegete more literally, but he feels he has biblical authority to sanction his more abstract approach:

> One should not look with a jaundiced eye, to be sure, on anyone who wants to take everything that is said here absolutely literally, and who can avoid blasphemy in so doing, and present everything as in accordance with Catholic faith; on the contrary one should hold up such a person as an outstanding and wholly admirable understander of the text. If, however, no other way is available of reaching an understanding of what is written that is religious and worthy of God, except by supposing that it has all been set before us in a figurative sense and in riddles, we have the authority of the apostles for doing this.[9]

Augustine claimed he had not only apostolic authority for handling sexual difference allegorically but also the very words of Christ. He cites Luke 20:34 as a reason for believing that in the prelapsarian age, there would have been no begetting of physical children.[10] Augustine suggests that the verse means it is only the children of this age, and hence not the protological age Augustine is discussing in a Genesis commentary, who are born of fleshly sexual difference. Similarly, when Augustine comments on Genesis 2:24, the verse where a man leaves his father and mother and clings to his wife in one flesh, he writes, "I can find no way of referring this to history. . . . In fact the whole thing is a prophecy" of Ephesians 5. Along similar lines, Adam and Eve's unashamed nudity in Genesis 2:25 is considered noteworthy by Augustine not as a historical account or an insight into the relationship between actual male and female bodies but as signification of interior "simplicity of soul and chastity."[11] The pattern of what interested Augustine in this book is clearly abstract and allegorical, and he decided to keep his attention focused at that level. Although he professes openness to more concrete readings, he does not venture them, and he appears to believe that the biblical data cohere more readily with a less corporeal interpretation.

However, unlike other patristic protologies with a spiritualized sense of Eden, Augustine's does not regard the "tunics of skin" in Genesis 3:21 as a postlapsarian addition of sexual difference to humanity. Considering these garments, Augustine writes, "God changed their bodies into this mortal flesh" after "they themselves" ate from the tree of knowledge and attempted to hide their deception, and on account of their loss of interior simplicity.[12] Here the fall appears to be effecting an anthropological change, for it results in a type of flesh the couple did not previously have. Whether the change was from "no flesh" to "mortal flesh," or from "some unknown type of flesh" to "this mortal flesh," is unclear. However, a reader can see that, logically, whatever this new embodiment is, it is not necessarily a change from androgyny to sexual differentiation. On the contrary, Augustine has been comfortable speaking of the sexual differentiation, understood spiritually, of Adam and Eve prior to the fall. Mortal flesh, or the skin tunic, is thus not necessarily the bearer of sexually difference, for its acquisition is subsequent to comments about the creation of the two sexes. Of course, this is merely logical inference, based on Augustine's structure. Augustine himself does not make this point. It is simply a logic he does not deny: if male and female precede the fall, and if the fall brings about mortal bodies, then sexual difference is more anthropologically basic than mortal flesh. More than that—for instance, whether sexual difference is necessarily linked to having some kind of body or not, a body of some other flesh than "mortal"—one cannot safely infer, and even this inference is speculative.

Several decades later, Augustine himself seemed to realize that this treatise was filled with possibilities and confusing implications. In *Retractationes*, Augustine wrote that if his words in *Gen. Man.* are taken to say "those two human beings would not have had human children unless they had sinned, [then] I totally repudiate it."[13] By that date, he did not want readers to entertain the idea that physical procreative sexuality was only a postlapsarian phenomenon. He must have surmised that his words in *Gen. Man.* allowed these beliefs and associated questions, so perhaps our reading and questioning of this document is only doing what Augustine eventually realized its readers would do. In the forty years after *Gen. Man.*, Augustine's own position evolved to the point where he could speak with precision and confidence about matters that only invite speculation at this early stage. It seems that we should expect, on the basis of Augustine's own words, clarifications and development of thought about sexual difference as his career progresses, and so questions and tentativeness at this stage are appropriate.

## De Genesi ad litteram opus imperfectum

This short unfinished work is commonly dated between 393 and 395.[14] It ends before Augustine reaches Genesis 1:27 and the creation of the two sexes. Not surprisingly, it does not discuss sexual difference except for a minor side reference to 1 Corinthians 11:3. In this instance Augustine tries to explain how the Creator "is rightly called [creation's] head."[15] Here he appears comfortable with the hierarchies of his previous work. However, Augustine felt so awkward exegeting Genesis that he abandoned this commentary, and he did so before he would have been required to devote sustained attention to male and female.

We might also infer an implicit opinion about sexual difference from Augustine's comments about the *imago Dei*. Again, consistent with what he says in *Gen. Man.*, Augustine says the image is "the innermost and principal element in humanity," by which he means to refer to "the mind . . . which holds the leading place in human nature."[16] As regards other aspects of humanity, among which a reader would reasonably assume the sexed body is included, Augustine says "though beautiful in their kind" they "are still common to us and animals, and therefore in us are to be priced cheaply."[17] It would seem that corporeal sexual difference, while "beautiful" by implication, is not a place where significant human or theological meaning resides.

## Expositio epistulae ad Galatas liber unus

Written at nearly the same time as *Gen. imp.*, in either 394 or 395,[18] this commentary very briefly treats Galatians 3:28, a verse which invariably puts the question of sexual difference in Christ before its interpreters. Augustine's argument is that there is no distinction between male and female insofar as there is a common baptism and regard for Christ as Lord, or a common belonging to "Abraham's seed."[19] As a criterion for admission into the eschatological polity, sexual difference is erased and irrelevant. However, in the present era, "the body is still dead on account of sin," and differences such as sex, although "removed in the unity of faith," nevertheless remain "in this mortal life."[20] On this basis, we might infer a presumption that sexual difference is linked to mortality and the effects of sin. But the idea is not pursued, and if Augustine believes in a protological or eschatological androgyny, he does not press the point. Augustine's own interests are more this worldly, affirming that there is now at this time an "order . . . to be observed on this life's journey" that is taught by the apostles, "who hand down very salutary rules as to how Christians should live together with regard to differences of people (Jews and Greeks), status (masters and slaves), sex (husbands and wives), and the like; and it is also the teaching of the Lord himself, who said earlier: 'Give to Caesar the things that are Caesar's, and to God the things that are God's.' "[21] In other words, sexual differences are apparently overcome in social life from an eschatological perspective, but, like Caesar, they persist for the time being and merit respect as part of a legitimate secular order. For Christians, the sexes are not differentiated in that everyone has Christ as the head of the common body ("all are one in Christ and receive the inheritance through faith" and are no longer "under a disciplinarian"[22]), but they remain differentiated in the life God wishes for mortals as natural creatures. Gerald Bonner, exegeting different works of Augustine, but on a similar point, provides an apt summary: "In things spiritual, considered as *homo*, she [woman] is man's equal; in the natural order, considered as *femina*, she is inferior to him. . . . Secular conventions must receive their due."[23]

## Confessionum libri XIII

Written from 397 to 400,[24] *Confessionum* again offers sexual difference as a complex illustration of hierarchy side by side with an affirmation of sexual equality:

And as in his soul there is one element which deliberates and aspires to domination, and another element which is submissive and obedient, so in the bodily realm woman is made for man. In mental power she has an equal capacity of rational intelligence, but by the sex of her body she is submissive to the masculine sex. This is analogous to the way in which the impulse for action is subordinate to the rational mind's prudent concern that the act is right. So we see that each particular point and the whole taken together are very good.[25]

In other words, in the bodily realm, it is taken for granted that women are submissive, while in the mental realm, men and women are equal. But the mental realm is higher ranking and relates to the bodily as men relate to women in the physical world. Put another way, the difference Augustine sees between the sexes is only in the external, bodily aspects of a human person, that is, the differences of mortal flesh. These external bodily differences can lead to the hierarchical social roles of husband and wife—"You [God] made its [the soul's] rational action subject to the superiority of the intellect, as if symbolized by a woman's submissive role with her husband"[26]—but these external differences do not imply internal differences of spirit: "For 'you made man male and female' in your spiritual grace to be equal."[27] Thus the capacity of a human to be a member of the church and to do quintessentially human things, such as to be a judge over the other animals, is not contingent upon being one or the other sex,[28] but the external aspects of bodily sexual differences give rise to some interpersonal or intrahuman significance.

But are those external or bodily differences products of the fall, or part of God's good prelapsarian creation? It can be hard to tell in *Confessionum*. Clearly Augustine believes that the intellectual and spiritual realm is more beautiful and closer to God than the bodily: "For priority goes to your spiritual creation rather than the physical order, however heavenly and full of light."[29] Heaven is said to be an incorporeal place.[30] Thus some sort of hierarchy is still in place, but what does that imply for the lower end of the hierarchy? It is not necessarily associated with the fall just because it is lower. But Augustine's references to the lower, bodily, sexually differentiated realm are ambiguous: "If Adam had not fallen from you, there would not have flowed from his loins that salty sea-water the human race—deeply inquisitive, like a sea in a stormy swell, restlessly unstable."[31] Is Augustine saying that if Adam had not fallen, then some other race, a nonrestless race, would have flowed from Adam's procreating loins? That would be the simplest interpretation. But what if we read this passage in light of the sentiments expressed ten years earlier, in *Gen. Man.*, when Augustine believed that in the prelapsarian age there would be no physical begetting of children. Could this passage in *Confessionum* then be taken to imply that if Adam had not fallen, then his loins would not have been associated with procreation at all? In other words, Augustine appears to be less than clear on whether or not sinless human persons would have used sexually differentiated organs for procreation. This possibility raises a further question: Would the prelapsarian Adam and Eve have possessed those external, bodily organs that differentiate the sexes even if they were not using them for reproduction? *Confessionum* can stimulate such questions, but on its own terms, the answers are elusive.

Nevertheless, for *Confessionum*, sexual difference clearly exists significantly in the postlapsarian world. One of the well-known themes in *Confessionum* is the exploration of Augustine's personal existential and psychological situation. Augustine confesses that his appetite for the opposite sex was a major factor that delayed his wholehearted embrace of Christianity. He believed that were he "deprived of the embraces of a woman," he would "become very miserable."[32] He could not imagine a life ordered according to theological priorities because the delights of erotic encounters with women were so strong that he believed they would necessarily and always dominate his attention: "I believed continence to be achieved by personal resources which I was not aware of possessing," and "it was out of my power to live a celibate life."[33] Against a friend who insisted Augustine could muster the sexual self-control to make progress in matters of wisdom and religion, Augustine objected that his friend's sexual experience must have been meager and furtive, a pale imitation of "the delights of my own regular habit," or else the friend would not suggest such impossibilities.[34] One must conclude that Augustine believed that the physical, external aspects of sexuality, although only a feature of mortal flesh and perhaps protologically or eschatologically insignificant, were nevertheless significant in the present times. Augustine experienced the sexual appetite as a constraint on human freedom, a hunger that must always be fed and that is so deep it is impossible to conceive of life any other way. For that reason, he refers to himself as having been "in bondage" to his appetite and hence unavailable and not free for God.[35]

This bondage was real in the sense that it demanded so much of his attention that it obscured for Augustine where true happiness might be found:

The single desire that dominated my search for delight was simply to love and to be loved. But no restraint was imposed by the exchange of mind with mind, which marks the brightly lit path of friendship. Clouds of muddy carnal concupiscence filled the air. The bubbling impulses of puberty befogged and obscured my heart so that it could not see the difference between love's serenity and lust's darkness. Confusion of the two things boiled within me.[36]

For Augustine there could be no sanctuary in the realm of "mind with mind," where, as we have seen, he believed humans are not sexually differentiated, because the realm of the carnal, which is sexually differentiated, is compulsively attractive. Augustine does not condemn his desire to love and be loved, and he does not deny that "fleeting experiences of beauty" are possible in this "lower" realm of the mortal body.[37] But because this love for the visible is so strong and dominant, Augustine explains that it leads to an "intoxication" with creation rather than the Creator,[38] a perversity that prefers the penultimate to the ultimate, and his appetite for love is oriented around false priorities and a reversed hierarchy: "Each of the other senses has its own appropriate mode of response to physical things," yet in appreciating the physical, "one must not depart from you, Lord, nor deviate from your law." The problem with the sexual appetite, with lust, is precisely this loss of moderation, abandoning "the higher and supreme goods," replacing love for God with passion for "the bottom end of the scale of good." In this blindness, the sensually passionate cannot see that "there are no caresses tenderer than your [God's] charity, and no object of love is more healthy than your truth, beautiful and luminous beyond all things."[39]

For Augustine, the consequence of describing sexuality as a phenomenon in which he inevitably became disoriented from the true good is that sexuality requires a theologically based, ascetical reconfiguration. Unmediated sexual difference is an arena of internal chaos and disordered love. Sexuality therefore requires forms of life that can discipline the appetite and orient our loves rightly, because left to our own devices, our appetites will not lead us to the right places. In the strength of his human lust, Augustine reckons that he has been like a drowsy person, half-asleep and half-awake:

No one wants to be asleep all the time, and the sane judgement of everyone judges it better to be awake. Yet often a man defers shaking off sleep when his limbs are heavy with slumber. Although displeased with himself he is glad to take a bit longer, even when the time to get up has arrived. In this way I was sure it was better for me to render myself up to your love than to surrender to my own cupidity. But while the former course was pleasant to think about and had my notional assent, the latter was more pleasant and overcame me.[40]

Augustine, reasoning from his own experience, reckons that a person whose love is misdirected from its proper object becomes like a hungry person who loses his or her appetite for truly nourishing food: "The emptier I was, the more unappetizing such food became. So my soul was in rotten health. In an ulcerous condition it thrust itself to outward things, miserably avid to be scratched by contact with the world of the senses. Yet physical things had no soul. Love lay outside their range."[41] In such an environment, where the soul is so tempted to go wrong, some form of life will be required to contain and redirect the passions or appetites. The stakes are high because the human capacity for self-mismanagement is so great; sexuality is significant and complex in human experience because, among other reasons, it has so much power to overwhelm and distort. Unlike eye color or shoe size, for example, the sexually differentiated aspects of a person are visibly part of social organization, sin, and the divine address. Thus for the Augustine of *Confessionum* sexual difference is a physical feature, but it is related to potential spiritual chaos. Sexuality of all sorts requires discipline to keep the libido from usurping the rightful place of love for God.

In later works Augustine elaborates his practical proposals for ascesis that are based on these sorts of anthropological observations, but already in *Confessionum*, there are hints of what is to come. The "acts of the Sodomites" should be avoided because "the social bond which should exist between God and us is violated when the nature of which he is the author is polluted by a perversion of sexual desire."[42] It is unclear in this passage precisely what Augustine believed the "acts of the Sodomites" to have been, but he has made it clear in an earlier passage that he believes the law of which God is author requires that sexual union should be for children.[43] Thus, on the basis of this procreative requirement, we can say he believes that rightly ordered sexual activity is sexually differentiated activity, or, put differently, that sexual difference is a necessary but not sufficient condition for godly sexual union. Furthermore, Augustine believes that cultures where sexual activity is pursued without procreation as its end should change to accord with God's law: "But when God commands something contrary to the customs or laws of a people, even if that has never been previously done, it has to be done."[44] That Augustine calls attention to the possibility of conflict between God's law and natural, culturally sanctioned sexuality is significant, for it commits Augustine to the sovereignty of a theological perspective. Cultural custom or natural knowledge is regarded as penultimate or insufficient for inferring the meaning of sexual difference, and, in any case, the soul's relationship with God should always be primary in fashioning sexual practices.

Augustine believes that continence is also an appropriate way to live in a sexually differentiated world, for it is a way of life that unifies the loves of a person; a commitment to continence is an appeal to the Holy Spirit for help in resisting "the weight of cupidity pulling us downwards" and drawing "us upwards in a love of freedom from anxiety."[45] As such, as an exercise in love and the spiritual life, it is, on Augustine's terms, not an activity of the sexually differentiated aspects of the person but an attempt to prioritize a certain way of life in sexually differentiated circumstances. Augustine explains that continence is so difficult that it truly cannot be accomplished through human power, but he adds that it can be granted through God's grace: "O charity, my God, set me on fire. You command continence; grant what you command, and command what you will."[46] God can penetrate and perform such interior reordering in a way the unaided human soul cannot: "Grant what you command. . . . I cannot easily be sure how far I am cleansed from that plague. I have great fear of my subconscious impulses which your eyes know but mine do not."[47] But we should pray and long for such grace-infused transformation, because its fruit, in turning from being lustful to being continent, is a new internal unity of our loves, a unity which might also be interpreted as a social unity of persons united around love for the same thing: "By continence we are collected together and brought to the unity from which we disintegrated into multiplicity."[48] Continence is a pathway for the sexually undifferentiated grace that refuses and retrains the chaos of a lusting, restless heart. Continence is Augustine's proposal for the most fruitful way of managing the tensions of sexual difference by appealing to a love that transcends these differences. Reproduction of children is a theologically permitted practice that brings some acceptable results from sexual difference, but since Augustine knows how difficult it is to be sexually active and confine one's self to procreative desires—if "the stormy waves of my youth would have finally broken on the shore of marriage . . . I could not have been wholly content to confine sexual union to acts intended to procreate children"[49]—and that gives him a motive for preferring continence.

## *De bono conjugali* and *De sancta virginitate*

Shortly after writing *Confessionum*, in 401, Augustine wrote two works back to back that elaborate his practical proposals for marriage and continence.[50] Much of his language about virginity in *Virginit.* appears aimed at women, and one might think that in this rhetoric lies an implicit theory of sexual difference. For instance, virgins, who are free from begetting "the sons of men," are enjoined to look on Christ as their lover.[51] Such talk might seem to be advising that women should practice continence in a way distinctive to their sex. Similarly, examples of virginal role models are more likely to be female biblical characters (Mary, Susannah) than male.[52] Sociologically and historically, it is also possible that virginity in Augustine's era held more unique promise for women—for instance, as a means of escaping arranged marriages at a young age and achieving greater social independence.[53] But this feminine-specific rhetoric and background does not appear to shape Augustine's overt argument and professed theory. He never goes so far as to describe virginity as a distinctly female occupation, or to describe female virginity in contrast with male virginity. Not only has he already offered himself as a continent subject in *Confessionum*, but in *Virginit.* there are frequent appeals to "saintly boys and girls," "males and females, unmarried men and women," and "many men and many women."[54] We can conclude, then, that despite a rhetorical bias in favor of female virginity, in purely logical terms, Augustine's proposals for the practice of virginity do not appear to seek or to find significance in sexual difference. Yet *Virginit.* never argues that one should become a virgin because sexual difference is bad. Augustine never suggests, as some of his predecessors do, that sexual difference is not part of God's good creation and is something we should aspire to flee.

In *Bon. conj.*, however, we find some explicit treatment of sexual difference, although Augustine is still tentative, deferring conclusions:

> It is not necessary at this time to search out and to deliver a definitive judgement on how the offspring of the first human beings could have come into existence if they had not sinned. It was only then that their bodies by sinning deserved to undergo the fate of death, and sexual intercourse can take place only between mortal bodies. There have been several different theories on the matter, and if we had to investigate which of them most closely accords with the truth of the divine scriptures, it would involve lengthy discussion.[55]

The other theories he has in mind include procreation through nonsexual means, that the injunction to fill the earth was entirely metaphorical or mystical, or that the bodies of the first humans were indeed mortal and sexually procreating but obtained immortality and transcended sexuality in this life through virtuous living.[56] Among these many options, Augustine is obviously not excluding the possibility that reproductive sexual intercourse as the telos of sexual difference is a postlapsarian phenomenon, but neither can he be seen to prefer that interpretation, as he might have done in earlier works.

Instead of pursuing such speculation, in *Bon. conj.* Augustine tries to explain how "in our present situation of birth and death, which we experience and in which we were created, marriage between male and female is something good."[57] Augustine's famous three goods of marriage—"offspring, fidelity, sacrament"—are enumerated here for the first time.[58] However, *Bon. conj.* also mentions other goods of marriage, which are not included in his future works. In the opening paragraph of *Bon. conj.*, Augustine claims that human beings are naturally social, with "a capacity for friendship," and that the first link in human society is "that between husband and wife." The fact that Eve was created from Adam's flesh, and that they were not created therefore as entirely separate individuals, is meant, according to Augustine, to signal "the strength of their union." The next "link in the chain is children, the sole worthy outcome not of the union between male and female, but of sexual intercourse."[59] In other words, in this sentence and in this paragraph, we see a distinction being made between reproductive coitus and the union between male and female spouses. They are two distinct links in a chain of sociality: "The explanation of why marriage is a good lies, I think, not merely in the procreation of children, but also in the natural compact between the sexes. . . . Even without such sexual association [i.e., that which produces children], there could exist a true union of friendship between the two sexes, with the one governing and the other obeying."[60] The sense of a hierarchy has been retained from *Gen. Man.*, but now it can be more clearly linked with actual, lived, bodily life. Augustine says that the natural compact between the sexes is exemplified in elderly married couples, past the age of reproduction, who nevertheless remain married: "In a good marriage between elderly partners, though the youthful passion between male and female has withered, the ordered love between husband and wife remains strong."[61] Thus the distinct fruits of sexual difference include the governing hierarchy of an ordered marriage, the youthful passion between the sexes, the love between spouses, the act of procreation, and the protological bond of friendship between Adam and Eve. Marriage is necessary for all of these relationships between the sexes, even when procreation and coitus are not occurring, which suggests that sexual difference has significance beyond procreative intercourse.

Indeed, sexual activity, even for procreating children, appears to Augustine as a potential threat to the compact between the sexes. The possibility of intercourse creates the temptation to go beyond what is necessary for procreation, and any activity that is "no longer subject to reason, but lust," is a threat to marriage.[62] Such intercourse is an example, for Augustine, of a lack of self-control and the antithesis of where marriage should lead. To possess a spouse in the unfreedom of self-satisfying desire is the very opposite of the logic that creates marriage in the first place, a logic that is oriented to God's purposes. By contrast, when a couple agree together to abstain from sexual intercourse, then "the chastity of souls truly united continues the purer . . . and the safer."[63] Such abstinent marriages are, or so it seems Augustine believes, more likely to be unified marriages. For him, nonprocreative sexual intercourse promotes virtuous relations between the sexes only insofar as submitting to a spouse's request for intercourse reckons the submitting spouse to be honorable;[64] to consent to a spouse's lust and to keep sexual activity within marriage is to "shoulder each other's weaknesses."[65] The shouldering of the weakness, or perhaps acknowledging that one is not sovereign over one's own body, builds up the marriage and honors the compact between the sexes—not the coitus itself. The meaning of sexual difference is partly contained in this opportunity for self-sacrifice and mutual submission.

Finally, in *Bon. conj.* and *Virginit.* the significance of sexual difference can be seen to change according to developments in salvation history.[66] Once upon a time, "in the early days of the human race it was the duty of the saints to exploit the good of marriage to multiply the people of God, so that through them the Prince and Saviour of all peoples would be predicted in prophecy and then born."[67] In those days, then, sexual difference could be assimilated into a vocation to participate in divine providence for the social life of Israel. Ancient men and women were summoned to procreative marriages in order to create a people for God and a race from which Christ would come. But after Christ, once that child has been born, the meaning of sexual difference changes. As procreation loses its divine necessity, the significance of sexual difference changes too: "The interval which separates our eras brings such discretion to act rightly or otherwise that nowadays the man who does not take even one wife acts for the better unless he cannot control himself."[68] Nowadays, intercourse in marriage has become something secular. Rather than assisting with the divine plan, "intercourse in marriage . . . when undertaken to beget children" either "carries no blame" or is the opportunity to shoulder the partner's weakness.[69] In this logic, Christ is the pivot point for interpreting all history, including the history of sexual difference. Before Christ, sexual difference had a role in God's work that, after Christ, it appears not to have any longer. Augustine will never lose this sense that, *post Christum natum*, marriage has changed relative to the divinely ordained role it once had.

## *De Genesi ad litteram*

Some scholars believe that when Augustine wrote *Bon. conj.*, he deferred speculation about protological sexuality because in 401 he was already beginning *Gen. litt.* and knew the latter work would be his protology.[70] Probably *Gen. litt.* was not completed until as late as 416, although the first nine books were likely completed by 410.[71] Given this history of composition, begun with *Bon. conj.*'s relatively unformed views as a point of departure, it is not surprising that a reader can sometimes detect subtle shifts of opinion even within *Gen. litt.* But as a generalization, *Gen. litt.* offers a view of sexual difference that is more focused on procreation as the purpose of sexual difference than *Bon. conj.* Perhaps that is to be expected in a commentary where Augustine repeatedly insists he wants to read Genesis historically and literally, and not figuratively or metaphorically.[72] Certainly as Augustine grew more confident with historical or literal exegesis, the reproductive elements of the protological sexually differentiated relationship came to the fore.

In *Gen. litt.*, we find Augustine speculating directly about God's motives for creating sexual difference prior to the fall:

> If the question is asked, though, for what purpose it was necessary for this help [Eve] to be made, no more likely answer suggests itself than that it was for the sake of procreating children. . . . This reason for the setting up and joining together of male and female and this blessing did not fall away after the man's sin and punishment. [73]

Here the claim is that sexual difference was created *not* for the sake of the fellowship between the sexes, which was clearly at least considered in *Bon. conj.*, but instead was created for the sake of reproduction. Sexual differentiation is likened to soil: "For what other reason was a helper like him sought in the female sex, than that a wife by her very nature should assist him, like fertile soil, in sowing and planting out the human race?"[74] As Augustine goes on to say:

> So then, when you ask what help that sex was made to provide the man with, the only thing that occurs to me after carefully considering everything to the best of my ability is that it was for the sake of having children, so that the earth might be filled from their stock; and a stock not engendered, what is more, in the way human beings are engendered nowadays, when the law of sin is

in their members fighting back against the law of the mind, even when by God's grace they virtuously overcome it.[75]

In other words, sexually differentiated and procreating humanity has its origins prior to the fall, but with differences to today. The difference between procreation before and after the fall is that before sin the two sexes could be "wedded with honor,"[76] without lust, whereas today's coitus is marred by a fight between the fleshly members and the mind:

> Why should we not suppose that . . . those two human beings were able to control and command their genital organs for the procreation of children in the same way as their other limbs, which the soul moves for all kinds of action without any trouble or any sort of prurient itch for pleasure?[77]

But this difference derives from changes in the way the will relates to the body; the body's sexual anatomy was the same before the fall, but the will's relation to it has changed. Augustine has therefore repudiated a view that, once upon a time, he clearly took seriously. In *Gen. Man.*, he entertains the possibility that Adam and Eve would not have reproduced biologically without a fall. He had been agnostic on this point in *Bon. conj.* and had treated the point ambiguously in *Confessionum*. But now the matter appears settled. In terms of the gross anatomy of the organs that enabled the two sexes to procreate, Augustine believes there was no difference between before and after the fall.

Augustine considers the issue of nonprocreative companionship between the sexes in *Gen. litt.*, but only in order to minimize it:

> Or if it was not for help in producing children that a wife was made for the man, then what other help was she made for? If it was to till the earth together with him, there was as yet no hard toil to need such assistance; and if there had been the need, a male would have been a better help. The same can be said about companionship, should he grow tired of solitude. How much more agreeably, after all, for conviviality and conversation would two male friends live together on equal terms than man and wife. . . . For these reasons I cannot work out what help a wife could have been made to provide the man with, if you take away the purpose of childbearing.[78]

Thus *Bon. conj.*'s loosely proposed "fourth good" of marriage, that of a natural companionship between the sexes, has been eclipsed. The formal three goods of marriage appear again in *Gen. litt.*, and indeed with more succinct definition than they had earlier. But these definitions, beyond procreation, are largely negative: fidelity means "neither partner should sleep with another person," and sacrament means that "the union should not be broken up, and that . . . neither should marry another even for the sake of having children."[79] Perhaps some fellowship between spouses is implicit, as their bond cannot be broken for the sake of having children. Augustine does say Adam followed Eve into sin on account "of a kind of loving concern for their mutual friendship."[80] But still, this fellowship is at best secondary for both Augustine's protological rationale for sexual difference and the goods of marriage. Unlike even the earlier *Gen. Man.*, Augustine does not appear to explore anymore how the interplay or addition of femininity to masculinity issues in a noteworthy or significant spiritual fertility; the allegorical or symbolic aspects of sexual difference have also receded. Sexual difference in *Gen. litt.* is entirely concrete. Typical for *Gen. litt.* are declarations such as "Man can only have been made male and female with respect to the body" and "The difference of sex between male and female can only be verified in bodies."[81] Sexual difference has no spiritual or intellectual significance between humans. Augustine continues to allow its symbolic significance for the internal life of a single individual—that is, the proposal we saw in earlier works, that each sex represents the "directing" and "conforming" relationship between intellect and act—but he never owns this idea as his own, preferring now to mention it with some distance, as an aside, as something put forward by "some people" or "anyone" who might "suggest" such an additional meaning.[82] He allows that the way in which Eve was created from Adam's rib might "signify something" that will become apparent in the future, but he postpones investigation, preferring to view Genesis "not as prefiguring things to come" but "of things that actually happened."[83] Now Augustine emphasizes that sexual difference pertains to the physical, visible body, and that it has been so from the beginning.[84]

There is, however, at least one significant continuity between the earlier *Bon. conj.* and the later *Gen. litt.* that is worth noting. In the later work, Augustine still believes that while the world once needed to be peopled, so that "in the resurrection of the saints" there could be multitudes to join the "countless millions" of angels in the heavenly city,[85] the requisite population of heaven has now been reached:

It is true that faithful and religious virginity now earns the great reward of being greatly honored by God . . . in this present *time to refrain from embracing* [Eccl 3:5], when the abundant supply of people from all nations is amply sufficient for filling up the number of saints.[86]

Marriage, as in *Bon. conj.*, is no longer mandatory. Procreation is still a good with its roots in prelapsarian creation, but its goodness is relativized by the ripeness of the population for heaven. Procreation, the chief significance of sexual difference in *Gen. litt.*, explicitly takes its changing significance relative to theological history. This theme is more thoroughly explored in *De civitate Dei*.

## *De Trinitate*

Begun around the year 400, Augustine did not complete and publicly circulate *De Trinitate* until 419.[87] This work is profoundly significant for some questions about theological anthropology, such as the nature of the *imago Dei* and the philosophy of mind and body, but it directly entertains the question of sexual difference only very briefly. Augustine is concerned generally in *Trin.* to explain how it is in "the rational mind where the knowledge of God can reside." This rational mind is, for Augustine, the *imago Dei*: "Man was made in the image of God, not according to the form of the body, but according to the rational mind."[88] As we have seen from earlier works, this intellectual aspect of humanity is not, for Augustine, sexually differentiated. Augustine reaffirms his spiritual interpretation of Galatians 3:28, saying that women cannot be excluded from Christian fellowship as they are "co-heirs of grace," which knows not the distinction of sex.[89] So Augustine appears firmly committed in *Trin.* to an interior, rational, spiritual lack of sexual difference between persons; human persons are homogeneous at this level.

But if that is so, Augustine feels obliged to explain the apparent tension between 1 Corinthians 11:7, which, in his reading, suggests that man is the image of God while woman is merely the "glory" of the man, and Genesis 1:27–28, where it says God created both sexes in the image of God.[90] Augustine puts the question bluntly: "Have the believing women, therefore, lost their bodily sex?"[91] Do women, when taking up heirship and grace with men, somehow become men? Augustine's answer is that women remain entirely distinct in their bodily sex from men, even in ecclesial life, because, as Augustine reaffirms, the image of God pertains to "the spirit of [a human person's] mind," where "there is no sex."[92] But there is another aspect to a person's mind, the lower aspect, to which the spiritual and rational mind delegates more temporal concerns. This aspect is subordinate and symbolized by woman. Augustine is making recourse to a figurative interpretation of sexual difference we first saw in *Gen. Man.* "Therefore in their [male and female's] minds a common nature is recognized; but in their bodies the division of this one mind itself is symbolized."[93] Thus Genesis 1 is taken to be an affirmation that the two sexes exist in the created order and have a common *imago Dei*; Galatians 3 is taken as an affirmation that the two sexes are not distinct in what they are given in grace; and 1 Corinthians 11 is understood as referring to those symbolic aspects of sexual difference that have to do with the internal dynamics of an individual's mind. Augustine summarizes, with reference to 1 Corinthians 11:

> But because she differs from the man by her bodily sex, that part of the reason which is turned aside to regulate temporal things could be properly symbolized by her corporeal veil; thus the image of God does not remain except in that part of the mind of man in which it clings to the contemplation and consideration of the eternal reasons, which, as is evident, not only men but also women possess.[94]

Despite the two sexes having common heirship to God's promises, their visible, sexual differences still retain significance. Furthermore, neither spiritual homogeneity nor physical differences between the sexes render allegorical differences obsolete. These different aspects of sexual difference can interact in complex ways. For instance, on Augustine's terms, if a woman wears a veil in order to symbolize the submission of action to reason, then sexually differentiated social practices, such as veiling, make visible theological truths that would otherwise be invisible. Herein might lie theological significance for sexual difference in addition to marriage, but Augustine does not elaborate this point or offer further examples.

## De civitate Dei

Augustine began *De civitate Dei* in 413 and completed it in 426.[95] The fourteenth book, which may have been written around 418,[96] weaves sexual difference particularly clearly into the larger theological narrative. This larger narrative attempts to explain the relationship between Creator and human creature, as well as internal psychological or spiritual dynamics within the human individual. Sexual difference is essential within this larger narrative as an enduring and significant feature of human personhood and as an instrument in God's plans for salvation history. But to understand this role, one must begin with the larger narrative itself.

The premise of *Civ.* is that there are two cities in the world: "In the one city, love of God has been given pride of place, and, in the other, love of self."[97] Everything that matters for the life of these two cities and their citizens flows from the respective love on which each city is founded. For Augustine, what we love or desire determines the city to which each of us belongs and the ends for which we act. To be ultimately happy and flourish, it matters that we should seek our citizenship in the heavenly city; put another way, it matters vitally for Augustine that we eschew self-love and cultivate love of God:

> When a man lives according to truth, then, he lives not according to self, but according to God. . . . It is because man was created righteous, to live according to His Maker and not according to himself, doing his Maker's will and not his own; falsehood consists in not living in the way for which he was created. Man does indeed wish to be happy; but he lives in such a way that it is not possible for him to be so.[98]

To love ourselves, or our own purposes and the appetites that are only accountable to human self-definition, is, for Augustine, the great human undoing: "For it is a perverse kind of elevation indeed to forsake the foundation upon which the mind should rest, and to become and remain, as it were, one's own foundation." Protologically, it was precisely this perverse and false love that resulted in "the transgression of eating the forbidden fruit" in the garden. "The first evil act of the will, since it preceded all other evil acts in man, consisted rather in its falling away from the work of God to its own works. . . . And those works of the will were evil because they were according to itself, and not according to God."[99] The fall was a substitution of autonomy for theonomy, an act of loyalty to the human self or earthly city at the expense of obedience to God and citizenship in the heavenly city.

Why would anyone live so perversely? Augustine answers that it is due to a sickness of soul, a disordered self-regard he names as pride: "For what is pride but an appetite for a perverse kind of elevation?"[100] But as we saw more briefly in *Gen. litt.*, if the origin of sin is firmly in the soul's propensity for pride and nowhere else, then a story can be told in which the body as created and hence sexual difference are theoretically immunized from suspicion. Augustine knows he is giving a different protology of sin than other theologians have given: "Now someone may say that the flesh is the cause of moral evils of every kind, because it is thanks to the influence of the flesh that the soul lives as it does."[101] "Someone" may say that having a body necessarily burdens a human being, but Augustine will not allow this suspicion of the flesh, and he rebuts the claim that the body receives the blame for sin: "The cause of our being pressed down is not the nature and substance of the body, but its corruption; and, knowing this, we do not wish to be divested of the body, but to be clothed with its immortality."[102] Thus, according to Augustine, we should not wish to be free of having flesh; rather, we should want our flesh to live according to a proper love for God. This is because our flesh, our bodies, are created by God for good purposes, and it is only our pride that gives us the will or appetite to use our bodies badly. It is our pride, our sickness of soul, that makes the body seem like a temptation or a burden, and not the body itself.

With this perspective on human sin—putting it firmly in the soul's pride or self-love rather than in the corporeal conditions of creaturehood—Augustine has prepared the way for a theological affirmation of sexual difference based on an affirmation or love for God's plans for creation. Augustine writes, "If no one had sinned there would have come into being a number of saints sufficient to fill that most blessed City: as large a number as is now being assembled, through God's grace, from the multitude of sinners, so long as the children of this world beget and are begotten."[103] In other words, from the beginning, from before sin, God had in mind a society of rightly ordered love, a heavenly city, and this city needed to be populated. To produce this city, the two protological humans needed to reproduce. As Augustine goes on to say in a subsequent book of *Civ.*, "The coupling of male and female is the seedbed, as it were, of a city."[104] Male and female would have therefore been necessary from the beginning. Sexual difference was always supposed to be a cornerstone of human social life. Being in the flesh in this way is no curse, but a divine blessing: "The procreation of children pertains to the glory of marriage, not to the punishment of sin."[105] Sexual difference is one way in which human creatures participate in divine providence.

This dynamism, this sense that male and female have a calling in God's purposes, a calling that requires their bodies to physically procreate, enables Augustine to make anthropological affirmations that contradict some of the positions we have seen in his own earlier works and in earlier theologians. Most notably, following from *Gen. litt.*, there is no need in *Civ.* to allegorize Eden in order to avoid exegetical difficulty. For the logic of Augustine's providential view of procreation to hold, Eden, and the man and woman in it, must mean that human origins are corporeal: "It is certain, then, that in the beginning, male and female were constituted just as we see and know that two human beings of different sex are now."[106] By implication, this belief repudiates the view, seen in *Gen. Man.*, that the "tunics of skin" in Genesis 3:7 might be bodies, the enfleshment of a hitherto disembodied soul. Indeed, as we would now expect, Augustine treats this verse as if the "aprons" or "loin-cloths" were merely clothes to cover actual, visible, male and female flesh.[107] Furthermore, he repudiates what has been a frequent refrain in earlier works and what he even hinted at as recently as *Trin.*: "We cannot, however, interpret 'male' and 'female' as symbolizing something else in each individual man: for example, the distinction between the ruling element and the ruled."[108] *Civ.*'s thesis requires tangible, visible, fleshly masculinity and femininity as part of human anthropology and God's history, and to strengthen that position, Augustine appears eager to repudiate alternatives.

However, although sin originates in the prideful soul rather than the sexual body, that does not mean that sin and sexual difference have no relationship with each other. Certainly human sin cannot change God's purposes, in which sexual difference is included; sin cannot infect sexual difference to derail God's intentions: "Man could not disturb the divine purpose by his sin: could not, that is, compel God to change what He had decreed."[109] But there is a further aspect to sexual difference in *Civ.*, for human pride means sexual difference is no longer innocent on the human side. "The first man, then, lived according to God in a Paradise both corporeal and spiritual." But the fallen man lives in the earthly city, which "is made up of men who live according to the flesh," as if mortal flesh were the highest good. There is no peace in this city, riven and divided against the real good. The retribution for disobedience is "disobedience itself." Man's pride and autonomy, man's hunger to please himself, has brought him what he desired: to be "handed over to himself" by God and to his own authority.[110] But if, as we have seen, Augustine believes that creaturely self-sufficiency is the primal lie, then no true freedom could be possible that is contingent on a lie; no true freedom of action is possible in a context whose first premise is disobedience. In the fall, disobedience is loosed upon the world. Man, in trying to be his own master, can no longer be any sort of master: "For who can count the many things that a man wishes to do but cannot?"[111]

In this context of sin, Augustine finds the sexually differentiated organs a particularly apt illustration of this disordered existential situation. He is not invoking a male-female allegory, claiming that male represents something in relation to a female something else. Rather, he is saying that the sex organs are one place where the effects of sin can be seen. Elaborating upon ideas in *Gen. litt.*, before sin Augustine says that man and woman could have used their sex organs for coitus under the governance of an ordered love and a rational will; as all their lives were ordered to the love of God, their sexuality would be no different. It would be used for its natural, created purposes of populating the heavenly city and thus undergirding the social life of the saints. In this context, when the time came to procreate, Adam and Eve could have employed their genitals with the same freedom of will with which we now move our other limbs:

> We move our hands and feet to perform their tasks when we so will, without any conflict and with all the ease that we observe in ourselves and others. . . . Why, then, with respect to the procreation of children, should we not believe that the sexual organs could have been as obedient to the will of mankind as the other members are?[112]

Sexuality could have been—should have been and would have been—an aspect of human life lived in freedom, "in tranquillity of mind" and "without any corruption of her [Eve's] body's integrity."[113] But now, postfall and with the root of disobedience in our will, sex is different. Now the sexual organs are efficacious only in conditions of lust or passion in which our willful freedom is overcome by passion: "But the sexual organs have somehow fallen so completely under the sway of lust that they have no power of movement at all if this passion is absent, and unless it has either arisen of its own accord or been aroused by another."[114] If once sex organs could have moved "at the command of his [Adam's] will," now, for both men and women alike,

> sometimes the urge arises unwanted; sometimes, on the other hand, it forsakes the eager lover, and desires grow cold in the body even while burning in the mind. Thus strangely, then, does lust refuse to serve not only the desire to beget, but even the lust for lewd enjoyment.[115]

The notion of a divided will, the notion of a person divided against himself or herself, has been a feature of Augustine's anthropology ever since, at least, *Confessionum*, when Augustine speculated about his own mixed and confused motives as an adolescent stealing pears for no real reason.[116] But this theme comes to the forefront in *Civ.*, for the psychological claim is combined with an argument about the place of sex within the social order of corporate humanity. All of human social life is plagued by the chaos of pride, but sexual life is a particularly apt example of chaos at work.

However, chaos and sin are not the last word for human social life, the human individual, or sexual difference. All are bound together in creation, and so all will be redeemed. If nothing "pertains more closely to a body than its sex," if bodies are "not an ornament" or a garment but "belong to the very nature of man," if spiritual flesh is not spiritual because it is incorporeal but because it serves the spirit, then sexual difference cannot be left behind in heaven. "He, then, who instituted two sexes will restore them both."[117] Augustine is not claiming that our restored, eschatological bodies will be the same as mortal bodies—indeed, he believes the final body will be "better then than it was here even when in perfect health; it will also be better than those bodies which the first human beings had before they sinned."[118] But because sexually differentiated embodiedness is so essential to human identity, Augustine is led to suggest a radically transformed eschatological body. Perhaps this suggestion is a rhetorical by-product of Augustine's main concern, which is to argue for the good-ness of the created body; certainly his comments on this point have the quality of being asides. But nevertheless, these asides open up a certain logic. "The sex of a woman," he writes, "is not a vice, but nature," so why should it be shed in heaven?[119] Augustine knows that eschatological sex-ual difference will not be ordered to marriage and procreation, for he takes seriously Christ's claim in Luke 20 that in heaven there is no mar-riage: "There will be no generation there, when regeneration has led us thither."[120] But if sexual difference had one significance at creation, which was relativized *post Christum natum*, then there is no reason why it can-not adapt for heaven. In heaven,

> they [the sexual parts of a woman, but also of a man] will then be exempt from sexual intercourse and childbearing, but the female parts will nonetheless remain in being, accommodated not to the old uses, but to a new beauty, which, so far from inciting lust, which no longer exists, will move us to praise the wisdom and clemency of God.[121]

Once upon a time in salvation history, sexual difference existed only for procreation. Once upon a time in the works of Augustine, the signifi-cance of sexual difference ended there. But Augustine's logic and rhetoric now include sexual difference among that which will be redeemed, mak-ing it thinkable to include it in the worship of heaven and giving sexual difference an inexhaustible telos.

### *De bono viduitatis, De continentia,* and *De incompetentibus nuptiis*

Written between 414 and 420,[122] these works are concerned with how postlapsarian sexuality can be socialized or lived according to the vision and love of the heavenly city. They do not elaborate a theological anthropology as does *Civ.* or *Gen. litt.*; rather, they are examinations of and exhortations toward the sort of practical living that is a consequence of Augustine's theological anthropology, which has now been more or less settled. However, in these explorations of Christian practices, a few more implications regarding sexual difference become apparent.

*Vid.* is written to a woman and counsels her on widowhood and her daughter's professed virginity. As such, it refers to virgins with mostly feminine pronouns and names. However, as with *Virginit.*, this audience does not mean Augustine believed continence was the preserve of women. *Incomp. nupt.* is written to a man, and its rhetoric assumes a masculine perspective. Both works reflect on the conditions necessary to maintain chastity in either marriage, widowhood, or virginity in ways that apply to both sexes, even when the rhetoric in one particular instance might seem to be sexually specific. *Incomp. nupt.* in particular goes out of its way to say, "Bear in mind that I am saying these things as applying to both sexes,"[123] lest the reader not realize that the same standards and practices of sexual purity apply to both men and women. Augustine observes that eunuchs for the sake of the kingdom of heaven exist among "both sexes." He argues that what constitutes adultery is "the same for men and women," and gives as his reason what Paul says in 1 Corinthians 7:4: "The wife does not have authority over her own body, but her husband does. . . . And likewise the husband does not have authority over his own body, but his wife does."[124] Thus, for Augustine, the logic of marriage joins a man and woman together in a system of mutual submission. Like the practice of virginity, the virtues proper to this rationale are not differentiated by sex. The call to follow Christ in purity of heart and love for God knows no distinction of sex, for it works in the soul, where there is no sexual difference. Yet this undifferentiated call to virtue does not render sexual difference obsolete. For the later Augustine of this period, spiritual qualities cannot exist in abstraction from creaturely flesh. The common, undifferentiated and internal submission of will is manifested in the medium of differentiated flesh. As husband and wife, they are in roles that build upon sexual difference, even as they are enacting a charity that is not differentiated. "He [the Apostle Paul] said that the bodies of the faithful are both members of Christ and also the temple of the Holy Spirit, and unquestionably this refers to the faithful of both sexes."[125] The Spirit that unites the sexes is not itself differentiated. There is no spirit for men and another spirit for women; neither is there segregation in the body of Christ. Yet the two sexes remain differentiated and distinct as two sexes, for Augustine (and Paul) never speak as if there were only one sex.

Evidently Augustine knew of men who would object to this equality in Christ and the Spirit, men who believed that they should have greater liberty than women in matters such as adultery, and he rebukes them in the male-oriented *Incomp. nupt.*[126] Augustine explains that if male leadership means anything, it undermines male license. About Ephesians 5:23, where man is given a sort of headship over the woman, Augustine says the conclusion must be that unfaithful men "ought to have been punished more severely, since it is their role to surpass women in virtue and guide them by example."[127] Augustine believed that this kind of sexual differentiation—in which men are given leadership responsibility along with an exhortation toward the imitation of Christ, in which leadership is really servantship—is a practice unique to the heavenly city. He says that in "the earthly city," in regard to issues of chastity, "the laws of the courts do not seem to place the same restrictions on men as they do on women." But "subject to the laws of . . . Christ" the situation is otherwise, and "the same rule of chastity" applies to both "husband and wife." Augustine has particularly pointed comments for "men, who consider themselves to be superior to women in not having to maintain the same standards of chastity. They should in fact have higher standards, so that women may follow their lead."[128] In other words, men and women are equal, but there are areas of inequality, such as when men are to lead by being under more pressure to be chaste.

That the hierarchy between men and women is a hierarchy about care and responsibility, always modified by a sense of mutuality, is confirmed by *Contin.*'s exegesis of Ephesians 5, where "superior and inferior, they are all good."[129] Here again, there is for Augustine a "beauty and orderliness of one being superior and in charge and the other honourably subordinate,"[130] but to be on the leading side of this theological hierarchy is not an opportunity to exercise privilege. In ordinary, fallen life, it may indeed be that we experience only hierarchies that are exploitative and self-interested, but Augustine explains that this sort of hierarchy is not what he finds in Ephesians 5. For instance, we know in the postlapsarian world that the spirit often "has desires opposed to the flesh" and the flesh "with desires opposed to the spirit and rebellious does not look after either the interests of the spirit or its own interests."[131] Thus Augustine advises that the contemporary relationship between spirit and flesh, modeled so disastrously in the earthly city, cannot be our model. Rather, we should look to the model of Christ and the church, an analogous hierarchy where "both entities point to God being the maker of both of them."[132] In a series of rhetorical questions that conclude his exegesis of Ephesians 5, which are directed against Manichaens, Augustine affirms by implication that as Christ appeared in a real mortal body, all mortal bodies, including both the bodies of male and female, are the works of the same God, and that spirit and flesh are joined together as two good substances.[133] These christological, ecclesiastical, and anthropological affirmations interpret Ephesians 5 for him and enable him to read this sexually differentiated hierarchy as an opposition to the hierarchies of the earthly city. Proper hierarchy is only known through such theological premises, and through no appeal to experience, and only the theological hierarchies of prelapsarian spirit and flesh or the eternal relation of Christ to the church enable Augustine to explain the sort of sexually differentiated living he prefers. This sexual difference upends natural hierarchies and replaces them with hierarchies that press the "superior" to greater deeds of love.

## De nuptiis et concupiscentia ad Valerium comitem and Contra Julianum

The two books of *Nupt.* were written from 418 to 421, and the six books of *C. Jul.* were written shortly afterward. These two works are the most important in a series of anti-Pelagian treatises that occupied Augustine until his death in 430.[134] In this debate, the Pelagians alleged that Augustine's critique of sexual desire was evidence that he had not really abandoned his youthful Manichaen disdain toward marriage and the body. To disprove this charge, Augustine is as specific as possible in his critique of desire, to show how his objection is against the unfreedom associated with fallen desire and not against marriage or the human body. Thus in these works we can see Augustine repeating the history of sexual anthropology we have already seen in works such as *Civ.*—including how the two sexes were protologically intended to marry and procreate—but this time that story is told in such a way as to locate it even more clearly in relation to sexual desire.

Here the three goods of marriage are reiterated,[135] as are the protological foundations of bodily sexual difference.[136] Augustine reiterates that the sexual difference he is describing is not allegorical: "The difference of the sexes has to do with the organs of the parents."[137] Rival interpretations, such as the view that male and female in paradise might not have had fully animal bodies, or that these bodies were so spiritual that they might have subsisted only on wisdom rather than food, are again repudiated: "I agree with those who understand this statement [Gen 1:27–28] in terms of bodily and visible sexuality."[138] Augustine believes that these Edenic bodies needed to draw near to the opposite sex and beget children "with some motion of the body."[139] Sex in paradise would have been a matter of generating new human births by means of "the union of the two sexes . . . without shame,"[140] or, similarly, "even if no one had sinned, children could only be born through the union of the two sexes."[141] In one summary declaration, Augustine ties together the physical nature of sexual difference, the procreative purpose of sexual difference, the relationship between procreation and marriage, and the divine authorship and blessing of all these things: "The difference of the sexes has to do with the organs of the parents, and their union pertains to the conception of children, and fertility is part of the blessing of marriage. All of these come from God."[142]

The Pelagians, wanting to discredit Augustine with the Manichaen label, thought they could challenge Augustine on whether sexual difference was good, godly, and for the purpose of uniting in procreation, but Augustine has granted these things, and he would seem to have diffused their argument.[143] Yet Augustine wants to go on the offensive as well, and here he turns to the nature of sexual desire. Augustine argues that what is unfallen should be a matter of "freedom's choice" rather than "necessity."[144] Pauline verses—such as 1 Thessalonians 4:3–5, where each Christian should know "how to possess his own vessel in holiness and honour"—lead Augustine to believe that not only should the married not commit adultery or lust but that true sanctification means living freely and not living possessed "in the disease of carnal desire." Carnal concupiscence is termed a disease or a threat to freedom because it "resists the law of the mind."[145] To claim such is an attack on the Pelagians, for they had argued that this desire is good, that it can easily be kept under control, and that rational choice is adequate for governing one's erotic longings. To the contrary, Augustine's case is that concupiscence resists being ruled by anything but itself, for it "yearns to derive pleasure, whether from something forbidden or from something permitted. . . . What concupiscence itself does, namely, to set one ablaze with no concern about whether it is for something permitted or for something forbidden, is surely an evil."[146] Because it is oriented entirely toward its own satisfaction, such appetite is immoral; indifferent to all considerations save self-satisfaction, one cannot be free, and one cannot claim continuity with prelapsarian sexuality.

Concupiscence and unfreedom are of particular concern in the realm of sexuality because now procreation "cannot take place free from the heat of sexual desire. . . . It is only that passion which arouses, as if by its own command, the members which cannot be aroused by the will. . . . It shows that it is a servant which has to be moved, not by free choice, by some seductive stimulus."[147] Postlapsarian sexual procreation cannot occur, according to Augustine, without some sort of nonrational, affective, or appetite-inducing arousal associated with concupiscence. Thus the sexual act cannot occur without the human person at some point giving himself or herself over to a force that is inherently chaotic, inherently in tension with the rational or ordered will. Moreover, "no one is set free from this chain of slavery" except by grace.[148] It is this internal dissonance, this discord between appetite and will, that Augustine believes Paul was describing in Romans 7 and that leads him to conclude, "The disobedience of sexual desire is evil."[149] Pointedly, it is not sexual desire per se that concerns Augustine, but rather the disobedient or ungovernable aspects of desire as we now experience it. There might have been sexual desire before sin, Augustine admits, but he insists "it would not be as it is now, but would obey the least indication of the will." The penis, for example, would have been capable of arousal before sin, "but it was not then indecent so that it caused shame, because the command of the will aroused it, not the flesh with desires opposed to the spirit."[150] Women are no different, for they too could have experienced obedient desire in paradise even as they now experience disobedient desire. At the fall Eve "did not cover a visible arousal, but in those same members she experienced in a more hidden way something like what the man experienced."[151] The problems with sexual desire are not sexually differentiated. The point is rather that once upon a time, men and women lived in freedom, joining together sexually when their will disposed them to do so and not when their lusts compelled them to do so. But after their primal disobedience in the garden, men and women are no longer their own masters and can procreate only by entertaining an appetite that knows no master, "the disobedience which is the recompense for disobedience."[152]

This argument sheds light on sexual difference because as Augustine locates the flaw in sexuality in concupiscence, a postlapsarian phenomenon, he is locating the flaw in a place that is clearly segregated from sexual difference. As we saw in *Gen. litt.* and *Civ.*, sins, not male or female bodies, are attributable "to an evil source."[153] In Augustine's way of speaking, our desires are one thing, but our sexual identity is another and the two can be thought separately: "We ought . . . to want those desires not to exist, even if we cannot attain that goal in the body of this death."[154] Human maleness and femaleness are conceptually distinct from concupiscence. Our sexually differentiated organs have existence and beauty prior to their association with desire. The fact that certain bodily parts "are beautiful" and that they also "arouse desire or are aroused by desire" are two distinct matters, the first pertaining to creation, the second pertaining to sin.[155] Put more dramatically, Augustine says that even if human beings were dominated by the evil of sexual desire to the point that without the goodness of marriage they all had intercourse promiscuously and everywhere like dogs, the making of their bodies, of which God is the author, would not be deformed. . . . Even now in an adulterous union, which is certainly evil, the work of God in making the bodies is good.[156]

In sum, while the current exercise of sexual difference in the act of union is not known free of concupiscence, at the anthropological and theoretical level, to have a sex and to have desire are not necessarily the same thing. One is more profoundly human than the other.

Furthermore, these sorts of distinctions mean that the logic of marriage relies more fundamentally on sexual difference than it does on desire: "The union of male and female for the sake of having children is . . . the natural good of marriage. But one makes bad use of this good if one uses it like an animal so that one's intention is directed toward the pleasure of sexual desire, not toward the will to propagate."[157] Marriage, for Augustine, maintains its created purpose of bringing the procreative potential of sexual differentiation to fruition and is not altered by the presence or absence of desire. The absence of desire does not mean the absence of marriage; continent couples, such as Mary and Joseph, are still fully married.[158] And the presence of desire does not taint the fundamental purpose of marriage; the pursuit of sexual pleasure within marriage is pardoned because "the weakness of a lack of self-control is rescued" by the three goods of marriage. In either case, the teleology of sexual difference is firmly rooted in the procreation of children and not pleasure: "The procreation of many children, not the . . . arousal of their members" is the essence of married coupling. The seeds of each sex, which in Augustine's biology commingle to produce the child, are not produced by pleasure or for pleasure, and it is only contingently that they are "aroused and spilled forth with pleasure."[159] Marriage can exist without desire, but it cannot exist without sexual difference: "After all, who has ever imagined any marriage without the movement of bodies and without need of the sexes?"[160]

Augustine's emphasis on sexually differentiated procreation is not a form of biological naturalism. Augustine condemns rape, adultery, or visiting a prostitute, all of which are biologically procreative.[161] Employing sexual difference for its God-given purpose means socializing male and female with procreation as a central reference point; the natural, biological potential of sexual differentiation is the cornerstone of why sexual difference exists. But procreation is not sufficient, and other, nonbiological goods are necessary to socialize sexual difference. In this way, for Augustine, nature and theology are linked and interwoven. In this link we see how nature can be socialized and how theology relies upon the material creation.

## Summary

In this chapter, we have surveyed Augustine's work over a roughly forty-year period. We have seen an evolving set of arguments, concepts, and suggestive possibilities for the significance of sexual difference. As we have witnessed repeatedly, this mixture is the fruit of polemical encounters and intellectual asides, as well as deliberate reflection.

First, in *Gen. Man.* sexual difference has allegorical significance, revealing the hierarchical relationship between that which decides and that which obeys in any one individual. Perhaps mainly as a result of his anti-Manichaen polemical concerns, Augustine described a well-ordered hierarchy that could issue in a spiritual fertility, the birth of divine praise. Augustine is, from his very earliest treatises, impelled to move beyond a Manichaen disdain for creation, and this means, among other things, thinking in ways that allow some significance for sexual difference as an aspect of God's good creation.

Next, at midpoint in the forty-year span under consideration, a variety of ideas about sexual difference were still negotiable for Augustine. Augustine's agenda at this stage was not to produce a theory of sexual difference in its own right; rather, he was answering a variety of other pastoral, theological, and polemical concerns, and along the way, various theses carried implications for sexual difference. With this caution in mind, we have seen how in *Confessionum* or *Bon. conj.*, for instance, while the corporeal realm is more confidently investigated than it had been in the early Genesis commentaries, the protological status of sexual differentiation was still unresolved and may or may not have been corporeal. But clearly Augustine is proposing procreative marriage as a way of fulfilling divine providence, as a precondition for social life, both in terms of populating heaven and in terms of redeeming the individual's sexual desire. It is apparently procreative marriage that discloses whatever meaning Augustine was prepared to find in sexual difference. In *Gen. litt.*, the protological status of sexual difference is more settled, and sexual difference is said to have an unambiguously procreative telos from the beginning. But the eschatological destiny of sexual differences remains unsettled, and several works consistently emphasize that the most spiritual aspects of a person (reason, or the *imago Dei*) are not sexually differentiated. Meanwhile, the more spiritual vocation of continence seems to make no appeal to sexually differentiated aspects of personhood; on the other hand, continence in Augustine is not born of disdain for sexual difference but rather as a unity and focus of love for Christ.

Later works, from *Civ.* onward, resolve the eschatological fate of sexual difference for Augustine. Again, this resolution happens without making the topic a priority, but largely as a logical implication of other arguments. In these works, maleness or femaleness is an important part of a person that must be retained for the sake of continuity with mortal identity. Whatever meaning sexual difference has in salvation history, it shifts according to what God calls people to do at that stage. That means procreating prior to Christ for the sake of populating the kingdom, and either procreating after Christ (for the sake of honoring creation's teleology) or being celibate (as a way of unifying the loves and not seeking concupiscent pleasure). In a quiet way, which is never emphasized but which is nevertheless stated as an aside in *Civ.*, sexually differentiated bodies might have their part to play in heavenly worship. That a new, eschatological role would be found for sexual difference is, in a sense, the logical mirror image of Augustine's claim that the sexually differentiated organs are a unique illustration of pride and sin: if sexual difference bears the scars of disobedience, then we can also expect it to be healed in redemption. Never does sexual difference itself become a programmatic theme for any of these works, but, nevertheless, all of the points I am noting are either present in Augustine's asides or arising from his mature logic and anthropology from *Civ.* onward. By the end of his career, it is as if something of the spiritual fertility of male and female from *Gen. Man.* has, in a sense, been recovered, or at least that the wholly procreative emphasis of sexual difference in *Gen. litt.* has been modified.

What is at the fore of these later works, however, is a general anthropology clearly and robustly grounded in all three eras of salvation history: creation, the earthly pilgrimage, and eschatology. For in these later works we meet an anthropology that allows Augustine to make the distinction between sinful, prideful concupiscence as presently experienced, on the one hand, and sexual life theologically conceptualized, on the other hand. With this contrast firmly grasped, "we may learn to be cautious about supposing that we can take our own sexual experience as a guide to right order."[162] The works on marriage, concupiscence, continence, adultery, and widowhood that follow *Civ.* are the fruits of this mature sexual-theological anthropology. Augustine now has a theological model for sexuality that is distinct from the natural model followed in the earthly city, and this model leads Augustine to imagine corporeal sexual difference as an arena in which God works for redemption. The logic of marriage and thus of sexual difference is not dependent on the logic of concupiscence, and in fact, the former logic critiques and condemns the latter.

How does our study of Augustine orient us for the rest of this book? Oliver O'Donovan has written about sexual difference that "it is not possible to negotiate this fact about our common humanity; it can only be either welcomed or resented."[163] Prior to Augustine, it was evidently unclear which of these two alternatives was more genuinely Christian. But Augustine has supplied the rationale for much of the subsequent Christian tradition, implicitly and explicitly arguing and explaining why Christians should welcome sexual difference and seek forms of life that socialize it in theological ways. When we welcome sexual difference, Augustine has argued implicitly and explicitly that we are welcoming God's creation, that we are affirming the corporeality of our own creaturely identity, and that we are assuming a vocation to certain ways of relating and loving one another. As we saw in chapter 1, prior to Augustine, there was disagreement on all these points. Augustine's predecessors disputed the relationship between physical reality and creation, or the relationship between our bodies and our own ontological identity and eschatological fate, and how practical, daily life should be shaped accordingly. But after Augustine, as we shall see in subsequent chapters, a rough consensus emerged in Western Christendom on Augustinian lines. Not every detail and potential development was assimilated equally by all of his successors. But having understood Augustine, we are much better prepared to evaluate the theological adequacy of subsequent arguments.

## Notes

1. See Augustine, *On Genesis: A Refutation of the Manichees; Unfinished Literal Commentary on Genesis; The Literal Meaning of Genesis* (ed. John E. Rotelle; trans. Edmund Hill; The Works of Saint Augustine: A Translation for the 21st Century, vol. 1/13; Hyde Park, NY: New City, 2002), 13.

2. For instance, Augustine, *On Genesis: "Two Books on Genesis against the Manichees" and "On the Literal Interpretation of Genesis: An Unfinished Book"* (trans. Roland J. Teske; The Fathers of the Church: A New Translation, vol. 84; Washington, DC: Catholic University of America Press, 1991), 74, §1.17.27. Teske's introduction discusses this point.

3. *Gen. Man.*, 83, §2.12.17.

4. Ibid.

5. Ibid., 82, §2.11.15.

6. Ibid., 91, §2.18.28; 99, §2.27.40; 82, §2.11.15.

7. Ibid., 81, §2.11.15.

8. Ibid., 99, §2.27.40.

9. Ibid., 72, §2.2.3.

10. Ibid., 58, §1.19.30.

11. Ibid., 84, §2.13.19.

12. Ibid., 93, §2.21.32.

13. *Retractationes*, 37, §1.10.2, in Augustine, *On Genesis: A Refutation of the Manichees*.

14. Ibid., 105–6.

15. Ibid., 117, *Gen. imp.*, §3.7.

16. Ibid., 149, §16.60.

17. Ibid.

18. Augustine, *Augustine's Commentary on the Galatians: Introduction, Text, Translation, and Notes* (trans. Eric Plumer; Oxford: Oxford University Press, 2003), 3–4.

19. Ibid., 175, *Exp. Gal.*, §28.

20. Ibid.

21. Ibid.

22. Ibid.

23. Gerald Bonner, "Augustine's Attitude on Women and *Amicitia*," in *Festgabe für Luc Verheijen, Osa zu seinem 70. Geburtstag* (ed. Cornelius Mayer and Karl Heinz Chelius; Würzberg: Augustinus-Verlag, 1987), 262–63.

24. Augustine, *Confessions* (trans. Henry Chadwick; Oxford: Oxford University Press, 1998), xi–xiii.

25. Ibid., 302, §13.32.47.

26. Ibid., 303, §13.34.49.

27. Ibid., 293, §13.23.33.

28. Ibid.

29. Ibid., 41, §3.6.10.

30. Ibid., 255, §13.15.19.

31. Ibid., 289, §13.20.28.

32. Ibid., 106, §6.11.20.

33. Ibid., 106, §6.11.20; 107, §6.12.22.

34. Ibid., 107, §6.12.22.

35. Ibid.

36. Ibid., 24, §2.2.2.

37. Ibid.

38. Ibid., 27, §2.3.6.

39. Ibid., 29, §2.5.10; 30, §2.5.10; 31, §2.6.13.

40. Ibid., 141, §8.5.12.

41. Ibid., 35, §3.1.1.

42. Ibid., 46, §3.7.15.

43. Ibid., 25, §2.2.3.

44. Ibid., 46, §3.7.15.

45. Ibid., 277, §13.7.8.

46. Ibid., 202, §10.29.40.

47. Ibid., 214–15, §10.37.60.

48. Ibid., 202, §10.29.40.

49. Ibid., 25, §2.2.2.

50. Augustine, *De bono conjugali and De sancta virginitate* (trans. P. G. Walsh; Oxford: Clarendon, 2001), ix.

51. Ibid., 145, *Virginit.*, §55.

52. Ibid., 67–75, §2–7; 89, §20.

53. Ibid., xiii, xiv.

54. Ibid., 117, *Virginit.*, §36; 101, §27; 133, §46.

55. Ibid., 3, *Bon. conj.*, §2.

56. Ibid., 3–5, §2.

57. Ibid., 7, §3.

58. Ibid., 59, §32.

59. Ibid., 3, §1.

60. Ibid., 7, §3; 3, §1.

61. Ibid., 7, §3.

62. Ibid., 25, §11.

63. Ibid., 7, *Bon. conj.*, §3.

64. See, e.g., ibid., 13, §5.

65. Ibid., 15, §6.

66. See ibid., 75, *Virginit.*, §9. The idea that Augustine's sexual ethics are most coherently understood in relation to salvation history is famously argued by Paul Ramsey, "Human Sexuality in the History of Redemption," *Journal of Religious Ethics* 16 (1988): 56–88.

67. Augustine, *Bon. conj.* 23, §9.

68. Ibid., 35, §17.

69. Ibid., 15, §6.

70. See ibid., 2–3n4.

71. Augustine, *On Genesis: A Refutation of the Manichees*, 164.

72. See ibid., 157–62, for an explanation and examples of what he meant by "literal."

73. Ibid., 378, *Gen. litt.*, §9.3.5.

74. Ibid., 384, §9.9.15.

75. Ibid., 386, §9.11.19.

76. Ibid., 378, §9.3.6.

77. Ibid., 385, §9.10.18.

78. Ibid., 380, §9.5.9.

79. Ibid., 382, §9.7.12.

80. Ibid., 463, §9.42.59.

81. Ibid., 237, §3.22.34.; 307, §6.7.12.

82. Ibid., 237, §3.22.34.; 307, §6.7.12.

83. Ibid., 389, §9.13.23; §9.14.24.

84. Ibid., 307, §6.7.12, says that what was created on the sixth day is "realized visibly."

85. Ibid., 384, §9.9.15.

86. Ibid., 382 §9.7.12.

87. See Serge Lancel, *Saint Augustine* (trans. Antonia Nevill; London: SCM Press, 2002), 368.

88. Augustine, *On the Trinity: Books 8–15* (ed. Karl Ameriks and Desmond M. Clarke; trans. Stephen McKenna and Gareth B. Matthews; Cambridge: Cambridge University Press, 2002), 91, §12.7.12.

89. Ibid.

90. Ibid., 89, §12.7.10.

91. Ibid., 91, §12.7.12.

92. Ibid.

93. Ibid., 92, §12.8.13.

94. Ibid., 91, §12.7.12.

95. Augustine, *The City of God against the Pagans* (trans. R.W. Dyson; Cambridge: Cambridge University Press, 1998b), xi.

96. Lancel, *Saint Augustine*, 396.

97. Augustine, *City of God*, 609, §14.13.

98. Ibid., 586–87, §14.4.

99. Ibid., 608, §14.13; 604, §14.11.

100. Ibid., 608, §14.13.

101. Ibid., 584, §14.3.

102. Ibid., 585, §14.3.

103. Ibid., 623, §14.23.

104. Ibid., 667, §15.16.

105. Ibid., 620–21, §14.21.

106. Ibid., 622, §14.22.

107. Ibid., 616, §14.17.

108. Ibid., 622, §14.22.

109. Ibid., 605, §14.11.

110. Ibid., 605, §14.11; 581, §14.1; 612, §14.15; 611, §14.15.

111. Ibid., 612, §14.15.

112. Ibid., 623, §14.23.

113. Ibid., 629, §14.26.

114. Ibid., 619, §14.19.

115. Ibid., 614–15, §14.16.

116. Augustine, *Confessions*, 29, §2.4.9.

117. Augustine, *City of God*, 195, §5.6; 22, §1.13; 566, §13.20; 1152, §22.12; 1145, §22.17.

118. Ibid., 566, §13.20; 573, §23.

119. Ibid., 1145, §22.17.

120. Ibid., 669, §15.17.

121. Ibid., 1145, §22.17.

122. For dates, see Augustine, *Marriage and Virginity: The Excellence of Marriage, Holy Virginity, the Excellence of Widowhood, Adulterous Marriages, Continence* (ed. John E. Rotelle; trans. Ray Kearney and David G. Hunter; The Works of Saint Augustine: A Translation for the 21st Century, vol. 1/9; Hyde Park, NY: New City, 1999), *Vid.*, 111; *Incomp. nupt.*, 139; *Contin.*, 189. Dating *Contin.* is somewhat difficult. See Gerald Schlabach, *For the Joy Set before Us: Augustine and Self-Denying Love* (Notre Dame, IN: University of Notre Dame Press, 2001), 200n18.

123. Augustine, *Marriage and Virginity*, 183, *Incomp. nupt.*, §2.20.21.

124. Ibid., 181, §1.17.18; 147, §1.8.8.

125. Ibid., 117, *Vid.*, §6.8.

126. See, e.g., ibid., 183, *Incomp. nupt.*, §2.20.21.

127. Ibid., 170, §2.8.7.

128. Ibid., 171, §2.8.8; 183, §2.20.21.

129. Ibid., 207, *Contin.*, §23.

130. Ibid.

131. Ibid., 208, §23.

132. Ibid.

133. Ibid.

134. Augustine, *Answer to the Pelagians, II: Marriage and Desire, Answer to the Two Letters of the Pelagians, Answer to Julian* (ed. John E. Rotelle; trans. Roland J. Teske; Hyde Park, NY: New City, 1998), 13–14 and 223; and Augustine, *Against Julian* (trans. Matthew A. Schumacher; Washington, DC: Catholic University of America Press, 1977), xi–xii.

135. See, e.g., Augustine, *Answer to the Pelagians, II*, 34, *Nupt.*, §1.10.11; 40, §17.19; or 43, §21.23. In *C. Jul.*, see 356, §3.16.30; 372, §3.25.57; or 462, §5.12.46.

136. See, e.g., ibid., 31–32, *Nupt.*, §1.5.6.

137. Ibid., 61, §2.5.14.

138. Ibid., 419, *C. Jul.*, §4.69.

139. Ibid., 87, *Nupt.*, §2.31.53.

140. Ibid., 77, §2.22.37.

141. Ibid., 457, *C. Jul.*, §5.36.

142. Ibid., 61, *Nupt.*, §2.5.14.

143. Augustine refutes Julian's objections with simple syllogisms (ibid., 347, *C. Jul.*, §3.16).

144. Ibid., 33, *Nupt.*, §1.8.9.

145. Ibid., 33, *Nupt.*, §1.8.9; 91, §2.58.

146. Ibid., 383, *C. Jul.*, §4.7.

147. Ibid., 45, *Nupt.*, §1.24.27.

148. Ibid., 57, §2.8.

149. Ibid., 415, *C. Jul.*, §4.63.

150. Ibid., 412, §4.11.57; 415, §4.13.62.

151. Ibid., 415, §4.13.62.

152. Ibid., 69, *Nupt.*, §2.13.26.

153. Ibid., 62, §2.6.16.

154. Ibid., 47, §2.27.30.

155. Ibid., 413, *C. Jul.*, §4.12.58.

156. Ibid., 347, §3.16.

157. Ibid., 30, *Nupt.*, §1.4.5.

158. Ibid., 35–36, §1.11.12; 462, *C. Jul.*, §5.12.46.

159. Ibid., 40, *Nupt.*, §1.16.18; 68, §2.12.25; 69, §2.13.26.

160. Ibid., 372, *C. Jul.*, §3.25.57.

161. Ibid., 361, §3.40; 349, §3.9.18; 75, *Nupt.*, §2.20.35.

162. Gilbert Meilaender, "Sweet Necessities: Food, Sex, and Saint Augustine," *Journal of Religious Ethics* 29, no. 1 (2001): 11.

163. Oliver O'Donovan, *Transsexualism and Christian Marriage* (Grove Booklets on Ethics 48; Bramcote, England: Grove Books, 1982), 6.

# Chapter 3
# BERNARD OF CLAIRVAUX'S
# SERMONS ON THE SONG OF SONGS

In the last chapter we saw that the later Augustine believed that corporeal sexual difference was part of God's original prelapsarian intentions for creaturely life in Eden, and, furthermore, that sexual difference is a feature with divinely bestowed meaning and purpose for anthropology at every stage of salvation history. The main teleology of sexual difference Augustine actually discussed was reproductive marriage for the sake of populating the heavenly city, but, in light of this teleology, he made additional arguments about how Christians should habituate and assess their erotic desires. Furthermore, and more subtly, Augustine also claimed that sexual difference continued to be significant even after its created teleology had been fulfilled. This ongoing significance was usually not explored thoroughly or even self-consciously by Augustine. In large part, probably this inattention is due to the fact that these eschatological openings are expressed mainly as asides in various polemical contexts, and an occasion for more systematic elaboration on these ideas never arose. Still, this theological rationale is present, even if often only by implication.

In this chapter we will study Bernard of Clairvaux's sermons on the Song of Songs. Bernard is arguably the greatest theologian between the patristic and scholastic eras, and he is the apogee of the ancient tradition of allegorical commentary on the Song of Songs. This tradition explored the nature of love between God and Israel, the church, and the soul using the sexually differentiated imagery of bride and groom.

We will see how Bernard's sermons presuppose Augustine's framework for sexual difference. However, sexual difference, as a topic in its own right, is not Bernard's priority in these sermons. His priority is to discuss the relationship between God and the soul, or Christ and the church. But for this purpose, he did elect to use a sexually differentiated allegory, privileging the language of brides and grooms, when he could plausibly have chosen other allegorical images of love. This particular sexually differentiated relationship is evidently more apt for Bernard's purposes than others, and his choice is not simply a neutral fact but an implicit valuation of brides and grooms. Bernard does not offer much explicit argument to justify this valuation; he mostly presupposes it. However, and somewhat tentatively, this chapter will suggest that by examining the logic of Bernard's allegories in light of his Augustinian beliefs about creation and sexuality, we can identify an implicit rationale. Painstaking exegesis strongly suggests that, for Bernard, sexual difference in marriage is privileged material for his allegories because sexually difference uniquely posits two persons who are noninterchangeable, hierarchically related, and created for covenant.

## Bernard's Augustinian Beliefs about Sexual Difference

Among other things, Bernard would have presupposed most of Augustine's beliefs about sexual difference. He follows Augustine's account of creation, believing that "the Holy Spirit spoke of the distinction of sex," that is, that sexual difference is of God's beneficent authorship, for the sake of marriage prior to the fall.[1] "It is the difference in sex which is meant by the saying 'Male and female he created them' . . . for it is the difference in sex which is the essential element in marriage."[2] When men and women become husband and wife, they are fulfilling the teleology of having been given a sex. When one speaks of brides and grooms, one speaks of the reason why God made male and female. Furthermore, like Augustine, Bernard believes that there would have been sexual difference in paradise and that virginity would have been inappropriate at that stage of salvation history: "From the very beginning this voice [the 'preaching of chastity'] was not heard on the earth, but instead that other: 'Be fruitful and multiply and fill the earth.'"[3] At that time, God's purposes still required the peopling of Israel. Thus when Bernard invokes the language of brides and grooms, it is as one who believes that to be married is to fulfill the vocation implicit in the creation of sexual difference but that the significance of sexual difference should be understood relative to the stages of salvation history.

Furthermore, and again as with Augustine, Bernard believes that sexual difference after the fall provokes concupiscence. Marriage as a remedy for incontinence is indicative of a "venial fault."[4] Rebuking some heretics who preached nonmarital cohabitation between the sexes, Bernard said, "Every day your side touches the girl's side at table, your bed touches hers in your room, your eyes meet hers in conversation, your hands meet hers at work—do you expect to be thought chaste? It may be that you are, but I have my suspicions."[5] Yet, as with Augustine, Bernard does not think that such dangers should lead to a denunciation of the body or sexual difference. He follows Augustine in believing that it is sin and wrongly ordered desire, not our bodies, which cause the problems and make us exiles from God's presence.[6] Bernard does not long for an escape from the body or sexuality; he longs for its redemption and reconfiguration in rightly ordered relations. A "spiritual and immortal body, a perfect body," is not disembodied but a body "beautiful and at peace and subject to the spirit in all things."[7] About the eschatological body, Bernard says, "I do not say that the substance of the flesh will not be there, but that every carnal need will be absent, that the love of the flesh will be absorbed in the love of the spirit, and that what are now weak human affections will be transformed into divine powers."[8] Thus Bernard as well as Augustine believes in the changing significance of sexual difference across every era of salvation history: God creates the two sexes before the fall, and after the fall the two sexes can tempt and lead one another down false paths, but the solution is not the oblivion of the sexes but their transformation into obedience.

## God's Love Is Bernard's Priority

There is an apparent irony in Bernard's project. On the one hand, he is wary of sexual desire for the Augustinian reasons we have examined. On the other hand, by using the text of the Song as a means for illustrating the love of God, his message relies on vivid descriptions of sexual desire. If we want to understand how this irony is not incoherence, and if we wish to do so without committing anachronism, then it is prudent to ensure that we understand Bernard's project according to its explicit purposes as well as its Augustinian background. What did Bernard think his allegory was explaining? Only by understanding what he thought he had described can we work backward to see the complete range of possibly implicit beliefs that might have underwritten and enabled his project, and only by understanding the limits of what he claimed to have achieved can we safely suggest implications of his argument that he might not have foreseen.

For Bernard, the Song of Songs is the "splendid and delicious" climax to the previous books of Solomon—to Ecclesiastes, which he presumes has already taught the monk "how to recognize and have done with the false promises of this world," and to Proverbs, which has already "amended and enlightened" the monk's life and conduct.[9] But more broadly for Bernard, a dominant feature of the Old Testament is the "intense longing" of Israel for the consummation of its covenant with God, or "the burning desire with which the patriarchs longed for the incarnation of Christ."[10] Bernard acknowledges other songs and themes in Scripture,[11] but this one, captured in this Song, he claims to be the crown and glory of them all:

> We must conclude then it was a special divine impulse that inspired these songs of his that now celebrate the praises of Christ and his Church, the gift of holy love, the sacrament of endless union with God. Here too are expressed the mounting desires of the soul, its marriage song, an exultation of spirit poured forth in figurative language pregnant with delight.[12]

Thus it is this ancient ache and pull toward the fruition of divine purpose that Bernard believes leads the bride to burst forth in the ejaculations of the Song's opening petition: "Let him kiss me with the kiss of his mouth!" The Song opens with this cry, and from then onward, in Bernard's hands, the Song's dialogue of intimacy and absence, of consummation and longing, becomes the plea of the soul "thirsting for God," as well as of the whole people of God seeking Christ "with a desire that is intense, a thirst ever burning, an application that never flags."[13]

Crucially, however, this desire is not only reciprocated on God's side but is actually instigated by God. Bernard reads the whole Trinity, or often specifically Christ, as the groom to the bride, who can be either the soul or the church. This is the groom who declares his love in the Song, for this is the one who became flesh "to recapture the affections of carnal men who were unable to love in any other way."[14] In fact, it is this overture of God's which inaugurates the whole cycle of affective relationship, for in these songs, the lovers are often separated, and only the groom's gracious initiative can reunite them. God longs for "the consummation of the Church," or "to see the prosperity of his chosen ones, to rejoice in the gladness of his people, to glory with his heritage."[15] For Bernard, this love affair is of cosmic significance. Everything depends on God drawing his people close to him, on the implications of God's one work of love:

> You must not think that this is a small matter. I tell you that none of his [the Lord's] works will reach perfection if this one fails. Does not the end of all things depend on the condition and consummation

of the Church? Take away this, and the lower creation will wait in vain for the revelation of the sons of God. Take away this, then neither patriarchs nor prophets will come to perfection, for Paul says that God has ordained for us that apart from us they should not be made perfect. Take away this, and the very glory of the holy angels will be impaired if their numbers are not complete, nor will the City of God rejoice in its wholeness.[16]

Thus the heavenly bridegroom longs for his bride, and the fate of the universe depends upon this aspiration being consummated. This passion interprets and guides every subsequent passion. Bernard's eighty-six sermons are commentary on this love affair, using the language of the Song of Songs to illustrate a dynamic that will sweep his audience of monks into the passion between God and God's people.

## The Logical Structure of Bernard's Use of Allegory: Its Precedents and Implications

Marital language is not the only language Bernard uses to describe the spiritual dynamics to which he wants to call attention; it is merely the dominant image in the service of the dominant theme, which is God's affective love. But these sermons are choked with countless minor allegories to cover subsidiary points, and the way in which these allegories are employed confirms a pattern of presupposing certain natural relations in order to probe supernatural priorities.

For instance, in a sermon on the second verse of the Song ("Your name is oil poured out"), oil is reckoned a suitable image for Jesus' name because oil is a liquid which "floats above all other liquids with which it mixes" and so can designate "a name that is above all names."[17] Obviously Bernard is not interested in describing oil, but he does believe that a particular quality of oil, which he presupposes, can be relied upon to say something about Christ. Similarly, in another sermon, when Bernard says it is appropriate to refer to faith as "the vine, the virtues the branches, good works the cluster of grapes, and devotion the wine," and goes on to state the obvious, that "without the vine there is no wine," he is invoking the logic of one set of natural relationships in order to make the less obvious point that "without faith there is no virtue."[18] Such images proliferate endlessly in these sermons: A garden is seen to represent the historical sense of Scripture, a storeroom represents its moral sense, and a bedroom the mysteries of contemplating God; for Bernard, these different levels of intimacy in a house indicate stages of virtue and spiritual understanding.[19]

This continues: Pharaoh's chariots can stand for malice and avarice. A neck can signify an intellect. A visit to the divine "wine cellar" inspires holiness. At one moment the church is like flowers (recent converts) and fruits (mature Christians), but later on the communion of saints is like a conglomeration of stones making a good and suitable wall.[20] In each case, Bernard makes an argument justifying the analogy, appealing beyond the text to a theological relationship that is formally congruent to a recognizable extent with some item from everyday observation. In this way, Bernard proposes "to penetrate the obscurity of these allegories and reveal the secrets of Christ and his Church." He believes that to do otherwise, to fail to read allegorically, would be to read like the "stupid" and "mentally dull" who read Song 2:15 (a verse about foxes ruining a vineyard) and conclude that the Bible offers practical lessons "on how to care for earthly possessions," as if strategies for making wine and protecting vineyards from wild animals were a biblical subject.[21] To fail to press for the hidden meaning beyond this surface meaning is to condemn oneself to theological obtuseness, with those who take "the veil covering the mystery for the mystery itself."[22] Thus whenever we encounter one of Bernard's allegories, we have to be careful. We would not want to make the same mistake and overemphasize the natural qualities of what is only a veil, but, at the same time, presuppositions about the relevant natural qualities are not entirely irrelevant.

For the purposes of learning about sexual difference, then, we must be careful not to read these sermons as some sort of marriage manual; they are not, primarily, an attempt to offer practical techniques for right living between the sexes. At least twice, Bernard specifically disavows any possibility that he intends to speak prescriptively of actual men and women.[23] However, even if that is the case, we can still read these sermons for clues to presupposed beliefs about sexual difference. Bernard believed that certain things about oil and water were true, and he could appeal to this relation in order to make certain points. Similarly, Bernard must have believed that certain things were true about marriage, and hence perhaps sexual difference, in order to think it was suitable allegorical material.

In one of the earliest sermons in the series, Bernard explains which qualities he is presupposing for marriage and why he turns to it for his dominant image:

> In order to clarify for you the characteristics of the bride, I shall deal briefly with the diverse affective relationships between persons. Fear motivates a slave's attitude to his master, gain that of

wage-earner to his employer, the learner is attentive to his teacher, the son is respectful to his father. But the one who asks for a kiss, she is a lover. Among all the natural endowments of man love holds first place. . . . No sweeter names can be found to embody that sweet interflow of affections between the Word and the soul, than bridegroom and bride. Between these all things are equally shared, there are no selfish reservations, nothing causes division. . . . Therefore if a love relationship is the special and outstanding characteristic of the bride and groom, it is not unfitting to call the soul that loves God a bride. Now one who asks for a kiss is in love. It is not for liberty that she asks, nor for an award, not for an inheritance nor even knowledge, but for a kiss.[24]

"No sweeter names can be found . . . than bridegroom and bride," and so it is to this way of speaking that Bernard makes resort. Years later, in one of the final sermons, Bernard offered basically the same summary rationale: "What other bond or compulsion do you look for between those who are betrothed, except to love and be loved?"[25] The reason for choosing the Song to illuminate the affection between God and creature is therefore clear: A variety of hierarchical relationships might apply between two subjects (master-slave, employer-worker, teacher-student, parent-child), but it is the affective dynamics of the betrothal that illustrate the theological relationship most aptly. For rhetorical purposes, this theological relationship is still opaque, and it is the object of Bernard's teaching. The formal and logical parallel of betrothal is thus invoked for pedagogical reasons, following the pattern we have been led to expect:

Where, I ask, can you find the words to pay worthy tribute to that majesty, or properly describe it, or adequately define it? But we speak as well as we can of that which we do our best to understand, as the Holy Spirit reveals. We are taught by the authority of the Fathers and the usage of the scriptures that it is lawful to appropriate suitable analogies from the writings we know, and rather than coin new words, to borrow the familiar with which these analogies may be worthily and properly clothed. Otherwise you will make an absurd attempt to teach the unknown by the unknown.[26]

In other words, when confronted with the dilemma of how to speak about relations with an unseen God, Bernard borrows a known language. He reaches for that part of the biblical canon which, in terms of its relational dynamic, already bears the burden of his point.

The resort to marital imagery is not original to Bernard. Not only are there centuries of predecessors and colleagues writing similar sermons, but the Old Testament itself is strewn with the language of sexually differentiated eros, of wooing and alluring, betrothal and fidelity, as well as adultery and prostitution, to evoke the relationship between Yahweh and Israel, to the point of it being one of the central motifs for describing the relationship. In Hosea, God posits himself as husband or groom to Israel's bride:

> I will now allure her,
>     and bring her into the wilderness,
>     and speak tenderly to her.
> From there I will give her her vineyards,
>     and make the Valley of Achor a door of hope.
> There she shall respond as in the days of her youth,
>     as at the time when she came out of the land of
>     Egypt.

On that day, says the LORD, you will call me, "My husband," and no longer will you call me, "My Baal." (Hos 2:14–16 NRSV)

Israel is often notoriously unfaithful in this relationship, and Hosea and other Old Testament prophets tend to use the marital imagery not only to explore the delight between husband and wife but also to explore God's faithfulness in spite of Israel's promiscuity. But the bride and groom in the Song are a different instance, for they are faithful, and, in any case, the point for understanding Bernard's use of the Song is that exegetes like him who approach the Song allegorically have intrabiblical precedents. The dynamic between lovers is elsewhere established in God's own words as a vivid and recurring motif for exploring the complexity of relations between God and God's people, a precedent inviting the same approach to the Song. In Ezekiel, for instance, God speaks with a sensual richness about the nation of Israel that could have come straight from the Song itself:

> You grew up and became tall and arrived at full womanhood; your breasts were formed, and your hair had grown; yet you were naked and bare.
>     I passed by you again and looked on you; you were at the age for love. I spread the edge of my cloak over you, and covered your nakedness: I pledged myself to you and entered into a covenant

with you, says the Lord GOD, and you became mine. Then I bathed you with water and washed off the blood from you, and anointed you with oil. I clothed you with embroidered cloth and with sandals of fine leather; I bound you in fine linen and covered you with rich fabric. I adorned you with ornaments: I put bracelets on your arms, a chain on your neck, a ring on your nose, earrings in your ears, and a beautiful crown upon your head. You were adorned with gold and silver, while your clothing was of fine linen, rich fabric, and embroidered cloth. You had choice flour and honey and oil for food. You grew exceedingly beautiful, fit to be a queen. (Ezek 16:7–13 NRSV)

Thus the allegory of the Song is a sustained elaboration of the precedent already established by numerous other similar allegories within Scripture. Sexually differentiated love and erotic interaction are well established within the Christian tradition as being capable of modeling love between God and God's people. Bernard presupposes not just any sexual attraction but a loving one, one in which "all things are equally shared, there are no selfish reservations, nothing causes division," and on this basis he appeals to that marital relationship in pursuit of other, theological interests.[27]

But can we go any further than this? Surely there are other examples of loving, sharing, and mutually attractive relationships in Scripture. Why choose the loving relation between bride and groom? What is it about sexual differentiated marital love that makes it especially suitable material for theological interpretation of this sort? If Bernard's interest is really in the love dynamic, is it possible that in theory sexual difference is not a necessary ingredient to the allegory? Or does sexual difference itself contribute something indispensable?

Bernard is of course able to cite other biblical images for loving union in God. His friend and fellow Cistercian, Aelred of Rievaulx, had written on spiritual friendship.[28] Perhaps it would have been wise, in a monastic context, to have used the literature on friendship in order to discuss relationships of love between two persons. That would have allowed Bernard to avoid the potential hazards of using erotically charged language to speak to an audience of celibates. In the sermons, Bernard does consider using other types of asexual love imagery, such as adoption: "Living in the Spirit of the Son, let such a soul recognize herself as a daughter of the Father, a bride or even a sister of the Son, for you will find that the soul who enjoys this privilege is called by either of these names."[29] "Bride" and "sister" are not mutually exclusive terms when the references are to dynamics between God and creatures. Both are valid for gesturing toward the dynamics Bernard wants to describe. But Bernard eventually rejects adoption as the privileged motif, claiming that the affective bond between two who are betrothed is stronger than other affections and, citing Matthew 19:5, "stronger even than nature's firm bond between parents and children."[30] Or again:

> Love is the being and the hope of a bride. She is full of it, and the bridegroom is contented with it. He asks nothing else, and she has nothing else to give. That is why he is the bridegroom and she the bride; this love is the property only of the couple. No-one else can share it, not even a son.[31]

But here again, our question about the reasons for sexually differentiated marital imagery are still begged. Bernard appears to answer the question of why there are not other examples of loving relationship not with an answer that appeals to sexual difference but with an answer that appeals to the love dynamic. Is sexual difference potentially beside the point in Bernard's sermons, appearing simply as the relic of previous tradition and pointing to no significance in itself? Could the couple in the Song, in theory, be replaced by a non–sexually differentiated couple who also felt strong and exclusive love? Yet that did not happen in Bernard or in his tradition.

## Why Bernard's Eros Must Be Set in Sexually Differentiated Marriage

We have just seen how Bernard and his tradition have identified love as the enabling premise that makes a groom and a bride suitable allegorical material for relations with God. But why this sexually differentiated marital love and not other kinds of love? What implied and presupposed beliefs about sexual difference and marriage are at work? Is there something necessary about sexual difference itself? Bernard does not answer these questions directly. But a close reading of Bernard's texts, in light of his Augustinian beliefs about sexual difference, suggests some of the beliefs about sexual difference that are, arguably, latent and efficacious.

As one who would have agreed with Augustine's exegesis of Genesis, Bernard would have assumed that marriage was a God-given practice that fulfills the created purpose of sexual difference. Take away marriage and one takes away the essential habitat for using our sexual differentiating features in holy ways. In these sermons, Bernard condemns sexual practices that are not shaped by this teleology: "Take from the Church the honourable estate of marriage and the purity of the marriage-bed, and you will surely fill it with concubinage, incest, masturbation, effeminacy, homosexuality—in short, with every kind of filthiness."[32] Bernard believes in a particular protology of sexuality that makes the marriage bed honorable, and a particular eschatological anthropology as well. The sexual practices named in this list are not prescribed by the protology, and neither can they be described as foreshadowing the eschatology. They therefore lack a theologically derived justification or referent and, on Bernard's terms, are incapable of testifying to God's purposes. Bernard's conclusion can only be that these bodily practices must be autonomous human innovations. But the attempt to self-author the meaning of creation, the attempt to treat God's work as if it were theologically indifferent and available for human self-fashioning, is a version of rejecting relationship with God and, hence, Bernard's use of the word "filthy."

Later on in the same sermon, Bernard mentions how these same heretics who are against "the honourable estate of marriage" happen also not to eat meat because of its association with sexual intercourse. In explaining why this contempt for God's creation is wrong, Bernard refers to Augustine's polemic against the Manichaens:

> But what is the reason for this wholesale avoidance of everything produced by copulation? This close scrutiny of food, these detailed instructions, arouse my suspicions. If you commend it to us on medical grounds, we will not censure you for taking care of your body—for no one ever hates his body—provided it is done in moderation. If you give as your reason the disciplinary value of abstinence, that is the routine of spiritual therapy, we will even approve it as laudable, so long as by bringing the flesh into subjection you curb its lusts. But if you limit the goodness of God after the insane manner of the Manichaean, so that what he has created and given to be received with thankfulness, you, ungrateful, thoughtless and censorious, judge to be unclean and shun like the plague, then I certainly do not commend your abstinence. On the contrary, I condemn your blasphemy.[33]

In other words, what God has given is not to be shunned, but received with thankfulness. What God has created is not meaningless or offensive, but something that should evoke gratitude, something we might term a gift, a blessing, or a promise. We can also apply this logic to sexual difference. Bernard believes the created origins and the eschatological future for human male and femaleness have been given by God, as part of the "goodness of God," and so should be included among that which should be received with thankfulness and not shunned.

On this basis, we are able to infer why, for Bernard, there is a latent but essential theological mandate for using a sexually differentiated and married relationship for allegorizing the erotic encounter between God and God's creatures. To use another embodied and sexually charged human relationship for this allegory would have been to insert the "manner of the Manichaean" in the service of explaining God's love. To do that—to use some other relationship that also has strong longing, sexual desire, and attraction but that does not have its roots in God's creation and purposes—would be to appeal to an erotic illustration Bernard would have regarded as disobedient at its core. Such an allegory would undermine itself, for it would appeal to a form of life that did not welcome the creation as it has been given in order to explain a form of life in love with the Creator. One would be disobeying God in order to testify to the glory of relationship with God. By contrast, we can infer how a sexually differentiated marital allegory actually fosters the project of learning about being in love with the Creator. If we consider that it is the purpose of these sermons to argue that the human creature is created for covenant with God, and if we further consider that Bernard believed that male and female were created for covenant with one another, we can see how there is a consistent momentum, logically and rhetorically, to these sermons. As the sexes are created for one another, and as the creature is created for its Creator, in both cases, the momentum is from creation toward fellowship. In both cases, a covenant of love fulfills the rationale for the existence of the relevant persons. For Bernard, no other relationship but a sexually differentiated one could have served such purposes.

## Further Reasons Why Sexual Difference Is the Right Analog

There are probably further reasons why Bernard would have found sexual difference necessary and helpful for his allegory. We shall examine a moment in the eighth sermon as a revealing case study. This sermon is devoted to explaining how and why Bernard believes that the cry of the Song's first verse—"Let him kiss me with the kiss of his mouth"—is a cry of invocation for the Holy Spirit. It is a sermon about the interior dynamics of the Trinity and how we might participate in them.

Bernard begins this sermon by clarifying whom he believes the Spirit is. Bernard appeals to Matthew 11:27, saying,

"No one knows the Son except the Father, just as no one knows the Father except the Son and those to whom the Son chooses to reveal him." For the Father loves the Son whom he embraces with a love that is unique; he who is infinite embraces his equal, who is eternal, his co-eternal, the sole God, his only-begotten. . . . Now, that mutual knowledge and love between him who begets and him who is begotten—what can it comprise if not a kiss that is utterly sweet, but utterly a mystery as well?[34]

Bernard is convinced that "no creature, not even an angel, is permitted to comprehend this secret of divine love."[35] The secret of this union is not reducible to propositional knowledge. Rather, taking us to this threshold and witnessing this kiss, we are actually encountering the presence of one of the irreducible persons in the Trinity: "If, as is properly understood, the Father is he who kisses, the Son he who is kissed, then it cannot be wrong to see in the kiss the Holy Spirit, for he is the imperturbably peace of the Father and the Son, their unshakable bond, their undivided love, their indivisible unity."[36] The mutual relations between the Father and the Son are held together in the Spirit, for which the kiss is a symbol. Therefore Bernard can conclude, when the Bride in the Song asks for the kiss of the Bridegroom, that she is asking "actually for that Spirit in whom both the Father and the Son will reveal themselves to her. For it is not possible that one of these could be known without the other."[37] To ask for the Spirit is to ask for the presence of the triune God in his fullness. To ask for the Spirit is to ask for an affective force that will make two persons more present to one another than they could possibly otherwise be. It would be incorrect to reduce the Spirit to such an affective force or presence, but it is precisely such uniting affective efficacy—such erotic power—which the Spirit can grant as a gift.

But the Spirit not only unifies, it also preserves differences between persons as it unifies. The Father does not stop being the one who begets, and the Son does not stop being the one who is begotten as they are united in the Spirit. As Bernard says later in the same sermon, the Father sends and the Son obeys, and the Holy Spirit "is nothing else but the love and the benign goodness of them both."[38] In the Holy Spirit's kiss, identities between persons remain distinct even while their union is palpable and concrete. Even an apparently hierarchical difference, of sending and obeying, of begetting and being begotten, is not exploitative. Here we are learning something theologically. The Holy Spirit's kiss is not the postlapsarian passion that aroused Augustine's suspicion. Here we are seeing what a kiss is like when it happens within the Trinity.

In a similar vein, in the same sense of a love that unites even as it respects hierarchical differences, God extends his internal dynamic of love to love his creaturely bride. The kiss that unites even as it respects distinctions condescends to unite Creator and creature, even as it insists on their differences. In a much later sermon, Bernard describes the move of love from God's groom to the human bride, and here too there are dissimilarities and differences within the union:

> The stream of love does not flow equally from her who loves and from him who is love, the soul and the Word, the Bride and the Bridegroom, the Creator and the creature—any more than a thirsty man can be compared to a fountain. Will the Bride's vow perish, then, because of this? Will the desire of her heart, her burning love, her affirmation of confidence, fail in their purpose because she has not the strength to keep pace with a giant, or rival honey in sweetness, the lamb in gentleness, or the lily in whiteness? Because she cannot equal the brightness of the sun, and the charity of him who is Charity? No. Although the creature loves less, being a lesser being, yet if it loves with its whole heart nothing is lacking, for it has given all. Such love, as I have said, is marriage, for a soul cannot love like this and not be beloved: complete and perfect marriage consists in the exchange of love.[39]

God establishes what love is, but the creature can genuinely return it, and the inequality is no blot against this reciprocity of love. "Such love ... is marriage," even if elsewhere, reflecting on our fallen experience, marriage is associated with sin. "Such love" is the paradigm, not our natural experience. "The Bridegroom is our God, and we, I say in all humility, are the Bride—we, and the whole multitude of captives whom he acknowledges. Let us rejoice that this glory is ours; we are they to whom God inclines. But how unequal a partnership!"[40] That God initiates, inclines and acknowledges, and extends the grace of eros to a partner who lacks ontological equality is no obstacle to the creation of this new thing, this marital intimacy between God and "captive" creatures. Here again is a love in which differences stay different, in which similarities of love are noted even as the persons involved and their capacities are known to be different:

> Love is the only one of the motions of the soul, of its senses and affections, in which the creature can respond to its Creator, even if not as an equal, and repay his favor in some similar way. For example, if God is angry with me, am I to be angry in return? No, indeed, but I shall tremble with fear and ask pardon. So also, if he accuses me, I shall not accuse him in return, but rather justify him.

Not, if he judges me, shall I judge him, but I shall adore him; and in saving me he does not ask to be saved by me; nor does he who sets all men free, need to be set free by me. If he commands, I must obey, and not demand his service or obedience. Now you see how different love is, for when God loves, he desires nothing but to be loved, since he loves us for no other reason than to be loved, for he knows that those who love him are blessed in their very love.[41]

Thus by following Bernard's description of love between Creator and creature, we are following contours similar to Bernard's description of love within the Trinity. In both cases, we are seeing that his language of kissing and betrothal is a language where differences are not threatening or obscured. Just as Creator and creature maintain a whole host of significant differences, and just as it is no fault but a glory that their love does not merge them into one another, neither does a bride stop being a bride and merge into being a groom. The Spirit enables love between different, noninterchangeable, and hierarchically related persons. No conflation is possible or desirable in these relations of intimacy. Real marital love, after the pattern of the Spirit revealed in the Song, is a reconciling language, analogously suitable for mysteries between triune persons; genuine marital love renders unthreatening the potential imbalance created by difference between God and human creature. Speaking in marital terms of the unity between God and creature, Bernard writes in ways that could also be taken to evoke the relation between divine Father and Son: "Truly this is a spiritual contract, a holy marriage. It is more than a contract, it is an embrace: an embrace where identity of will makes of two one spirit."[42] But in such embrace, the distinctions between persons of the Trinity are never elided, just as in Bernard's portrait of relations between Creator and creature and between husband and wife.

The point of Bernard's sermons is to proclaim that God's eros seeks and effects intimacy with us, even as we are utterly different from and subordinate to him. For this purpose, Bernard needs to speak of erotic relations that reconcile differences while maintaining them, in which otherness cannot possibly be confused or obliterated. Sexual difference apparently suits this purpose, although to explain why has required a very close reading, and offering a rationale Bernard does not make as explicit as he might have done. But whether it is an explicit or an implicit rationale, it is nevertheless a logic on which he seems to rely, and it coheres perfectly with his purposes in these sermons. It would seem that Bernard's silence or lack of explicit argument about sexual difference is not because he thinks sexual difference is insignificant, but because he thinks its significance is so obvious it could be presupposed. Oil floats on water, and so it is suitable allegorical material for discussing a name that rises above other names; Bernard can take for granted that his audience does not need persuading about the properties of oil and water, and he can focus on his true priorities. Brides and grooms love one another, but their roles remain distinct and cannot be confused, and so Bernard takes for granted that they are suitable allegorical material for discussing a love that seeks union but that does not obscure particularity.

In other words, it is not only the element of love or desire, or even the element of being consistent with the purposes of creation, that makes marriage suitable allegorical material for Bernard's sermons. It is also the fact that marriage, as Bernard understands it, presupposes particular persons who are, due to visible somatic differences and the roles that follow from those differences, irreducibly different. Marriage, as Bernard understands it, relies upon an ontology of maleness and femaleness, for marriage relies upon two modes of being human that are utterly distinct and yet created for partnership. Staying within Bernard's terms, it only underlines the point if we discern male hegemony in Bernard, or the presupposition that men and women relate hierarchically. For Father and Son, and Creator and creature, are hierarchical relations, and so perhaps to use sexual difference as an analog for God's ways of relating depends upon an inequality between the sexes. Bernard would not have seen that as a problem or a criticism, and its internal logic is consistent. Sexual difference, held together in the bond of marriage, is a counterpart to intra-Trinitarian difference and divine-human difference, for all three types of difference are held together in the bond of the Spirit. As such, sexual difference in marriage is particularly suitable allegorical material for Bernard's purposes.

## Conclusion:
## Redeemed Sexual Difference Includes More Than Fertility

Bernard was well aware of fallen relations between the sexes. As we have seen, Bernard could follow Augustine in suspecting that, after the fall, quotidian contact between the sexes usually led to at least some type of lustful dynamic. Bernard is also capable of passing asides that reflect uncritical assimilation of various gender stereotypes: He can use "manliness" as a synonym for bravery and constancy, and he can use women as a cipher for that which is either sensual or humble and meek.[43] In his discussions, femininity can be a synonym for nurture and safety, as revealed in images of breasts or wombs.[44] But whether these various gender stereotypes are true or not, whether quotidian contact leads to concupiscence or not, whether or not marriage as we experience it involves sin or not, in these sermons Bernard has also painted a portrait of love between the sexes in which desire, attraction, disparities, and differences between the sexes need not be threatening. The problems between the sexes do not have the last word and are only a minor motif.

By far the greater motif in these sermons is the kiss with which the Holy Spirit unites the Father and the Son, or the passion with which God pursues the creature, or even the desire that goads the human bride to beg for the "kiss of the mouth." But these things are not the same type of concupiscent desire that Augustine accused as a manifestation of pride and disorder. For the former kind of kiss is the kiss of God himself, in the service of God's purposes in creation, while the latter kind of desire is an exercise in human pride. Similarly, that the creature's unequal but nonetheless wholehearted love for the heavenly groom might be such that Bernard can call it marriage means that this marriage has dynamics that cannot be contained by a focus on procreation. This marriage is one in which sexual difference has significance other than, or in addition to, procreation.

In Bernard's sermons, sexual difference, although clearly conceivable as an occasion for lust and stereotype, can also be conceptualized theologically as a difference that is meant to be reconciled without being homogenized. We saw that in Augustine the very same sexual organs are examples of both obedience and pride, before and after the fall—similarly in Bernard. He did not deign to speak of actual relations between the sexes, except to warn of their dangers. Nevertheless, he has painted a portrait, using an imaginative exegesis of Scripture, of sexually differentiated relations untainted by sin. Our focus on this portrait has gone beyond Bernard's explicitly stated priorities but in ways that are nevertheless faithful to the implications of his arguments. The significance of sexual difference in these sermons appears to be its clarity as a harbinger of otherness, as a human feature that simply cannot be rendered interchangeable and that is created and structured for encounter as well as fertility. These characteristics seem to be necessary and presupposed, in addition to the love and desire Bernard more directly discusses, in order for marriage of man and woman to be ripe for his theological symbolism.

## Notes

1. SCC 66.4. The translations in this chapter are taken from the following series: Bernard of Clairvaux, *On the Song of Songs I* (trans. Kilian Walsh; Shannon,

Ireland: Irish University Press, 1971); *On the Song of Songs II* (trans. Kilian Walsh; Kalamazoo, MI: Cistercian Publications, 1976); *On the Song of Songs III* (trans. Kilian Walsh and Irene M. Edmonds; Kalamazoo, MI: Cistercian Publications, 1979); and *On the Song of Songs IV* (trans. Irene Edmonds; Kalamazoo, MI: Cistercian Publications, 1980).

2. SCC 66.4.

3. SCC 59.8.

4. SCC 57.7. See Emero S. Stiegman, *The Language of Asceticism in St. Bernard of Clairvaux's 'Sermones Super Cantica Canticorum'* (Ann Arbor, MI: University Microfilms, 1973), 154 and 159, for more, similar references.

5. SCC 65.4.

6. SCC 56.3.

7. Bernard of Clairvaux, *Bernard of Clairvaux: Selected Works* (trans. Gillian R. Evans; New York: Paulist Press, 1987), 196, *De diligendo Deo*, §9.29.

8. Bernard of Clairvaux, *The Letters of Saint Bernard of Clairvaux* (trans. Bruno Scott James; Stroud, England: Sutton Publishing, 1998), 47, "Letter to the Prior of the Grande Chartreuse," §9.

9. SCC 1.1.

10. SCC 2.1.

11. SCC 1.7.

12. SCC 1.8.

13. SCC 7.2; 3.2.2.

14. SCC 20.6.

15. SCC 68.4.

16. SCC 68.4.

17. SCC 16.15.

18. SCC 30.6.

19. SCC 23.3.

20. SCC 39.6–8, 41.1, 49.4, 51.2, 62.1.

21. SCC 80.1, 63.1.

22. SCC 73.2.

23. SCC 61.2, 75.2.

24. SCC 7.2.

25. SCC 83.3.

26. SCC 51.7

27. See above, note 24.

28. See Aelred of Rievaulx, *Spiritual Friendship* (trans. Mary Eugenia Laker; Kalamazoo, MI: Cistercian Publications, 1977).

29. SCC 8.9.

30. SCC 83.3.

31. SCC 83.5.

32.  SCC 66.2.
33.  SCC 66.7.
34.  SCC 8.1.
35.  SCC 8.2.
36.  SCC 8.2.
37.  SCC 8.3.
38.  SCC 8.4.
39.  SCC 83.6.
40.  SCC 68.1.
41.  SCC 83.4.
42.  SCC 83.3.
43.  SCC 38.4, 71.4.
44.  SCC 10.1, 66.4.

# Chapter 4
# THOMAS AQUINAS

The previous three chapters established that often in the Christian past, sexual difference was not a topic of direct and sustained theological argument. However, certain beliefs about sexual difference were latent and enabled other arguments, or were mentioned as rhetorical asides, or were occasionally discussed as main themes. Chapter 1 established that such beliefs were often contradictory in the earliest patristic theology. Chapter 2 described an emerging framework for thinking about sexual difference that arose over the course of Augustine's career. With a completeness and consistency lacking in his predecessors, the mature Augustine understood relations between man and woman in terms of creation, fall, and the coming of the heavenly city. This history led him to conceptualize sexual relations as beset by sin, yet not as the source of sin. On these terms, Christian marriage and celibacy testify to the goodness of primordial creation and its coming redemption. Chapter 3 examined Bernard of Clairvaux's sermons on the Song of Songs. These sermons presupposed that sexual difference is privileged material for allegories of God's love. Possible reasons for why that might be the case include the fact that sexual difference uniquely allowed Bernard to explore the dynamic between two different, noninterchangeable types of persons who are nonetheless created in order to be united in a covenant.

This chapter studies Aquinas, who does not develop Bernard's allegories but who does refer to the pre-Augustinian views on sexual difference as well as Augustine's established views. However, in this chapter, I will exegete Aquinas in his own right. We shall see that once again, to study a classic theologian's views about sexual difference one must gather relevant material by means of discussion of other subjects. In Aquinas's case, that means noting the Aristotelian influence on Aquinas's anthropology, as well as Aquinas's beliefs about marriage and celibacy.

## The Good of the Species, the Teleology of Sexual Difference, and the Anthropology of the Body

Commenting about Gregory of Nyssa and other "ancient Doctors of the Church," Aquinas concludes that they were so concerned about the lust that "besmirches copulation in the present state" that they made errors of judgment. For example, he says that Gregory was wrong to believe that the human race would have reproduced by asexual angelic means in paradise. Gregory was also wrong, says Aquinas, to believe that sexual difference exists only because of God's foreknowledge that some sort of postlapsarian procreative strategy would be needed. Instead, Aquinas argues that "the rhythm of nature demands that male and female should mate in copulation for procreating" and "everything that is natural to man is neither withdrawn from nor given to him by sin." Aligning himself with Augustine, Aquinas believes that God instituted corporeal procreation "even in the state of innocence" and that it remained in our present fallen state. Aquinas cites *De civitate Dei* 14.26, quoting to the effect that prelapsarian procreation could have occurred in freedom from lust, in tranquility of mind, but by means of the same physical organs as today.[1]

Believing that sexual difference is natural and God-given creates a modest intellectual tension for Aquinas, as he is also committed to Aristotelian biology. Aristotle had taught that woman is a "misbegotten male," and Aquinas is thus bound to explain how the defining features of a woman as a woman could be described as natural if those same features had their origin in a defect in the reproductive process. Aquinas poses the Aristotelian proposition:

> Now the female sex is beside the intention of nature, through a fault in the formative power of the seed, which is unable to bring the matter of the foetus to the male form: wherefore the Philosopher says [*De animal.* xvi, i.e., *De generat. animal.* ii] that "the female is a misbegotten male."[2]

To circumvent this potential impasse, Aquinas derives the perfection of a woman from the overall pattern of "universal nature" of which God is the author; sexual difference refers to the collective welfare: "Although the begetting of a woman is beside the intention of a particular nature, it is in the intention of universal nature, which requires both sexes for the perfection of the human species."[3] In other words, in the postlapsarian era, the begetting of a woman may be due to imperfection and uncontrollable flux—"as the Philosopher says, 'a north wind conduces to the procreation of males, a south wind to the procreation of females'"[4]—but this vulnerability to happenstance is nevertheless part of God's overall plan of nature, who providentially arranges that the two sexes should exist for the perpetuity of the species. Moreover, in the prelapsarian era, Aquinas claims that "when the body was more subordinate to the mind . . . the sex of the progeny would have been settled by the decision of the progenitor." In that time, when it was natural for all to procreate, what now happens by providence would have happened by choice: humanity's unfallen desire to cooperate with God's will and to procreate would have ensured that "as many females would have been engendered as males."[5] The "universal nature . . . requires both sexes for the perfection of the human species"[6] and hence that an individual might exist as one sex or the other is part of the protological dispensation that continues after the fall. This account allows Aquinas to have both the Aristotelian biology and the Augustinian protology.

Aquinas also agrees with Augustine that at the resurrection and in heavenly life, procreation will happen no longer but that sexual difference will continue to exist. Aquinas frames his discussion with reference to another argument, in which he had explained why an individual would be resurrected according to the height or stature "which would have been his at the end of his growth if nature had not erred or failed."[7] Here Aquinas reasons that sexual organs, like an individual's ideal size, are something that will be manifested in the resurrection, for that is when individual bodies are brought to the perfection of their natural state:

Since defects of nature are to be repaired in the resurrection, the bodies of those who will rise from the dead will lack none of the things that belong to the perfection of nature. Now, just as other members of the body belong to the integrity of the human body, so do those that serve the purpose of generation, both in man and in woman. Therefore bodies will rise again with these members.[8]

In other words, since nature has bestowed a sex upon an individual, that sex is now part of his or her individual integrity. In Aquinas's anthropology, "man is no mere soul, but a compound of soul and body."[9] Our uniquely individual particular bodily materiality, which includes the sexual aspect, is intrinsic to our personhood: "It belongs to the very conception of 'this man' that he have this soul and *this* flesh and bone."[10] If a human being does not "have a body consisting of flesh and bones and parts of this kind as he has now," then he is no longer a human being.[11] Thus our sex cannot be forfeit even in our ultimate heavenly destination, when the need to procreate becomes obsolete.[12] Our sex may originate in reasons that arise from the need of the species for collective perpetuity, but because sex is part of our bodies and our bodies are part of our identity, our sex is also personally and individually significant, and it cannot be dissolved without doing violence to our identity.

From some perspectives, it might seem curious for Aquinas to believe sexual difference has such significance, since he also believes that what is most spiritually significant about a human person, the *imago Dei* with which we are all created, is not sexually differentiated. One might imagine Aquinas believing that the "real" person lies underneath the sexual aspect, hidden in the sexless *imago*. However, a counterexplanation exists. Aquinas believes, again influenced by Aristotle, that the soul "actuates" and gives life to the body, yet on the other hand the soul is also distinct from the body, subsisting in its own right and incorporeal.[13] For Aquinas, humans are composites of body and soul; in the body we have sex, but in the soul the sexless *imago Dei*.[14] On these premises, Aquinas believes that humans are a composite of both sexed bodies and sexless souls, and, to the extent that these premises are sustainable, one can imagine how there need be no contradiction in saying that sexual difference is both significant and insignificant in different respects. For Aquinas, we enjoy and contemplate God in our soul, where there is no sexual difference because there is no body; but where we enjoy and live our human social life, our sexual existence is real and material. For our purposes, then, we need to note that Aquinas believes that our bodily participation in sexual difference, our existence as one sex or another, is vital for us to be the composite creatures we are. Without the soul we would be animals, without the body we would be like angels. We are humans, sharing common bodily characteristics with animals. To be faithful to our vocation as the sort of creatures we are, we must not aspire to be disembodied souls or act as if we were, for that is the provenance of angels, a different order of creation.[15] Thus, on Aquinas's premises, it follows that sexual difference is part of our natural existence without which we cannot be human, but sexual difference is also not sufficient to make us human and it does not in itself enable or bring us to our supernatural, beatific destinies. Our ultimate destiny is, according to Aquinas, something first and foremost enjoyed by the contemplative soul, which is where the *imago Dei* exists. Beatitude or eschatological fulfillment is a gift of grace bestowed on the soul by God. Eventually, at the general resurrection, our sexed bodies participate and are present in this supernatural end, but they do so on account of God's act and not due to the achievements or experiences of sexual difference. In the Thomistic metaphysical anthropology, the soul is incomplete without the body and longs to be united with it. But the sexed body is, in itself and on its own terms, not the vehicle for our final end. Thus Aquinas's theory of the sexless image of God in the soul does not relegate the sexed body to insignificance, but it helps to specify what limited significance sexual difference does have.

As evidence that this inference is correct, we might see how well our summary explains how Aquinas sounds egalitarian at some moments with regard to sexual difference, and yet hierarchical with regard to the difference at other moments. On the one hand, he cites Galatians 3:28 and Colossians 3:11 for the sake of affirming that there is no sexual difference in spiritual relationships and in our rebirth in Christ. He claims that "in matters pertaining to the soul woman does not differ from man."[16] Yet, on the other hand, he also claims that woman is naturally subject to the rule of man and "the female needs the male, not merely for the sake of genera-tion, as in the case of other animals, but also for the sake of government, since the male is both more perfect in reasoning and stronger in his pow-ers."[17] At first it might seem there is a contradiction in affirming equality and hierarchy at these alternate moments. But as our inferences should have led us to expect, and as was the case with Augustine, the denial of sexual difference in spiritual matters is no denigration or minimiza-tion of sexual difference at the biological level. As one feminist reviewer of Aquinas's sexual anthropology explains, "Both sexes join together to form the Church [mystical body of Christ], but this does not mean to say that there are not two different sexes."[18] In Aquinas's terms, where we enjoy God, there are no sexual differences, but where we live together with each other, we live as men and women. On Aquinas's description, at this latter, creaturely level, whether the differences are fruitful for pro-creation or social government, the differences are significant and can-not be ignored. As befits creatures who are both body and soul, the two levels are constantly interacting; as we shall see in the next section of this chapter, the spiritual or immaterial level helps to interpret and order the animal or material level.

## How Sexual Difference Is Morally Ordered in the Present Era

That sexual difference was created for the good of the whole species is reinforced by Aquinas's description of celibacy. Aquinas says that virginity is praiseworthy not because it transcends procreation or the two sexes but because it leaves the continent more free "to be devoted to divine things."[19] But for Aquinas, this vocation cannot be open to everyone in the present era of history, for that would pose problems for the perpetuity of species. If everyone were virginal and contemplative, what would become of the human race? Men "were bound to marry in olden times. . . lest the human race should cease to multiply." Yet individuals are clearly bound by this precept no longer, since Aquinas also believes that "a special reward, namely the aureole, is due to virgins."[20] Aquinas resolves the apparent contradiction by appealing to a division of labor for the sake of a common good, such that some are called to procreate, while others "undertake other functions, such as the military life or contemplation."[21] Insofar as marriage contrasts with celibacy, then, humans are either breeders or nonbreeders, their lives allocated either to the perpetuity of species or to some contemplative good. For Aquinas, it is mandatory that some humans be apportioned to the ranks of those who procreate, lest the natural teleology go unfulfilled, but it is not obligatory that each member of the species needs to be deployed this way. Some can be virgins and seek the aureole. So long as some are "multiplying" or breeding, the good purposes and precepts arising from sexual difference, which were always seen as arising from the perspective of the species, have been fulfilled. Thus, as with his explanation for the origin of woman, a possible conceptual impasse is overcome by redescribing the problem from the perspective of the whole species.

For those men and women who are going to procreate, Aquinas is committed to making an argument about how the raw biological potential of sexual difference, that is, the ability of male and female to reproduce, should be socialized and made humane through ethical practice. As Augustine also noted, Aquinas acknowledges that unions of incest, adultery, and fornication are all biologically as effective as marriage at simply producing children.[22] Thus if one form of procreation is to be preferred over another, a nonbiological rationale must be offered. One such rationale for Aquinas is to control concupiscence. Concupiscence is a problem demanding control because "concupiscence is most incompatible with spirituality, inasmuch as it makes a man to be wholly carnal" and thus contrary to his true nature as a composite of body and soul.[23] For instance, the problem with incest is not biological, for "brute animals copulate even with their mother," and children can be reared from such a union.[24] The problem is that if any blood relation were a potential sexual partner, "a wide scope would be afforded to concupiscence if those who have to live together in the same house were not forbidden to be mated in the flesh."[25] Similar concerns explain why a priest should not have intercourse with a woman whose confession he hears: "Relations between priest and penitent are most intimate, and consequently in order to remove the occasion of sin this prohibition was made."[26] Godparents, due to their spiritual consanguinity, are forbidden to procreate with their candidates for baptism and confirmation.[27] The biological possibility of procreation, which is for Aquinas the raison d'etre of sexual difference, is thus not self-interpreting.[28] How we are meant to live and actualize the vocation to procreate, which for Aquinas is implied by the existence of sexual difference, is subject to spiritual interpretation.

In another and very similar argument, Aquinas notes that the purpose of sexual difference, revealed in God's command to "increase and multiply," is something humans share with animals.[29] But that claim gets its theological nuance when Aquinas adds in the same passage that the way in which the human couple are meant to procreate, through marriage, is something that separates humans from animals: "Although this was said also to the other animals, it was not to be fulfilled by them in the same way as by men."[30] Therefore it is again not biological naturalism Aquinas is commending, but a particular kind of humanized or ethically deliberate use of biology. He would appeal to marriage as the natural form of human procreation and insist that it is just as natural as the biological processes, but this appeal would be to nature understood in a certain acculturated sense in which the natural and the biological are not synonyms. He makes a distinction between nature as resulting from necessity ("thus upward movement is natural to fire") and says, "In this way matrimony is not natural."[31] Matrimony is natural in the way that virtue is natural, as that which inclines to the flourishing of humans according to their fundamental or natural characteristics, and these "things . . . come to pass at the intervention or motion of the free-will."[32] This distinction gives his readers the leeway to deepen the distinction between the biological and the ethical, with both coming under the category of "the natural." The former makes sexual difference good as animal, but the latter is what makes it good as human. The two are related, for the animal facts of sexual difference make certain demands on how the human virtues will be construed, yet the two are conceptually distinct.

For these reasons Aquinas will argue, in effect, that marriage owes its significance to the possibility of biological procreation but its superiority to other procreative activity for reasons rooted in neighbor love and human sociality. The argument is that the procreation marriage intends also includes not merely producing the child but bringing up the child well, with good moral instruction, something Aquinas argues is impossible "unless there be a tie between the man and a definite woman, and it is in this that matrimony consists."[33] Thus while fornication or concupiscence is wrong for the injury it does to one's own self (turning the person into something "wholly carnal," as noted above), it also leads to injuring the offspring, as any resulting child would be born into a transient environment in which proper parental nurture is impossible.[34] Promiscuity is an offense to potential children, who need a father and mother "for a whole lifetime" for both earthly needs and the development of character: "Simple fornication is contrary to the love we should bear our neighbour, for, as we have indicated, it is an act of generation performed in a setting disadvantageous to the good of the child to be born."[35] A brute biological fact—the emission of semen—is given human meaning through context: semen should not be "emitted under conditions such that generation could result but the proper upbringing would be prevented." Proper upbringing includes the "education of the [child's] soul."[36] In sum, for Aquinas, given the procreative potential of sexual difference, marriage is the human institution that builds upon sexual difference properly, because through marriage alone it is possible for the sexes to procreate in a way that meets obligations to oneself, neighbor, and offspring.

This process of making meaning, of giving raw biology a moral shape, applies to all humans, Christian or not, because Aquinas maintains that it is natural (in the second sense, bearing in mind the exercise of free will) for any parent to look after the good of their offspring body and soul.[37] But the procreative root of marriage is given further and specifically Christian theological determination when he goes on to say that the begetting of offspring should aim to perfect the offspring in the realm of grace.[38] Intending offspring as a way of perpetuating the species makes marriage and sexual difference coherent goods even for nonbelievers, but this biological perpetuity is brought to perfection by Christians who should procreate intending the offspring as a new child of God, a new person for fellowship with Christ.[39] In this way, we can see again how the Thomistic teleology of sexual difference is a case of grace building on biology and, indeed, bringing biological potential to its fruition in a way it could not do on its own terms.

## Conclusion, and a Contrast with Augustine

In this chapter, we have seen how Thomas Aquinas believed sexual difference exists from the prelapsarian era up to and including eschatological time. He believed that sexual difference is created by God to serve the perpetuity of species, and it is at the level of the whole species where the teleology of sexual difference demands to be fulfilled. This creates some space for a potential division of labor; not every man or woman must procreate. The good of the species can be maintained by delegating among breeders and nonbreeders. Among those who do procreate, the act of procreation should be ordered in ways that resist concupiscence and promote the welfare of children and neighbor. This ordering is natural for all, in and out of the church. But both those who procreate and those who do not are all human; nonbreeders still have the bodily and sexed features of their species. All humans are composites of body and soul; in the soul we are sexless, but we cannot be called human unless we have both body and soul. Therefore Aquinas believes that the continuity of individual identity demands the persistence of sexual difference in the eschaton, even when procreating is no longer necessary for the perpetuity of the species.

Aquinas's description of celibacy and the "division of labour" implies a significance for sexual difference that contrasts with Augustine.[40] Augustine, at least from mid-career onward, believed that with the birth of Christ, the vocation of celibacy opened, in principle, to all. For Augustine, the procreative teleology of sexual difference was never oriented to the species per se, but to populating the heavenly city. Now that Christ has come and the heavenly city has in some sense been inaugurated in history, the perpetuity of species and the production of one generation after another can no longer be mandatory. When the decisive event in history has occurred, no natural activity can be compulsory in the same way as it was previously, for now the church has everything it needs, in principle, for God's final call. Thus, on Augustine's terms, were the species to stop procreating, it need not matter. No teleology would necessarily be transgressed. But Aquinas, partly under the influence of Aristotle's biology, had not described the relationship between procreation and the church's social life in the same explicitly or narrowly theological terms as Augustine. For Aquinas, the significance of sexual difference is more closely tied to its reproductive functions in preserving the species, which is a different point of reference than populating the heavenly city. One might even go so far as to suggest that sexual difference is more "conservative" in Aquinas, in the sense that, for Aquinas, the significance of sexual difference is more stable; it always has the same function, whatever the moment in the heavenly city's history. In contrast, for Augustine, one can see that sexual difference is exclusively theological from the beginning and hence more liable to different theological meanings at different stages in history. In chapter 8, when we see how certain modern theologies of marriage appeal more to a Thomistic understanding of sexual difference than an Augustinian one, we shall see how these two different perspectives bear fruit in various attempts to revise the theology of marriage and to diminish the significance of sexual difference.

## Notes

1. Thomas Aquinas, *Summa Theologiae: Man Made to God's Image (1a. 90–102)* (trans. Edmund Hill; vol. 13; London: Blackfriars, 1964), 1a.98.a2.

2. Thomas Aquinas, *Summa Theologica: Third Part (Supplement): Treatise of the Resurrection (Qq. LXIX–LXXXVI)* (trans. Fathers of the English Dominican Province; vol. 20; London: Burns, Oates & Washbourne, 1922), 3a.81.a3.

3. Ibid.

4. *ST*, 1a.99.a2.

5. Ibid.

6. Aquinas, *Summa Theologica: Third Part (Supplement)* 3a.81.a3.3.

7. Ibid., 3a.81.a2.

8. Thomas Aquinas, *The Summa contra Gentiles: The Fourth Book* (trans. English Dominican Fathers; vol. 5; London: Burns, Oates & Washbourne, 1929), 4.83.

9. Thomas Aquinas, *Summa Theologiae: Man (1a. 75–83)* (trans. Timothy Suttor; vol. 11; London: Blackfriars, 1970), 1a.75.a4. Cf. Thomas Aquinas, *On the Power of God (Quaestiones Disputatae De Potentia Dei)* (trans. Fathers of the English Dominican Province; vol. 3 [Questions VII–X]; London: Burns, Oates & Washbourne, 1934), 9.1.r6: "Thus the definition of man which signifies his essence, includes flesh and bones."

10. Aquinas, *Summa Theologiae:Man* 1a.75.a4.

11. Thomas Aquinas, *Summa contra Gentiles: Book IV: Salvation* (trans. Charles J. O'Neil; Notre Dame, IN: University of Notre Dame Press, 1975), 4.84.5.

12. Ibid., 4.83.1, 2, 6, 7, 9, and 10.

13. *ST* 1a.75.a1, 1a.75.a2.

14. *ST* 1a.93.a6. Lyndon Reynolds, "Bonaventure on Gender and Godlikeness: Compared to Augustine, Albertus Magnus, and Aquinas," *Downside Review* 106 (1988): 186ff., notes that an *imago Dei* without gender distinction is the position of the mature Aquinas and not necessarily representative of his earlier position.

15. See Thomas Aquinas, *Summa Theologiae: Angels (1a. 50–64)* (trans. Kenhelm Foster; vol. 9; London: Blackfriars, 1968), for his discussion of angels.

16. Thomas Aquinas, *Summa Theologica: Third Part (Supplement): Treatise on the Sacraments (Qq. Xxxiv–Lxviii)* (trans. Fathers of the English Dominican Province; vol. 19; London: Burns, Oates & Washbourne, 1922), 3a.57.a1, 3a.39.

17. *SCG*, III/II, ch. 123, §4; §3.

18. Boerresen, *Subordination and Equivalence*, 231.

19. Thomas Aquinas, *Summa Theologiae: Temperance (2a2ae. 141–154)* (trans. Thomas Gilby; vol. 43; London: Blackfriars, 1968), 2a2ae.152.

20. *ST* 3a.41.a2.

21. Thomas Aquinas, *Summa Contra Gentiles: Book III: Providence Part II* (trans. Vernon J. Bourke; Notre Dame, IN: University of Notre Dame Press, 1975), 3/2.136.9. See also *ST* 2a2ae.152.a2, 3a.41.a2.

22. *ST* 3a.54.a3; 3a.41.a3, 3a.49.a1.

23. *ST* 3a.66.a1.

24. *ST* 3a.54.a3.

25. Ibid.; see also 3a.57.a3.

26. *ST* 3a.56.a2.

27. *ST* 3a.56.a3.

28. Cf. ibid.

29. *ST* 3a.42.a2, 1a.92.a2.

30. Ibid.

31. *ST* 3a.41.a1.

32. Ibid.

33. Ibid.

34. *ST* 2a2ae.154.a4.

35. *ST* 2a2ae.154.a2.

36. *SCG* III/II.122.6, III/II.122.8.

37. *ST* 3a.59.a2.

38. Ibid.

39. *ST* 3a.49.a5, 3a.56.a2.

40. Banner, *Christian Ethics and Contemporary Moral Problems*, 301–4, also points to the contrast between Aquinas and Augustine on the logic of celibacy and procreation.

# Chapter 5
# LUTHER AND CALVIN

My research to this point has often had to work on the basis of inference. For example, I have often had to deduce what beliefs about sexual difference would have to be implicit in order to enable a certain theology of celibacy or marriage, or what ideas about sexual difference are present but unstated in an argument that is more overtly concerned with some other subject. In this chapter, this approach is still sometimes necessary, but less often. Particularly in the case of Martin Luther, in this chapter we will find a new degree of explicitness and directness in various statements about sexual difference.

This chapter examines Luther's contention that God made the two sexes and his belief that human beings are commanded by God to order their lives on the basis of being male and female, that is, on the basis of how God has made them. Furthermore, Luther is convinced that to fulfill this command, and live rightly as a man or a woman, will almost always mean to live as a husband or a wife. Luther does not go so far as to argue that marriage is compulsory, for he can imagine certain exceptional or temporary cases of celibacy and vowed virginity, but he does maintain that celibates must also acknowledge God's purposes in creating sexual difference. He describes monasticism or fornication as inadequate responses to sexual difference, for they appear to him as either futile attempts to defy our created nature as male and female, or impious attempts to avoid worshiping and giving thanks to God for being made as male or female.

Luther more or less makes all of these arguments in an early series of works written between 1519 and 1523. But as we shall see, these various arguments were collected and made particularly clear in his commentary on Genesis in the late 1530s.

This chapter will also discuss John Calvin, who treats marriage and human sexuality in ways consistent with Luther. However, since his arguments are subsequent to Luther and add little that is novel, we will not consider him in as much detail.

## A Sermon on the Estate of Marriage (1519)

In this sermon, Luther argues that although sexual difference is something humans share with animals, in humans it has a particular and unique significance. Luther believes that this significance is recognized and visible in the estate of marriage, claiming that marriage integrates our sex to the work of Christ and the church.

The key text in this argument is Genesis 2:18–24. Luther says that "these words teach us where man and woman come from, how they were given to one another, for what purpose a wife was created, and what kind of love there should be in the estate of marriage." To the animals, Luther observes that God simply says (in Gen 1:22) to go, be fruitful, and multiply. Only in humans does God bring the female to the male and thereby institute marriage, which gives human sexual difference a theological status that is not simply creaturely procreation.[1] Sexual difference is shared with animals, but it is also the substratum for something not shared with animals.

Luther explains what is not shared with animals as he enumerates the three purposes or "goods" of marriage. As with Augustine, these three goods existed prior to the fall, but Luther's sequence reverses Augustine's order, bringing christological elements to the fore.

In Luther's ordering, the sacramental good is first: "a sacred sign of something spiritual, holy, heavenly, and eternal," which in this case refers to marriage as "an outward and spiritual sign of the greatest, holiest, worthiest, and noblest thing that has ever existed or ever will exist, namely, the union of the divine and human natures in Christ."[2] Or again:

> The holy apostle Paul says that as man and wife united in the estate of matrimony are two in one flesh, so God and man are united in the one person Christ, and so Christ and Christendom are one body. It is indeed a wonderful sacrament, as Paul says [Eph 5:43] that the estate of marriage truly signifies such a great reality. Is it not a wonderful thing that God is man and that he gives himself to man and will be his, just as the husband gives himself to his wife and is hers?[3]

Thus the first defining feature of marriage is its suitability as an analog for God's salvific activity. Augustine defined the sacrament of marriage negatively, as a synonym for marriage's indissolubility, saying that "the union should not be broken up, and that . . . neither should marry another even for the sake of having children."[4] In Luther, the same aspect of marriage is given a different emphasis, being described as something that helps to disclose and teach the nature of God's activity toward humanity. Human sexual difference, then, is significant because God has created it for this theological purpose.

The second good of marriage specifies one condition a sexually differentiated couple must meet in order for their life together to be an analog for God's union with his people. Fidelity, says Luther, is "the whole basis and essence of marriage. . . . Each gives himself or herself to the other, and they promise to remain faithful to each other and not give themselves to any other."[5] Again, Augustine had determined fidelity more reductively—he had defined it as "neither partner should sleep with another person"[6]—and what Luther offers, while consistent with his predecessor, is more expansive. Luther says that for sexual reproduction to be recognizable as human, that is, to be recognizably related to God's works on behalf of humanity, requires man and woman "binding themselves to each other, and surrendering themselves to each other." Luther has such a high view of this mutual surrender that he believes it is the reason why, for humans, God permits coitus between man and woman "even more . . . than is necessary for the begetting of children."[7] Fidelity is thus a specification of the type of love between the spouses, a type of mutual self-gift and surrender, which fulfills the command for human sexual difference to distinguish itself from the simply reproductive significance of animal sexual difference.

Luther contrasts this type of love with the false love that seeks selfish gain; in Luther's words, proper marital love is in contrast to the way

a man loves money, possessions, honour, and women taken outside of marriage and against God's command. It is also in contrast to natural love between father and child, brother and sister, friend and relative, and similar relationships. Over and above all these is the married love, that is, a bride's love, which glows like a fire and desires nothing but the husband. She says, "It is you I want, not what is yours: I want neither your silver nor your gold; I want neither. I want only you. I want you in your entirety, or not at all." All other kinds of love seek something other than the loved one: this kind wants only to have the beloved's own self completely.[8]

In other words, this distinctively human institution called marriage is defined by a love that sees the other person as a particular—as a *you* and not an *it*, that sees the other as a person rather than as a means to acquiring and possessing things. This love claims the whole self for itself and is driven by a type of desire, but a desire that allows the other independence because it is different from self-love or natural bonds toward one's kin, for this desire regards the other as genuinely different and not as an extension of self. As we saw with Bernard, who also described a variety of human relationships and who also singled out marital love as quintessentially analogous to God's love, this love unifies differences without collapsing or begrudging them.

For the third good of marriage, Luther names that feature of sexual difference which humans have in common with animals and which is therefore, in a sense, at the root of marriage, existing before its more uniquely human qualities come into play: "Marriage produces offspring, for that is the end and chief purpose of marriage."[9] This biological possibility, and no other, is what is integrated into a wider theological significance. Procreation is the chief or common purpose of marriage in the sense that it is so basic that the heathen too have offspring and seek heirs. But, as Luther also notes, the heathen cannot really fulfill this good properly, for they are by definition deaf to the call to "bring up children to serve God, to praise and honour him."[10] Sexual difference is thus the necessary precondition for sexual reproduction, something all humans and animals share, but even this shared good has a distinctly human and Christian meaning. In Luther's interpretation, the third good of marriage, like the first two, opens the relationship between the sexes into a spiritual exercise with implications for the whole church: "There is no greater tragedy in Christendom than spoiling children. If we want to help Christendom, we must certainly have to start with the children, as happened in earlier times."[11]

Thus from the very first good of marriage to Luther's Christianized view of the third, we can see how, for him, coming together as a sexually differentiated couple is theologically significant many times over. God made male and female specifically so that this type of covenant could happen; to be a man or a woman is to be a creature created for this type of encounter, and to be a husband or a wife is to fulfill one's created purpose.

For Luther, God's command that the human significance of sexual difference is to be realized in marriage is a fact of creation that is prior to sin, and it endures after the fall. But after the fall, marriage as we experience it changes as humanity's disposition toward God changes. With the fall comes lust, and lust is a threat to marriage and thus a threat to manifesting the theological significance of sexual difference. Lust is self-ish and contrary to the love that makes marriage, and lust is a passion that makes humans (particularly youth, according to Luther) careless about what God considers a weighty matter.[12] Under the influence of lust, we may fail to seek the goods of marriage; now we can be given over to our own desires, rather than God's purposes. We now need marriage not only for its original goods but also as a remedial measure to recall our sexuality back to the original teleology, which we are otherwise liable to ignore. After the fall, Luther calls this remedial aspect to marriage "a hospital for incurables which prevents inmates from falling into graver sin."[13] He summarizes, "Thus the doctors have found three goods and useful things about the married estate, by means of which the sin of lust, which flows beneath the surface, is counteracted and ceases to be a cause of damnation."[14] Luther views marriage, we might say, as medicine that allows the two sexes to be what they are created to be, that is, creatures in fellowship with God and with one another.

## Judgment of Martin Luther on Monastic Vows (1521/1522)

For Luther, the vows of monks to be celibates or virgins are both impious and impossible. We will see why Luther is so skeptical of these types of continence. But first we can simply note that Luther also does not look upon virginity as a witness to eschatological social life, as one might have expected from someone so well versed in Augustine's theory of sexual life. As with Augustine, he does not think virginity should be a rejection of the goodness of the two sexes or of marriage, but, unlike Augustine, he does not explain how virginity can still be good in its own right. He does not, for instance, develop a vision of how the two sexes might relate to one another as two sexes in the heavenly city, in the era without marriage.

Luther mostly regards celibacy and virginity with suspicion. He claims that "a vow of chastity . . . is diametrically opposed to the gospel."[15] But Luther does not argue for this conclusion as one might expect. Having read Luther's earlier work on marriage, one might expect him to argue that a vow of chastity denies God's purposes in creation. But in this 1521/1522 treatise, Luther instead focuses on the consequences of sin and the dif-ficulty of avoiding lust in a fallen world: "For instance, it is commanded not to lust. Yet there has never been a virgin or an unmarried person in the world who has been utterly free from lust." The premise here is the inevitability of concupiscence and the belief that "natural man is not in command of the situation, and works do not secure a good and certain conscience." Vows of celibacy fail to reckon with this power of lust, and so they fail to offer a viable solution: "You cannot bring the inward tyrant into subjection by any amount of effort, much less by words."[16] According to Luther, the attempt to vow continence presumes powers "natural man" does not have and to which he should not aspire; it is a vow that is both impossible to fulfill without God's intervention to dampen desire, and impious to attempt as an effort at self-salvation. Luther believes such vows are equivalent to declaring:

> Look, O God, I vow to thee that I no longer want to be a Christian. I revoke the vow made in my baptism, and will no longer depend on Christ or live in him. All these things are useless and outdated. I vow to thee, however, a new and much better vow, better than Christ and other than Christ, that is, to live by my own works of chastity, obedience, poverty and by this entire rule. For by these works I shall be justified and saved, and will help myself and others towards righteousness and salvation.[17]

Such vows, on Luther's terms, will and should flounder.

However, Luther does not go so far as to make marriage mandatory for all men and women. He argues that vows of continence are permitted if they are self-consciously limited and subordinated, knowing that they are optional and not necessary. He would have it that such vows are regarded like "farming or a trade," as a way of occupying the self for purposes of service and meditation, "because I must live in the flesh and cannot be idle." He sharply denounces the likes of Jerome, who treated "virginity as a thing existing in its own right" and who, in so doing, "perverts" the idea that scriptures such as 1 Corinthians 7:38 are anything but utilitarian or practical observations that "a young woman not encumbered by any responsibilities is more free to serve God."[18] A virgin should opt out of marriage only for practical reasons. Luther says such a virgin should reason,

> "Although I could marry, I am content to remain unmarried, not because it is commanded, not because it is advised, not because it is greater and more sacrificial than all other virtues, but because this seems to me to be the right way to live, just as marriage or farming may seem right to somebody else. I do not want the responsibilities of married life, I want to be free of responsibilities and have time for God." See here, this is what it means to be a virgin in Christian simplicity, for she glories not in her virginity, but in Christ.[19]

But Luther thinks such virgins will be rare, almost miraculously so, due to the relentless nature of postlapsarian desire. Most men and women will be like the man who "cannot master the nature of his sexuality so as to be able to do without sexual intercourse naturally." For such people, unable to sustain chastity, one alternative is to consort with harlots, or, as Luther prefers, to take a wife as a "middle course." Marriage as a remedy for sin is preferable for the "continual searing of lust which never dies out" among those who vow chastity but lack the power to resist corruption. It is simply foolish to refuse a spouse when the soul is full of passion: "How foolish it would be, even godless, if you were to kill yourself by hunger for fear of the law when you could steal food from the abundance of another and thereby save your life. You are just as foolish if you do not take a wife when passion stirs and you remain continent to the danger of your soul."[20]

We can see, then, that Luther believes a strong and unavoidable desire conditions the postlapsarian relations between the sexes, for neither men nor women are ordinarily free of it, and that one function of marriage is to be a provision God makes for the providential welfare of his creatures. Taming desire will be a ubiquitous task in our era of history, and part of the purpose of marriage is to assist in this project. For this reason, in Luther's thought, the practice of marriage can, at times, seem to be a virtual necessity arising from the experience of sexual difference in fallen times. But he never argues for that conclusion to the exclusion of other possibilities, and certainly in other treatises he emphasizes the prelapsarian goodness of the two sexes as the main basis for marriage.

## The Estate of Marriage (1522)

This treatise returns to the earlier theme of the goodness of sexual difference in creation, before sin. It contains an unusually direct statement about sexual difference, seen in Luther's exegesis of Genesis 1:27:

From this passage we may be assured that God divided mankind into two classes, namely, male and female, or a he and a she. This was so pleasing to him that he himself called it a good creation [Gen 1:31]. Therefore, each one of us must have the kind of body God has created for us. I cannot make myself a woman, nor can you make yourself a man; we do not have that power. But we are exactly as he created us: I a man and you a woman. Moreover, he wills to have his excellent handiwork honoured as his divine creation, and not despised.[21]

Here, directly and without reference to procreation or marriage, Luther says that differentiation of humanity into two sexes is good owing to the fact that it is the work of God's hands. In this passage, we do not need to make any inference, any deduction from an argument about marriage or some other topic, for Luther is explicit about sexual difference in its own right. We cannot and do not make ourselves male or female—only God does. This act in creating the two sexes is pleasing to God. "Each one of us" must be as God made us. Thus to be what we are, to welcome sexual difference, to honor God's handiwork rather than to despise it, comes to human beings as a divine command, which means the human response to being sexually differentiated can be framed in terms of obedience or disobedience. To respond appropriately to the fact of who we are, that is, to the fact of being male and female, becomes part of our obedience to God and is a universal summons.

How might one honor sexual difference and obey God's will? Luther points to Genesis 1:28:

> Now this [ordinance] is just as inflexible as the first, and no more to be despised and made fun of than the other, since God gives it his blessing and does something over and above the act of creation. Hence, as it is not within my power not to be a man so it is not my prerogative to be without a woman. Again as it is not in your power not to be a woman, so it is not your prerogative to be without a man. For it is not a matter of free choice or decision but a natural and necessary thing, that whatever is a man must have a woman and whatever is a woman must have a man.[22]

Some sort of encounter between the sexes is, on these terms, a matter of necessity. To be a man under God and to welcome the fact of being a man includes being with a woman, and vice versa; to be otherwise "is not my prerogative." To be one sex is to be in relation to the other sex. Thus not only are we made male and female, but included in being made this way is a relationship to the opposite sex. Sexual difference, and sexually differentiated relationship, is intrinsic to being human under God.

Luther goes on to explain that the pagans do not have this knowledge. They are blind to their own created nature, as is revealed in their resentment of sexually differentiated relations such as marriage. Luther believes that God has allowed this blindness for the reasons given in Romans 1: "He who is married but does not recognise the estate of marriage cannot continue without bitterness, drudgery, and anguish; he will inevitably complain and blaspheme like the pagans and the blind, irrational men.

But he who recognises the estate of marriage will find therein delight, love, and joy without end." To avoid similar blindness, Christians must hold fast "that man and woman are the work of God." Christians should be careful, lest they fall under influences that shape their imagination and beliefs in unchristian ways: "Young men should be on their guard when they read pagan books and hear the common complaints about marriage, lest they inhale the poison."[23] Christians must perceive their work of marriage with reference to their faith in God's creation of the two sexes, lest the work itself come to seem burdensome and pointless.

We see in this discussion that epistemology is linked with faithfulness; for Luther, the ability to know and rejoice at the possibility of marriage is a result of attentiveness to God rather than self. "We err in that we judge the work of God according to our own feelings, and we regard not his will but our own desire. This is why we are unable to recognise his works and persist in making evil that which is good, and regarding as bitter that which is pleasant." "That clever harlot, our natural reason" looks at marriage and childbearing and sees chores and drudgery; the natural question is "Should I make such a prisoner of myself?" The natural answer is "It is better to remain free and lead a peaceful, carefree life." But a Christian man will regard all these things as occasions to make God smile, saying, "I confess to thee that I am not worthy to rock the little babe or wash its diapers, or to be entrusted with the care of the child and its mother," but to perform these sorts of labors is why God made men to be husbands and fathers, and it is God's pleasure that men do these things.[24] In making his case for marriage, Luther does not mind citing "natural" arguments such as the benefits of marriage to the social life of cities and countries, or the physical harm that "physicians" believe the body suffers when it is not allowed to reproduce. But the resting place of his argument is resolutely theological: "I base my remarks on Scripture, which to me is surer than all experience and cannot lie to me. He who finds still other good things in marriage [from experience] profits all the more, and should give thanks to God."[25]

## Commentary on 1 Corinthians 7 (1523)

In this commentary Luther repeats several earlier arguments, confirming his view that distinctive theological knowledge is necessary to grasp the meaning of human sexual existence. Strong contrasts are drawn between pagan and Christian ways of shaping relations between the two sexes. Luther suggests that in pagan perspective, relations between the two sexes are fundamentally antagonistic and selfish, but that the Christian perspective leads to mutual service between the sexes.

Again, Luther begins his argument in Scripture. In Scripture, Luther says that we learn that God "does not create any woman for the purpose of fornication," and neither does God wish that "all women should be strangled or banished" for the sake of creating a fellowship of only one sex.[26] In other words, to believe that woman is an object for the self's pleasure, or is merely a necessary evil, is a mode of rejecting woman herself and hence God's gift in creation.

Yet, according to Luther, this antipathy to creation masquerades as wisdom among the pagans: " 'What a fool is he who takes a wife,' says the world, and it is certainly true . . . [,] for those who believe that there is no life after this one . . . act almost wisely in falling back on free fornication and not tying themselves to the labour of married life."[27] In other words, if there were no eschatological covenant with the Creator, if there were no teleological purpose for honoring the Creator's intentions, then Luther believes fornication would be "almost wise." It would be wise to use the other sex for pleasure and avoid the trials of marriage if our lives were not ordered teleologically to God. One of the distinguishing features of fornication, for Luther, is that it is an instance of interpersonal encounter "where none rules over the other or owes his partner anything, rather each seeks only his own in the other."[28] This selfish indifference is the opposite of why Luther believes sexual difference was created, but lusting pagans are blind to this summons because they do not have God's testimony in Scripture. For them, human beings are not created by and for God, and so it can only seem arbitrary to claim that human males and females are made for marriage.

However, before explaining his own Christian alternative in greater detail, Luther takes pains once again to rebuke the viability of monasticism. He notes that the premise of monasticism indeed opposes paganism, believing that some bulwark against lust is necessary. However, Luther believes that monasteries promise a false solution to the problem. In monasticism, Luther claims, the two sexes are physically segregated, as if "chastity could be put into people from without," as if the mere fact of separation cultivated purity. But Luther asks, "How does it help me if I do not see, hear, or touch a woman and still my heart is full of women and my thoughts are taken up with them day and night, thinking of the shameless things that one might do? And of what help is it to a girl to shut her up so that she neither sees nor hears a man, when her heart still sighs day and night, without ceasing, for a young man?"[29] Indeed, as his definition of fornication shows, Luther believes that sexual difference as it is now experienced poses an internal, spiritual threat to both sexes. Monastic celibacy and fornication can therefore be seen to be similar, insofar as they are both inadequate responses to the same problem—the problem of disordered, self-oriented sexual desire in the human heart.

The proper Christian solution to the problem of disordered desire, Luther reiterates, is marriage. "The state of matrimony is constituted in the law of love so that no one rules over his own body but must serve his partner, as is the way of love."[30] Here is where a man or a woman is given over to the authority of the other sex. Differentiation into the "male or female form" is indeed something that human beings share with "birds and all the animals."[31] But whatever may be the case with other creatures, among fallen humans "the heat of the flesh, which rages without ceasing, and daily attraction to woman or to man" can cause people to "suffer so severely that they masturbate."[32] The pain of unfulfilled desire can be so great that instead of leading to self-giving, the self acts to slake its own appetite. Marriage is the alternative, says Luther, because "in this relationship you are bound up with your neighbour and have become his servant." In marriage, a man's "body is not his own but his wife's, and vice versa." For that reason, "all these [who suffer from desire] ought to be in the married estate."[33] After the fall, marriage is the rebuke to what human selfish desires might otherwise propose. This view of marriage is, in a sense, ascetical, since it views marriage as a channeling of an otherwise chaotic force. This view of marriage evidently hopes that by giving the self to the other sex, by committing to an other-oriented discipline, the self itself will be changed in ways more "outward" solutions could not. This type of mutual subordination is, for Luther, a return to and fulfillment of sexual difference's created purposes, and it can happen only when the two sexes are understood in theological perspective.

## Lectures on Galatians (1535)

Luther does not discuss Galatians 3:28 at much length in these lectures. Perhaps the verse gets brief treatment because the two sexes, and the extent to which they have a homogeneity in the church, are a sustained theme in his lectures on Genesis, which were due to be delivered around the same time as the Galatians lectures. But whatever the reason, Luther claims that Galatians 3:28 indicates that although there is neither male nor female in Christ, this sexual indifference does not represent a rejection of the goodness of the two sexes. "Thus the magistrate, the emperor, the king, the prince, the consul, the teacher, the preacher, the pupil, the father, the mother, the children, the master, the servant—all these are social positions or external masks. God wants us to respect and acknowledge them as His creatures, which are a necessity for this life." Thus Luther does not read Galatians 3:28 as advocating any sort of Christian androgyny: "Male, female, slave, free, Jew Gentile, king, subject . . . in Christ, in the matter of salvation, they amount to nothing, for all their wisdom, righteousness, devotion, and authority." To live well in this order—to fulfill one's roles as a man and husband, or as a woman and a wife—is a good thing that requires the grace of God. But such things in themselves "do not avail anything toward righteousness in the sight of God."[34] Luther appears to conclude that the "external masks" of the social order are not in themselves salvific, although they are still good.

## Lectures on Genesis (1535/1536)

In these lectures,[35] Luther condemns some of Augustine's earliest beliefs about male and female, such as the attempt to read Genesis allegorically or to equate Eve with the lower orders of human rationality.[36] Other aspects of Augustine's work, such as the later belief that prelapsarian life would have been robustly physical, are accepted and form part of Luther's basic presuppositions. But as we shall see, Luther also significantly departs from Augustine in these lectures. He also treats at length a theme—the common foundation of the two sexes in the church—that we might have expected to see in his discussion of Galatians 3:28.

In the lectures, Luther's claim that humanity is created by God for life in the church is the clue to understanding sexual difference. Luther makes this claim on the basis of Genesis 1:16–17, in which God gives Adam the command not to eat of the tree of knowledge. Luther explains that this command constitutes the establishment of the church, for the command furnishes Adam with "an outward work of obedience toward God" and hence "an outward form of worship." Luther observes that "here we have the establishment of the church before there was any government of the home and of the state; for Eve was not yet created." Thus, even though sexual difference is about to be created and will be reckoned to be among God's primordial blessings for humanity, humanity's ecclesial identity is even more basic than this sexuality: "But the church was established first because God wants to show by this sign, as it were, that man was created for another purpose than the rest of the living beings."[37] The animals do not share the human ecclesiastical teleology, and this human uniqueness will have consequences when sexual difference is created. Because humans have this basic ecclesiastical orientation, all of their other significant features, such as sexual difference, are governed and determined by ecclesiology. If, at the most basic and determinative level of anthropology, God wants one thing from Adam—"that he praise God, that he thank Him, that he rejoice in the Lord, and that he obey Him by not eating from the forbidden tree"—then it follows for Luther that subsequent levels of anthropology, such as sexual differentiation, would also be created to enable and join in this project of praising, thanking, rejoicing, and obeying.[38]

For Luther, the determination to praise, thank, obey, and rejoice in the Lord becomes, in effect, what we might call the hermeneutic for a biblical anthropology of sexual difference. Consider this statement, by Luther, which reflects basic Augustinian orthodoxy:

[The prelapsarian] Adam was not to live without food, drink, and procreation. But at the predetermined time, after the number of saints had become full, these physical activities would have come to an end; and Adam, together with his descendents, would have been translated to the eternal and spiritual life. Nevertheless, these activities of physical life—like eating, drinking, procreating, etc.— would have been a service pleasing to God; we could also have rendered this service to God without the defect of lust which is there now after sin, without any sin, and without the fear of death. This would have surely been a pleasant and delightful life, a life about which we may indeed think but which we may not attain in this life.[39]

As we have seen, Augustine and his successors have argued all these same themes: the physicality of prelapsarian life, without the stain of lust and lived in some greater mode of glory for God, and that current physical life is but a meager shadow of this earlier way. The command to "be fruitful" was part of the original blessing and command of God for male and female, which is now "marred" but still extant.[40] Thus Luther's exegesis includes a recapitulation of familiar Augustinian proposals.

But the next step in Luther's reasoning departs from Augustine significantly and depends on the premise that humanity's basic determination is for life in the church. Augustine would not have disagreed that humanity is determined for life in the church, but he did not apply it to his exegesis of Genesis in quite the same way as Luther. For not only does the Genesis text lead Luther to reckon with sexual difference in its own right, but it also requires a discussion of the *imago Dei*, and, with regard to this concept, Luther innovates in ways that are consequential for sexual difference.

Regarding the *imago*, Luther writes, "Memory, will, and mind we have indeed," but "if these powers are the image of God, it will also follow that

Satan was created to the image of God, since he surely has these natural endowments . . . to a far higher degree than we have them." Therefore Luther looks beyond Augustine's notion of the *imago Dei* and beyond Adam's natural endowments to a "unique work of God," which humans share with no one else. He settles on the unique human relationship humans have with God, that aspect of humans which differentiates them from the animals, as itself the *imago Dei*: "Therefore my understanding of the image of God is this: that Adam had it in his being and that he not only knew God and believed He was good, but that he also lived in a life that was wholly godly; that is, he was without the fear of death or of any other danger, and was content with God's favor."[41] In other words, the *imago Dei* is located in the faithful relationship between God and the human creature, and is visible to the extent that this relationship of right regard for God is visible. The *imago Dei* is effectively a synonym for the determination for God which God gave to humanity when God called Adam into the church. The *imago Dei* is a synonym for the project of obeying, thanking, rejoicing, and praising that Luther takes to be the purpose of the church.

This interpretation of the *imago Dei* has implications for sexual difference since this account of the *imago Dei* unproblematically includes both sexes. Luther is confident that Eve is called to the church as well as Adam. "Adam alone" heard the first sermon, but Luther surmises "he later on informed Eve of it." Men and women differ "in no respect than in sex," and thus they do not differ in the *imago Dei*.[42] Thus Luther has a firm rationale for repudiating anthropologies that somehow regard the existence of women as either problematic or illusory:

> Lyra also relates a Jewish tale, of which Plato too, makes mention somewhere, that in the beginning man was created bisexual and later on, by divine power, was, as it were, split or cut apart, as the form of the back and of the spine seems to prove. Others have expanded these ideas with more obscene details. . . . This tale fits Aristotle's designation of woman as a "maimed man." . . . These pagan ideas show that reason cannot establish anything sure about God and the works of God but only thinks up reasons against reasons and teaches nothing in a perfect and sound manner.[43]

In sum, Luther's account of creation, ecclesiology, and the *imago Dei* accumulate and compel him to repudiate pagan views of sexual difference. Luther's reading of Genesis insists that man and woman were created originally by God and have always been genuinely different from each other with respect to sex, and so Luther is bound to reject an androgynous or one-sex view of humanity. Plato's Androgyne and Aristotle's "defective male" are both refuted when genuine differences between the sexes are confessed as part of God's original work. Woman is "a creature of God in which God Himself took delight as in a most excellent work," and so cannot be described as a derivative of man or as only one imperfect half of a prototype.[44] An anthropology premised on what Luther understood by Plato or Aristotle's view of the sexes might have trouble understanding how woman would be included in the *imago Dei*, but this problem is not Luther's.

Having framed sexual difference in terms of the common *imago Dei* and humanity's creation for life in the church, it also follows that changes and defects in the relationship between the sexes after the fall correlate to changes and defects in the relationship between humans and God. When Adam and Eve were right with God, they were right with each other, and when they went wrong with God, they went wrong with each other. The prelapsarian Adam "would not have known his Eve except in the most unembarrassed attitude toward God, with a will obedient to God, and without any evil thought." The prelapsarian Eve was "suited for the kind of life which Adam was expecting" and "would have been the equal of Adam in all respects."[45]

However, once Adam and Eve lose their right relationship with God, lust, shame, and inequality all come into their relationship with one another. After sin, Eve "is now subjected to the man." The protological Eve "was not like the woman of today; her state was far better and more excellent, and she was in no respect inferior to Adam, whether you count the qualities of the body or those of the mind." Furthermore, nudity between male and female was once "the glory of our bodies," the "greatest dignity," and a "unique prerogative of the human race over all the other animals." Now the shame of public nudity is "a witness that our heart has lost the trust in God which they who were naked had before sin."[46] We were once able to walk about naked together because we were "full of trust and assurance toward God," but now that this confidence is replaced by "distrust, fear, and shame" toward God, it is reflected in our bodies and the feelings we have about them. Thus the postlapsarian degeneration of sexual difference—the introduction of lust and hierarchy where before there was none, and the introduction of shame when there was innocence—is a function of our disordered relationship with God, an indication or datum of our lack of faith.

Luther argues that marriage, in helping to heal the wounds between the sexes, also helps to heal the relationship between God and humans:

"The purpose for which God gives us good health, wife, children, and property is not that we might offend Him by means of these gifts, but that we might recognize His mercy and give thanks to Him."[47] Marriage, theologically understood, calls men and women back to relationship with their Creator. Giving thanks for the material blessings of creation, among them the opposite sex, is an opportunity to live life as it was and to resist the breach between God and humanity that came through the fall. "We should fear God, and, while giving thanks to Him, we should not mis-use His gifts to become proud."[48] Welcoming the other sex in marriage is one way, for Luther, that we keep faith with God's commandments. We ought to be led to such conclusions, says Luther, by the testimony of Genesis that God created male and female, that the Lord brought Eve to Adam and inaugurated marriage, that the Lord commanded us to pro-create sexually, and that the Ten Commandments preach the honoring of father and mother (and hence look kindly on the "union of a man and a woman").[49]

As with Luther's earlier works on marriage, in these lectures on Genesis, Luther again takes the opportunity to critique various kinds of celibacy and monasticism for their defiance of what he believes God intends. Luther says that the followers of Tatian, as well as celibates who seem to "regard themselves as neither male nor female," hold all these glories of creation in contempt and thus show their pride.[50] Far better, argues Luther, to follow the example of the prelapsarian Adam. Luther believes that Adam knew Eve not "simply as a result of the passion of his flesh" but because he had faith in God's promise that from his flesh would come Christ, the "blessed Seed" who would restore life to mortal flesh and "crush the serpent's head."[51] In other words, Luther again points to the marriage of Adam and Eve as an example of how the right regard for sexual difference is a type of right regard for God's creation and God's intentions for creation's fruition.

Luther does not regard marriage as straightforwardly curative of all the ills that beset the two sexes: "Not even marriage, which was ordained by God as a remedy for our weak nature" can completely remedy the curse of lust, the existence of adultery, and the ambivalence many people feel about their spouses (Luther quotes an ancient proverb, "I can live neither with you nor without you," as evidence of that).[52] He appreciates that many people are unhappy in their marriages: "If one takes a wife, there follows a loathing of one's own and a passion for strange women."[53] That marriage fails to restore all the effects of the fall is no fault of mar-riage, however. It is again the effects of sin, or, more specifically, the fail-ure of postlapsarian man to honor the first tablet of the Decalogue. These commandments concern themselves with "contempt of God and of His Word," and when these are set aside, "it becomes possible for shameful deeds and sins of all sorts to prevail," even in marriage.[54] Thus marriage itself, albeit an institution that provides a habitat for honorable fulfillment of the teleology of sexual difference, is no substitute for continual reliance on and relationship with God. Marriage serves God's purposes, but it does not have freestanding status apart from them.

We can conclude our discussion of Luther's Genesis exegesis by noting his discussion of Noah's marriage, which is a concrete example of all that he has said thus far about sexual difference, marriage, celibacy, and the dependence of all these things on God.[55]

Luther reckons that Noah is initially "a virgin above all virgins" because he waited five hundred years before he begat children, according to Genesis 5:32.[56] During this time, Luther reckons that Noah was so busy preaching repentance to the wicked people of his era that he had no time for marriage. Noah's vigorous preaching, which was the preoccupation Luther says kept him aloof from marriage, was rooted in his hope for "a better and more God-fearing age" (and not in any rejection of creation and its goods). Eventually, however, in response to God's call, Noah decided to seek marriage: "The divine voice indicated to him that the definite time when the world would perish" was coming, and "then he was prompted by the Holy Spirit to turn his mind to marriage, in order that he might leave at least a seed for the new age." Luther notes that the world scoffed at Noah's preparations for the new age, both the building of the ark and his propagation of children.[57] They took the former as a folly and the latter as an indication that Noah had given up his expectation that the flood was coming. Thus Luther regards both Noah's chastity and Noah's marriage as great countercultural acts of faith in God, for he sees both choices as motivated by God's command to preach and serve the church. Noah organized his entire sexual life with reference to God's purposes, and, we might say, Noah is a case study for Luther's discussion of sexual difference, an example of how human beings were given a sex in order to live lives that render obedience and praise to God.

## Some Summarizing Thoughts about Luther

Luther's essential argument, from the 1519 treatise through the 1535 commentary on Genesis, has been that sexual difference is significant because God makes it and that God calls us to live in ways that evince gratitude for it. The main way men and women show their gratitude and contentment at being what they are is by embracing marriage. In other words, the material and sexual aspect of ourselves, which we share with animals at the biological level, is not only significant at that level. For Luther, it is in and through our bodies, as male and female, that human beings manifest their fellowship with God and one another in the church. The marriage of Adam and Eve is described by Luther as a prototypical instance of this fellowship. Noah is a further example of how Luther believes that all men and women are meant to recognize and acknowledge their maleness and femaleness in Christian ways.

All of this, Luther concedes in the Genesis lectures, "is extravagant fiction and the silliest kind of nonsense if you set aside the authority of Scripture and follow the judgment of reason."[58] To believe that Eve came from Adam's side, and that sexual difference has a definite beginning point in order to fulfill a specific purpose, is the opposite of what Luther believes Aristotle, the philosophers, and all wisdom can deduce. In philosophical terms, Luther points out that all we can know is the "material and formal cause" of our lives, that we have "this man for a father and this woman for a mother," and that such a chain of sexually productive unions extends infinitely backward. But such ignorance of our "efficient and final cause" Luther terms "a wretched situation" and "pitiable and inadequate wisdom."[59] Much more beautiful and truthful, according to Luther, is to regard sexual difference as having its origins and fulfillment in certain ordered relations with other humans and with our Creator.

## Calvin on Sexual Difference

Calvin also believed that God made the two sexes and that marriage is preferable to other possible human responses to this fact, such as celibacy or promiscuity, for reasons arising before the fall but that are transformed after the fall. First, from the prelapsarian perspective, on the basis of Genesis 2:18, Calvin says that marriage is God's initial response to man's solitude, that Adam may have a companion and "not lead a solitary life, but may enjoy a helper joined to himself."[60] But from the postlapsarian perspective, marriage has added purposes, for marriage is also God's provision and response to our concupiscence. Calvin believes that marriage is God's remedy for sin, for it gives a moderate sexual license that "keeps us from plunging into unbridled lust."[61] Yet both the original and redemptive purposes for marriage will someday be obsolete and fulfilled, for marriage lacks eschatological status; then we will be like angels, who are exempt from the requirements and problems of materiality.[62] Presumably in the eschaton, we will have other ways of being sociable than the way founded in Eden, although Calvin does not offer details. In the resurrection we will presumably still have sexual difference, for, following Christ, a person will receive again "the mortal body which he had previously borne," but in a "far more excellent" condition. In heaven Calvin suggests there will be no lust but rather "an enjoyment, clear and pure from every vice," and that to have all the joy of materiality but without the "illness" or "intemperance" of "corruptible life" will be "the acme of happiness."[63]

But why does Calvin believe that neither fornication nor celibacy are good options in the present era? Regarding celibacy, like Luther, Calvin is inclined to view it from the perspective of the fall and suggests that those who think themselves capable of celibacy are usually "forgetful of their own infirmity." Calvin believes that "the whole man is of himself nothing but concupiscence."[64] Sexual desire is too inexorable a force; we cannot recuse ourselves from its power simply on the basis of a vow, a hope, or a rational choice. Sexual activity is not actually mandatory for all humans, and present-day lives of continence are possible, but such lives are a "special gift of God" and reserved for only a very few.[65] For everyone, gifted or not, the choice to be celibate is "not in our hands," for we lack "the power to make up our own minds."[66] Only God can work it in us. Calvin concedes that one may desire such chastity from God, for he allows that it does provide more time and fewer distractions from the business of seeking God.[67] But normally, to opt out of the sexually differentiated social system, to prescind from marriage and its consequent duties, is to show prideful contempt for what is normally a "heavenly calling." Our own pleasure and convenience, in the absence of God's special dispensation and license, is not a valid motive for avoiding marriage.[68] To vow that one will not marry is "as if a householder should vow that, forsaking his life and children, he would undertake other burdens; or a man fitted to hold public office, when elected, should vow that he would be a private citizen."[69] To think that one might not need the institution of marriage is to flirt with defying a near universal vocation for sexual difference. That Adam ought not be alone is "a common law of man's vocation, so that everyone ought to receive it as if it were addressed to him. Solitude is not good except for those people whom God exempts by a special privilege."[70] Only an exceptional call from God can exempt a person from the common call.

Meanwhile, fornication is "accursed" in God's sight[71] and also not a viable alternative to marriage, and an incident recounted in Calvin's commentary on Jeremiah helps to explain why not. Here Calvin tells of a moment when the prophet condemns his fellow Jews because "their love never continued, but they lusted after any they met with; nay, they went here and there to allure them."[72] The arbitrary, episodic discontinuities of the purely erotic appetite fail to embody the faithfulness the Lord shows to Israel, as well as the solidarity between Adam and Eve in the protological era. Stating that while he does not believe "Plato's impure and obscene speculation" (that it takes the two sexes to join together to recreate a primal androgynous unity), Calvin nevertheless insists that husband and wife are meant to cherish one another in an "indivisible society" in which the other counts as "no less than as half of himself." The "intermingling of three or four" is a falsifying of this union. Unmet sexual appetites—due to disease, "inconvenience," or "boredom"—are no reason to avoid or betray marriage.[73] Again, as with celibacy, individual longing and preference is not a valid motive for avoiding the type of mutuality Calvin believes our sexual difference demands. While it is true that remedy for our sexual desires is one reason marriage exists, those desires cannot be given so much priority that they license the undermining of marriage. The union that is marriage is a "wonderful gift of God . . . for the common welfare of the human race."[74] Marriage serves God's will, models God's fidelity, and helps to organize society. In other words, marriage serves the good of meeting sexual desire, but, due to the fact that marriage places other goods alongside sexual desire, desire cannot be the only or chief motive for human coupling or marriage. It is this distortion of sexuality, this reduction to a single motive, which occurs in fornication.

For Calvin, once a man and a woman are living within the order of marriage, forces are at work that homogenize the sexes and yet also reinforce their differences. On the one hand, marriage orients both sexes to God. In this respect, the two sexes are alike. On the other hand, marriage preserves and requires certain sexually differentiated roles with respect to the opposite sex. In this perspective, the two sexes remain distinct.

With respect to God and the homogeneity of the sexes, both men and women alike are compelled to honor the social system founded on marriage because our bodies are instituted as temples (Calvin cites 1 Cor 6:19) and hence "we are not under our own jurisdiction. . . . The Lord has acquired us for Himself as His own private property."[75] For both sexes, our bodies are supposed to be part of the project of worshiping God and having fellowship with him. Both sexes should live in marriage as he would have us live, "lest we should drive Him away and He should abandon us."[76] Moreover, everyone in Christian society is implicated in "mutual servitude . . . even kings and governors, for they rule that they may serve."[77] Specifically with reference to marriage, the "husband and wife are . . . bound to mutual goodwill, and from that it follows that neither he nor she has power over his or her own body."[78] In the marriage bed, man and wife are equal, and from the beginning, "the obligation of both sexes is mutual."[79] Men and women share preeminence over the beasts, they share the *imago Dei*, and they share common sinfulness and mortality.[80] This similarity between the sexes extends to their eschatological destiny as well: "God has made no difference betwixt men and women, in giving them the doctrine of salvation, but his meaning was that this benefit and treasure, should be common as well to the one as the other. . . . God's meaning was to make men and women equal in this respect."[81] Thus under God, while the two sexes remain two sexes, their obligations to God, and in some senses to each other, are the same.

However, commenting on the Pastoral Epistles, Calvin comments on how the two sexes are also different. He says that in order to respect nature, the two sexes should dress distinctly—men clothing themselves as men, and women as women, lest "the order of nature" be turned "upside down."[82] Clothes are postlapsarian, but they providentially emphasize the prelapsarian visibility of the two sexes. The differences between the sexes are darkened on account of the fall, and clothing is necessary, when once simply nudity would have sufficed. After the fall, where there is modesty and concern for the neighbor, as opposed to self-seeking attempts to seduce and attract attention, both men and women will dress modestly.[83] Thus differentiated dress is not only simply to honor the distinctions of nature but also to be modest so as to avoid stimulating lust in the other sex.[84] Both men and women are obliged to avoid inducing concupiscence and to respect creation, but they meet this common obligation in different ways.

Sometimes in Calvin, differentiated dress codes and other social roles for the sexes can seem like general guidelines that are in the service of greater goods and therefore can be relativized when there are other compelling reasons. For instance, alluding to Paul's discussion of women covering their heads in 1 Corinthians 11 and women's silence in church in 1 Corinthians 14, Calvin asks sarcastically, "Does religion consist in a woman's shawl, so that it is unlawful for her to go out with a bare head? Is that decree of Paul's concerning silence so holy that it cannot be broken without great offense?"[85] He thinks that such sexually differentiating conventions should be observed, but in the same way as kneeling to pray is an observance of the church: as something of God "in so far as it is part of that decorum whose care and observance the apostle has commended to us," but not insofar as it is an absolute and exceptionless rule.[86] Calvin appears to be struggling to reach some sort of middle course: on the one hand, "these things are not necessary to salvation, and for the upbuilding of the church ought to be variously accommodated to the customs of each nation and age." On the other hand, "we ought not to charge into innovation rashly, suddenly, for insufficient cause."[87]

In a similar way, within marriage there are also gender roles, but again, the way in which Calvin prescribes them opens them up in a way that refuses to be fixed. The roles arise for a theological reason, and this rationale should undermine naïve, nontheological notions of gender hierarchy. For instance, Calvin says that woman's present subjection to man is "a present token of God's wrath" and so women should bear "with equanimity and calmness the necessity of being in servitude to their husbands."[88] Prior to the fall, there had been "a liberal and gentle subjection" of woman to man, but after the fall, after woman had "exceeded her proper bounds," she was "forced back to her own position." That this return is by means of force means that woman is no longer free.[89] To refuse this sexual role is to refuse to participate in the social order given for our redemption; it is equivalent to choosing one's own destruction. But meanwhile men are also implicated in the postlapsarian transformation of power between the sexes, for they must love their wives in a way that demonstrates a readiness to die for them, in imitation of Christ who "did not hesitate to die for the Church."[90] Men lead women, but in a way that constantly threatens them with death and puts their own will in question. In these various ways—in discussions of what women should wear, or in the ordering of the sexes within marriage—Calvin can seem both hierarchical and yet flexible at the same time. It is as if he wants to gesture toward the necessity of some sort of gender roles, but he stops short of offering theological justification for a completely stable conception of what those roles might be.

## A Concluding Thought on Both Reformers

For both Luther and Calvin, marriage is partially a response to the problems of postlapsarian lust, and celibacy is a synonym for impious solitude and a recipe for corruption. These are major themes to their discussions, and they represent a different emphasis from the priority given to marriage for the sake of procreation and the perpetuity of species we found in Aquinas's discussion of sexual difference.

Looking only at this aspect of Luther's and Calvin's theologies, a casual reader might therefore be tempted to conclude that for the Reformers, marriage and sexual difference might not be inextricably linked in principle. For if marriage were simply about companionship or managing erotic attraction, then one might be tempted to think that the Reformed view of marriage could withstand the separation of gender roles, such as husband or wife, from sexuality, such as being male or female. If marriage is primarily about resisting solitude and bridling desires, then a partnership between two men or two women could plausibly serve the same function. One can have a stable companionship and focus the sort of peripatetic desire Calvin condemned in his Jeremiah commentary without necessarily involving sexual difference.

But Luther and Calvin did not believe that marriage could be understood so narrowly or abstractly. Because of the Genesis creation stories and the Bible's ongoing testimony to the significance of sexual difference, they both believed that the two sexes are included in the unfolding of humanity's relationship with God. As is particularly clear in Luther's commentary on Genesis, God creates Adam and the church begins. God addresses humanity, and his life with his chosen people is launched. Both Luther and Calvin regard the creation of maleness and femaleness as a subsequent step in this same ecclesiological project. That humanity exists as male or female is a quality humans share with other creatures, but these other creatures are not part of the same covenant with God. Because of this covenant, sexual difference means something different in humans than it does in animals. For humans, sexual difference is involved in the project of obeying, thanking, and praising God. For humans, then, sexual difference cannot be cast aside in the pursuit of companionship and the restraint of lust. The goodness of companionship and the reasons why lust is wrong derive from God's covenant, and it is this same covenant that testifies to the goodness of creation. In other words, the various goods that make marriage good come as part of an integrated package; in the Reformers' eyes, fidelity without sexual difference makes no more sense than procreation without fidelity.

For Luther and Calvin, if marriage requires sexual difference, it also seems at times like sexual difference requires marriage. Calvin briefly speculated about the eschaton, a time when he believed we would be sexually differentiated even though we do not marry. Luther clearly approved of Noah's celibacy as a deliberate and limited choice to forgo the possibilities of sex. But generally speaking, both Reformers gave little consideration to how, without marriage, sexual difference is recognized with gratitude and obedience.

Partly this lack of consideration is deliberate, for their argument about creation is that the teleology of the two sexes comes to fruition in marriage. But one wonders what might have happened if they had seen in Augustine's account of virginity the possibility of being grateful for creation, yet living in a way that testifies to the eschaton. Had they considered virginity in this respect, would it have been possible for their theory of marriage to be integrated with an account of sexual difference in other eras of salvation history?

That is not a question Luther and Calvin answer. Luther and Calvin consistently refer to monasticism as this-worldly and sinful, and their treatment of marriage and the sexes is oriented toward creation. There appears to be little consideration of any eschatological dimension to sexual difference in the Reformers. They both clearly believe in Augustine's basic anthropology of sexual difference, which includes sexual difference in the eschatological era in which marriage no longer exists. But they appear less interested in Augustine's positive account of virginity. Thus, in principle, a premise for exploring sexual difference in relation to virginity and the eschaton might have been available to them, but that was a road not taken.

However, as we shall see in chapters 6 and 7, Karl Barth and John Paul II not only explore sexual difference with reference to creation, and come to similar conclusions about the centrality of marriage, but they also consider sexual difference in eschatological perspective.

## Notes

1. Martin Luther, "A Sermon on the Estate of Marriage (1519)," in *The Christian in Society I* (ed. James Atkinson; Luther's Works; vol. 44; Philadelphia: Fortress, 1966), 8.

2. Ibid., 10.

3. Ibid.

4. Augustine, *Gen. litt.*, §9.7.12; see p. 75n79.

5. Luther, "Sermon on the Estate of Marriage," 10.

6. Augustine, *Gen. litt.*, §9.7.12; see above, p. 75n79.

7. Luther, "Sermon on the Estate of Marriage," 11.

8. Ibid., 9.

9. Ibid., 12.

10. Ibid.

11. Ibid., 13.

12. Ibid., 8.

13. Ibid., 9.

14. Ibid.

15. Martin Luther, "Judgement of Martin Luther on Monastic Vows (1521/22)," in *The Christian in Society I* (ed. James Atkinson; Luther's Works; vol. 44; Philadelphia: Fortress, 1966), 262.

16. Ibid., 263, 278, 340.

17. Ibid., 293.

18. Ibid., 294–95, 307.

19. Ibid.

20. Ibid., 341, 369, 391.

21. Martin Luther, "The Estate of Marriage (1522)," in *The Christian in Society II* (ed. Walther I. Brandt; Luther's Works; vol. 45; Philadelphia: Muhlenberg, 1962), 17.

22. Ibid., 18.

23. Ibid., 36, 38.

24. Ibid., 39.

25. Ibid., 44, 45, 43.

26. Martin Luther, "Commentary on 1 Corinthians 7 (1523)," in *Commentaries on 1 Corinthians 7, 1 Corinthians 15, Lectures on 1 Timothy* (ed. Hilton C. Oswald; Luther's Works; vol. 28; St. Louis: Concordia, 1973), 6.

27. Ibid., 5.

28. Ibid., 13.

29. Ibid., 10.

30. Ibid., 13.

31. Ibid., 26.

32. Ibid., 28.

33. Ibid., 45, 46, 28.

34. Martin Luther, *Lectures on Galatians (1535) Chapters 1–4* (ed. Jaroslav Pelikan and Helmut Lehmann; Luther's Works; vol. 26; St. Louis: Concordia, 1963), 95, 354, 355.

35. Jaroslav Pelikan notes, in an introduction to Martin Luther, *Lectures on Genesis, Chapters 1–5* (ed. Jaroslav Pelikan and Helmut T. Lehmann; Luther's Works; vol. 1; St. Louis: Concordia, 1958), ix–xii, that the Genesis lectures as we have them are "not a product of Luther's pen or even a transcript of his lectures; it is a transcript that has been reworked and edited. . . . We have reason to be on the lookout for marks of redactorial additions and changes" (x). Nevertheless, we will proceed as if "the hands are sometimes the hands of the editors, but the voice is nevertheless the voice of Luther" (xii), for two reasons. First, Pelikan surveys the areas where innovations seem likely, and these are far removed from the priorities of this thesis. Second, this chapter has already established the basic contours of Luther's thoughts on our subject, and, as we shall see, these lectures are consistent with those earlier premises. There seems little reason to fear that, even if some redactors have left fingerprints on these lectures, that we are too far removed from what Luther himself believed.

36. Ibid., 121, 184.

37. Ibid., 109, 103, 104.

38. Ibid., 106.

39. Ibid., 56–57.

40. Ibid., 71.

41. Ibid., 61, 62–63.

42. Ibid., 105, 137.

43. Ibid., 70; see elsewhere, such as 84 and 123ff.

44. Ibid.

45. Ibid., 62, 115.

46. Ibid., 115, 141, 167.

47. Ibid., 245.

48. Ibid., 257.

49. Ibid., 238.

50. Ibid.

51. Ibid., 237.

52. Ibid., 168.

53. Martin Luther, *Lectures on Genesis, Chapters 6–14* (ed. Jaroslav Pelikan and Helmut T. Lehmann; trans. George V. Schick; Luther's Works; vol. 2; St. Louis: Concordia, 1958), 119.

54. Ibid., 8.

55. I would like to thank Brian Brock, currently a lecturer in practical theology at the University of Aberdeen, for suggesting that I read Luther on Noah's marriage.

56. Luther, *Lectures on Genesis, Chapters 1–5*, 355; and Luther, *Lectures on Genesis, Chapters 6–14*, 7.

57. Luther, *Lectures on Genesis, Chapters 6–14*, 57, 28.

58. Ibid., 123.

59. Ibid., 124.

60. John Calvin, *Institutes of the Christian Religion* 2.8.41 (trans. Ford Lewis Battles; Philadelphia: Westminster, 1960), 1:405.

61. Ibid.

62. Ibid., 3.25.11, 2:1006.

63. Ibid., 3.25.7, 2:1000; 3.25.8, 2:1002; 3.25.11, 2:1007.

64. Ibid., 4.13.3, 2:1257; 2.1.9, 1:252.

65. Ibid., 2.8.42, 1:406.

66. John Calvin, *A Harmony of the Gospels: Matthew, Mark, and Luke* (vol. 2; ed. David W. Torrance and Thomas F. Torrance; trans. T. H. L. Parker; Grand Rapids: Eerdmans, 1995), 249.

67. John Calvin, *The First Epistle of Paul the Apostle to the Corinthians* (ed. David W. Torrance and Thomas F. Torrance; trans. John W. Fraser; Grand Rapids: Eerdmans, 1996), 167–68.

68. Calvin, *Harmony of the Gospels*, 249, 250.

69. Calvin, *Institutes*, 4.13.3, 2:1257.

70. John Calvin, *Genesis* (ed. Alister McGrath and J. I. Packer; Nottingham, England: Crossway, 2001), 37.

71. Calvin, *Institutes*, 2.8.41, 1:405.

72. John Calvin, *A Commentary on Jeremiah* (vol. 1; Edinburgh: Banner of Truth Trust, 1989), 147.

73. Calvin, *Harmony of the Gospels*, 244, 247, 248.

74. Ibid., 248.

75. Calvin, *First Epistle of Paul the Apostle to the Corinthians*, 132.

76. Ibid.

77. John Calvin, *The Epistles of Paul the Apostle to the Galatians, Ephesians, Philippians, and Colossians* (ed. David W. Torrance and Thomas F. Torrance; trans. John W. Fraser; Grand Rapids: Eerdmans, 1996), 204.

78. Calvin, *First Epistle of Paul the Apostle to the Corinthians*, 137.

79. Calvin, *Harmony of the Gospels*, 247; Calvin, *Genesis*, 38.

80. John Calvin, *Sermons on the Epistles to Timothy and Titus* (Edinburgh: Banner of Truth Trust, 1983), 219, 215, 218.

81. Ibid., 199–200. I have modernized spelling.

82. Ibid., 203.

83. John Calvin, *The Second Epistle of Paul the Apostle to the Corinthians and the Epistles to Timothy, Titus, and Philemon* (ed. David W. Torrance and Thomas F. Torrance; trans. T. A. Smail; Grand Rapids: Eerdmans, 1996), 216.

84. Calvin, *Sermons on the Epistles to Timothy and Titus*, 203–4.

85. Calvin, *Institutes*, 4.10.31, 2:1209.

86. Ibid., 4.10.30, 2:1208.

87. Ibid.

88. Calvin, *Second Epistle of Paul the Apostle to the Corinthians and the Epistles to Timothy, Titus, and Philemon*, 219.

89. Calvin, *Genesis*, 48.

90. Calvin, *Epistles of Paul the Apostle to the Galatians, Ephesians, Philippians, and Colossians*, 205.

# Chapter 6
# KARL BARTH

In the last chapter we saw that Luther and Calvin believed that sexual difference is theologically and morally significant. Their reasons for this conclusion rest largely on exegesis of Scripture, to the effect that God made human beings as male and female and that God expects us to live as male and female. As is especially clear in Luther's writing, the Reformers concluded that sexual difference is included in the work of the church, which means that in humans, our gratitude and obedience to God will have consequences for how we live together as male and female. For these and other reasons, Luther and Calvin concluded that a Christian response to sexual difference will most often, but not always, lead to marriage.

These arguments and beliefs about sexual difference have been somewhat apparent in each chapter of this book since Augustine. However, the Reformers are arguably clearer and more direct than earlier theologians, from whose work we sometimes had to make deductions or inferences.

As we shall see in this chapter, this emphasis on sexual difference in relation to the command of God becomes even clearer and more central in the work of Karl Barth. Barth makes an argument that appeals consistently to basic christological premises. First, Barth claims that in Christ we learn that our created bodily forms are not meaningless or indifferent. Second, he claims that in Christ we learn that we were created for the sake of having relations with God and one another. Putting these two premises together, and buttressed by a range of scriptural observations, Barth concludes that when Genesis speaks of the *imago Dei*, it suggests to us an analogy between God's triune relationality and human sexual difference. In this chapter, we will examine all of these arguments, as well as their moral implications. For Barth, human beings must live their lives with some type of sexually differentiated relationship or encounter in order to recognize and embrace their humanity. Furthermore, because human beings are created for covenant with God and one another, sexually differentiated relationships will always revolve around the concept of marriage in some respect, even if marriage is not mandatory for each and every human person. The interrelationship of creation and covenant leads Barth to conclude that both homosexuality and fornication are inadequate human responses to sexual difference.

## Being and Knowledge in Christ: Creation for Covenant

When Barth makes an argument about sexual difference, it is dependent upon a previously argued claim that Jesus Christ determines what is true about and what we know about God, creation, and ourselves. This means, firstly, that creation has a purpose, and, secondly, that this purpose is revealed to be covenantal relations with God and other humans. Both of these points serve as key premises in the arguments Barth subsequently makes about sexual difference, and so it is important to understand them clearly from the beginning.

Barth begins by reasoning that if Jesus is the Word of God, then Christ's own lived solidarity and involvement with the world means that God's will or purpose toward mortal creatures is merciful and good: "It goes to work. It intervenes. It commits and exposes itself."[1] The Creator of the cosmos is the same as "*this* God," this God we have met in Christ, and so a partnership of mercy is necessarily implied within the purposes of reality itself.[2] It follows then that creation, or all that which really exists and which is not God himself, cannot exist indifferently or meaninglessly. God's Word, God's self-disclosure, has indicated that God has loving purposes, which include mutuality between Creator and created: "And the revelation is that the world is loved by God because it was created by Him, and that as His creation it may love Him in return."[3] In other words, the Father created for the purpose that this covenant of love might exist between him and his children: "Creation stands in a series, in an indissolubly real connexion with God's further works," and these further works are all oriented toward the gathering of a people in and through Christ. "Creation sets the stage for the story of the covenant of grace."[4] The God who exists in himself as a triune being-in-relationship creates for the sake of enjoying further relations with his creatures, with those who are not himself.

Significantly for Barth, Jesus as the Word of God discloses not only what we know about God and creation but also what we may know about ourselves. Who are human beings, these creatures with whom God has *ad extra* relations in the form of a covenant? Barth reasons, "As the man Jesus is Himself the revealing Word of God, He is the source of our knowledge of the nature of man as created by God."[5] Christ is the one man who fulfills the teleology all men have; Christ is the man who establishes and embodies the covenant with the Creator. Jesus is "the one Archimedean point given us beyond humanity," the one possibility available for "discovering the ontological determination of man."[6]

When Barth looks to Jesus in his humanity, he concludes that Jesus is not "man for nothing, nor for Himself." Jesus is "for God's own glory" by being the "man for man, for other men, His fellows." Such a determination is intrinsic to Christ's humanity; to be the Deliverer of men is for Christ an ontological and not an accidental orientation. It is "not a new duty and virtue which can begin and end," but a sympathy and relationship to his human neighbors in his innermost being.[7] But as Jesus' humanity is the standard for ours,[8] it is also true that to be for others, to exist on behalf of and in encounter with our neighbors, must constitute our humanity in a way that is ontological and not accidental: "A man without his fellows, or radically neutral or opposed to his fellows, or under the impression that the co-existence of his fellows has only secondary significance, is a being which *ipso facto* is fundamentally alien to the man Jesus and cannot have Him as Deliverer and Saviour."[9] But to be fundamentally alien to Christ's humanity is impossible, for humanity is "the being whose Kinsman, Neighbour and Brother is the man Jesus."[10] We are, in this christologically known determination, beings whose nature exists for the sake of relationships with God and with our neighbors and fellows.

## The *imago Dei* and Sexual Difference

These doctrines about both God and humanity are juxtaposed in Barth's discussion of the *imago Dei*, which, Barth argues, necessarily includes and interprets human sexual difference.

Developing the theme of creation for covenant, Barth deduces that the God we meet in Christ, the "Deus triunus," cannot have, as a covenant partner, a "homo solitarius."[11] God creates in his image in order that his partner in the covenant may be a creature who is distinct and yet not alien from him. For this purpose, God desires a creature who is also a being-in-relation. A solitary creature, a creature not also structured for relationships, would not be in God's image and would not be suitable for this covenant.[12] "God is in relationship, and so too is the man created by him. This is his divine likeness."[13] Barth cites Genesis 2:18 in support of this argument, where God says it is not good for man to be alone:

In this saying there is a radical rejection of the picture of man in isolation. And the point of the whole text is to say and tell—for it has the form of a story—who and what is the man who is created good by God—good as the partner of God in the history which is the meaning and purpose of creation.[14]

In other words, the story of God creating a creature in his own image is the story of God rejecting man as an isolated being. The story of God creating a creature in his own image is the story of God's blessing us by creating us also as beings-in-relation.

For Barth, it is no accident that not only does God reject human isolation in this story but also simultaneously creates sexual difference. The creation narratives of Genesis, which include the story of God's creation of the sexes, are witnesses to the fact that God reaches out for the sake of relationship. The "who and what" of humanity is revealed in the creation of Adam and Eve, the primordial repetition of the christological analogy of being for God by being for the other. When God creates man and woman, it is because God desires a partner in which his own divine form of life, in relationship, is not alien. It is not good for man to be alone because God did not himself want to be alone: "God willed to create man as a being corresponding to His own being—in such a way that He Himself . . . is the original and prototype, and man the copy and imitation."[15] This human correspondence to God as a being-in-relation finds its first concrete manifestation in Genesis 1:27. "By the divine likeness of man in Genesis 1:27ff. there is understood the fact that God created them male and female, corresponding to the fact that God Himself exists in relationship and not in isolation."[16] In the man-woman relation, a human is a Thou to another human "and therefore an I in responsibility to this claim."[17] It is only after this moment, in the light of the creation of sexual difference, that it is impossible to speak of abstract or solitary man. From that moment, "man never exists as such, but always as the human male or the human female."[18] It is only in the wake of the creation of sexual difference that man can confidently say that, like God, he is a being-in-relation.

For Barth, it is of enormous significance that this human likeness to God, the *imago Dei,* is first manifest in sexual difference and not in anything abstractly spiritual in the human self. The *imago Dei* makes "no reference at all to the peculiar intellectual and moral talents and possibilities of man."[19] The *imago Dei* is not found by searching for some inner disposition or possession that separates humanity from other creatures: "It is not in something which distinguishes him from the beasts, but in that which formally he has in common with them, viz. that God has created him male and female, that he is this being in differentiation and relationship, and therefore in natural fellowship with God."[20] Human beings find themselves addressed by God in their creatureliness, as male and female. It is in the biological difference between male and female, which is in itself common with other creatures and in which humans are in no way unique, that God speaks to men and women and calls them into a relationship that will model his own being as I and Thou. What humanity has in common with the animals is precisely the site and occasion for God's summons to come and emulate his own divine way of life: "And this strictly natural and creaturely factor, which is held in common with the beasts, is not in any sense an animal element in man but the distinctively human element—not in itself but because it has pleased God to make man in this form of life an image and likeness, a witness, of His own form of life."[21] In and through their male and female differences, humans are commanded to be and do something no other animals do, which is to witness to God's own form of relational life.

## Sexual Difference Is a Permanent and Necessary Part of Human Identity

If sexual difference is such a significant feature of human identity, it follows for Barth that it cannot be an optional or ephemeral human characteristic. Instead, Barth argues that sexual difference is a universal and timeless command for relationship. He believes that this command is confirmed by the Sabbath and has an eschatological aspect. In short, Barth is certainly prepared to say that there are other types of human relationship in addition to sexually differentiated ones, but he insists that there is always this one too. In and among the many other ways in which humans are beings in relationship, sexual difference abides and has a ubiquity other human differences do not.

To make this argument, Barth again begins by appealing to the purposefulness of creation. For Barth, the animal or biological aspects of sexual difference (such as procreation or the family) are significant, but on their own they do not fully account for the significance of sexual difference. "Creatureliness, and therefore creation, is the external basis of the covenant of grace in which the love of God for man moves towards its fulfilment. It is in this teleology that it is presented in the first creation narrative of the Bible."[22] This teleology, embracing animal materiality, is an ontology in which human creatureliness is summoned toward grace by God's love. The material form of creation for Barth cannot be irrelevant for this summons, "accidental and capricious," as if the covenant could "hang in the air," as something apart from "natural being and existence of the world and man."[23] "God the Creator" must not become "a vague factor which is meaningless in practice and therefore dispensable."[24] Instead, God the Creator calls and commands on the basis of our materiality, leading human males and females to be what they actually are, to be creatures in covenants with God and one another. How human beings should exist with others, how they should procreate, form families, and otherwise organize their lives arises from humanity's creation for covenant.

Barth reasons that if sexual difference is commanded to emulate God's being-in-relationship, then the relationship itself—the actual encounter between male and female, that is, the meeting, confrontation, and discovery of whatever is noninterchangeable between the sexes—is the theologically significant aspect. It is the relationship between specific different persons that humans are emulating; no abstract qualities that might be imputed to each sex are at stake. The significance of sexual difference cannot be expressed in terms of social roles or biological functions; sexual difference is not significant because masculinity and femininity are complementary in some psychological sense, or because it is through maleness and femaleness that our species procreates. Instead, Barth says the significance of sexual difference is expressed in the "conjunction and inter-relatedness of man as male and female which cannot be defined as an existing quality or intrinsic capacity, possibility or structure of his being, but which simply occur[s]. In this relationship which is absolutely given and posited there is revealed freedom and therefore the divine likeness."[25]

We might summarize Barth's case to this point by saying that the relationship between male and female may occur, that the juxtaposition and encounter should and does happen, and that this relationship is God's gift, determination, and command to humanity. However, what the content of this relationship will be, what men and women should do as they confront one another and live together, is left up to actual men and women to discover and unfold from what God has given. God has given them to be beings-in-relation in this aspect of themselves, and it is up to them to discover what this means. There are certain guidelines. In this encounter, man and woman cannot repudiate their creatureliness and resent the call to engage as a man or a woman with the other sex, but beyond that Barth is wary of prescribing or defining in advance what it means to be male in relation to female, or female in relation to male:

> Our present concern is not with the physiology and psychology of the sexes, and we shall not attempt to describe their distinctive structure. But we may perhaps be permitted to issue the following warning. . . . It is much better if we avoid such generalised pronouncements as that man's interests are more outward and objective and woman's inward and subjective. . . . Statements such as these may sometimes be ventured as hypotheses, but cannot be represented as knowledge or dogma because real man and real woman are far too complex. . . . In what the strength and precedence consists on the one side, and the weakness and subsequence on the other, what it means that man is the head of woman and not *vice versa*, is something which is better left unresolved in a general statement, and value-judgements must certainly be resisted. . . . What distinguishes man from woman and woman from man even in this relationship of super- and subordination is more easily discovered, perceived, respected and valued in the encounter between them than it is defined.[26]

In other words, Barth does not want to venture beyond where his theological premises entitle him to go. He is not interested in having a theory of the sexes that will answer all questions one might have about sexual life; he is interested in asking how a God whose being is relational can be analogized in a creature who is made by that God to be relational in its sexual difference.

Barth insists that the way in which God created male and female implies that there is some difference between the sexes, even if he cannot specify it beyond what he calls a "precedence" and a "subsequence" between men and women. What he means is that the two are not interchangeable, even if their difference cannot be defined once and for all. As we shall see, he explains this sequence in somewhat more detail, for he is eager to help men and women hear and discern the call of God upon their encounter. But initially and most importantly, it is simply a claim that male and female are not exchangeable, and that there is no such thing as a sexless human, a *humanum* which is somehow not implicated in the difference between male and female. He makes this claim because he wants to discipline his claims strictly theologically and resist filling in the gaps with nonchristological speculation. He is confident that if the man and the woman know themselves in their maleness and femaleness christologically, then they will discover and perceive what is required of them in their encounter. His broader point, though, is more simple: some encounter between the sexes is necessary in order for humans to be beings-in-relation.

Barth specifically lambasts fellow Swiss theologians for forgoing such theological discipline, for failing to keep maleness and femaleness accountable to the Word of God and nothing else in their explanation of the sexes, and for consequently overcharacterizing the content of male and female encounter. For example, Theodor Bovet draws Barth's ire for his attempt to draw dogmatic-sounding prescriptions for the sexes from the natural sciences. Barth quotes Bovet as saying, "In many animal species, young males and females fight whenever they meet; the hamster, for example, bites to death every female it meets outside rutting time."[27] Bovet evidently thinks scientific data and biological analogies will help illustrate the built-in tensions between the sexes as God created and intends. Similarly, Emil Brunner claims to have observed human relations, and Barth quotes Brunner's hypothesis that "the man is the one who produces, he is the leader; the woman is receptive, and she preserves life. . . . The man must build, the woman adorns; the man must conquer, the woman must tend; the man must comprehend all with his mind, the woman must impregnate all with the life of her soul."[28] Against both Bovet and Brunner, Barth replies that such things "obviously cannot be said or heard in all seriousness. For they cannot be stated with real security. . . . On what authority are we told that these traits are masculine and these feminine?"[29]

Essentially Barth is accusing Bovet and Brunner of failures in theological epistemology. He believes they lack discipline with regard to how theologians may know what they profess to know about sexual differences. How can theological statements retain their status as theological if they are based upon anything except theological premises? Barth is ready to say that general sexual typologies and observations may be arguable and more or less credible or useful in some spheres, but in terms of discerning the command of God and what God requires of man and woman, Barth will not depart from theological knowledge. Circumscribing his claims to that sphere, he says only that "all other conditions of masculine and feminine being may be disputable" except that God made the sexes for the covenant, that man and woman were not created differently in vain, and that they were created to be in relation to one another.[30]

But Barth's wariness of overprescription does not mean that his basic theological claims are without further implications. As man and woman encounter one another in response to God's call and command, then one

implication for Barth is that there can be no "higher synthesis" of humanity, no aspiration to "being of man above the being of male and female."[31]
Barth's reason is tied to seeing the story of creation in connection with
the Sabbath rest on the seventh day; after relations between the sexes
were created in the *imago Dei*, God rested:

> He did not continue His work of creation. . . . He was satisfied to
> enter into *this* relationship with *this* reality distinct from Himself,
> to be the Creator of *this* creature, to find in *these* works of His
> Word the external sphere of His power and grace and the place of
> His revealed glory. A limit was reached. . . . It is precisely this rest
> which distinguishes God from a world-principle self-developing
> and self-evolving in infinite sequence.[32]

God loves humanity as God made it; God is committed to enjoying
humanity as God has created it and not in demanding that human beings
become something else. The Sabbath cessation from further creation
means that God calls men and women into relation as they have been
made. God's love does not chase shadows in an infinite restless sequence,
for "love has a definite, limited object. . . . It is in this way that God loves.
And the reason why He refrains from further activity on the seventh day
is that He has found the object of His love and has no need of any further works."[33] God loves and is pleased to have created two sexes, nothing
more and nothing less, and for that reason, some difference between the
sexes must be observed by men and women.

Furthermore, Barth believes that God's creation of men and women
as men and women, that is, God's command for them to live in encounter
as male and female, will persist in the eschaton. Because God rested on
the Sabbath and inaugurated his relations with humanity on the basis of
sexual difference,

> man would not be man if he were no longer male or female, if his
> humanity did not consist in this concrete fellow-humanity, in this
> distinction and connexion. He has lived in no other way in time,
> and he can live in no other way in eternity. This is something which
> he cannot lose. For by it there stands or falls his creatureliness.[34]

Because the Creator and the Redeemer are the same God, in the eschaton
God will not abolish, but will confirm, what he has made in his own image:
"In all His future utterances and actions God will acknowledge that He
has created man male and female, and in this way in His own image and

likeness."[35] Of course there is a unity in Christ which transcends sexual (and all other differences), according to Galatians 3:28, but according to Barth, "Paul is not saying that the antitheses are simply set aside and done away by the being of Christians in Christ."[36] Barth quotes Calvin to the effect that Christ does not come to the world to abolish what his Father has made, and for that reason Barth concludes that "the fact that male and female are one in Christ does not mean that they are no longer male and female."[37] Barth cites Augustine too, arguing that what "is to be set aside in the resurrection is not nature itself, but the violation of nature."[38] Thus for Barth, the unity and homogeneity men and women possess in Christ is a political belonging, a sign of who is called to belong to Christ's polity, and has nothing to do with abolition of their creatureliness or their transformation into something abstract and sexless. Put another way, in Christ, male and female receive the common and homogeneous invitation to be constituted in relations with the other. But when we consider this invitation as it is to be fulfilled in the eschaton, we are not meant to imagine a heaven or place of spirit beyond sex, but a new earth in which creatureliness is reaffirmed; the covenant is sealed "not in heaven, but on the new earth under the new heaven."[39] In other words, there are no barriers of sex for belonging to Christ or being a citizen of heaven, but to belong together in Christ or in heaven is not to be rendered abstractly spiritual; one remains a creature in one's renewal and new life.

Having concluded that both the Sabbath and the eschatological perspective confirm the significance of sexual difference, Barth can return to his theme that creation and covenant go hand in hand. As he describes what it might mean to live in the covenant in the form of male and female creatures, he has no reason to imagine life beyond male and female and every reason to accept male and female as the well-defined and particular sphere in which humanity is commanded to become cohumanity:

> All is well so long and so far as man and woman, as they seek to be man individually and together whether in or outside the union of love and marriage, are not merely fully aware of their sexuality, but honestly glad of it, thanking God that they are allowed to be members of their particular sex and therefore soberly and with a good conscience going the way marked out for them marked by this distinction.[40]

In whatever customs or functions or roles humanity under God discerns for the sexes, some difference must be gladly and gratefully observed between male and female; male and female risk their humanity if they repudiate their maleness and femaleness and seek to exist as some abstract, neutered "third thing." Male and female, or sexual difference itself, is inviolably a call to a relationship and encounter, for this aspect of creatureliness, like creation itself, is created for covenant.

Barth is well aware that there are other ways of being persons-in-relation than simply male and female. Barth is quick to say that Christ's determination of human beings as persons made for the covenant reaches other spheres, in addition to the dimension of men and women. For instance, Barth has a great deal to say about the implications of theological anthropology for relations between parents and children,[41] or with our near and distant neighbors in our own culture and in distant lands.[42] But he wants to maintain the distinctiveness of male-female relations as the only irreversible structural human differentiation. By this he means that the male-female relationship is the basic differentiation that makes humanity ontologically determined to be cohumanity, because it is prior to the other differences and the one difference that is inevitably "one long reference to relationship."[43] It is inescapable, because one cannot refer to humanity without saying "male or female" and therefore "male and female." Other apparent human differences (such as race) are only based on or derived from this structure, and our relations with our neighbors are fluid and provisional.[44]

Barth briefly considers that he could have proposed the parent-child relationship as a relationship that is as fundamental and ontological as the relationship between the sexes. He notes various features of that relationship that could have been used to argue this case, such as the fact that everyone is a child of parents, the parent-child relationship is one from which it is impossible to resign entirely, and the relationship has biblical analogs such as Yahweh and Israel or the Father and his children.[45] But Barth ultimately appeals to the discipline of the Genesis text, which he says "is imperious in this respect." "The whole of Gen 2:18ff. points to the man who is fellow-human as such . . . [and] it speaks of the co-existence of man and woman as the original and proper form of this fellow-humanity."[46] "The radical, sexual duality of man . . . is at the root of all other fellowship," and to deny the primacy of "the whole field of sexual encounter" is to "know nothing of the I and Thou and their encounter, and therefore of the human."[47] "Every other differentiation and agreement will continually prove to be preliminary or supplementary as compared with the fact that they are male and female."[48]

## Bone of My Bones:
## A Portrait of the Recognition of Sexual Difference

On the basis of his argument that some sort of sexually differentiated encounter is intrinsic to being human, Barth proceeds to enumerate the practical and ethical consequences of his claims. For Barth, more can still be said about how male and female are meant to proceed in gladness and gratitude in "the way marked out for them." What does Barth mean by "precedence" and "subsequence"? How can this path be explained without exceeding the discipline of Barth's theological premises and without lapsing into typologies and stereotypes?

Continuing with Genesis, Barth notes that in Genesis 2:23, Adam greets the creation of Eve with an exclamation: "This is now bone of my bones, and flesh of my flesh."[49] Barth says this recognition is a paradigmatic indication of the appropriate response of man to woman. Adam's "expression of a recognition . . . is not just a kind of epilogue to the creation of the woman, and therefore the completion of man's creation, but it is with this express saying of man that the latter reaches its goal. . . . Apart from this act of human freedom, the supreme and final gift of God would not be what it is."[50] Apart from Adam's glad acceptance of God's gift, woman, and therefore creation in its finished form, would not have been acknowledged as a gift, and the covenant would be no true covenant. Apart from Adam's grateful acceptance of Eve, there would have been an imperfect relationship between God and humanity, for humanity would not have had the opportunity to say yes to God.

This pattern is still true today, says Barth, for man's recognition of woman today is as much "a choice and decision" as it is a recognition.[51] For that reason, Barth believes it is important to understand the nature of Adam's recognition and what was at stake in the choice that confronted Adam. Barth explains that Adam could have preferred solitude, or he could have ordered himself to some sort of compromised fellowship, such as the companionship of the animals. Rather than be half-satisfied in these ways, Adam chose to be unsatisfied, waiting until another creature was presented to him by God, whom he could rightfully address as a fellow "I," as a "Thou."[52] The "this!" exclamation is Adam's realization that this time of waiting has come to an end; here is an encounter and a relationship that God presents to him and that Adam accepts. Adam was asleep when Eve was created, and so he knows as little about her creation as he knows about his own.[53] Nevertheless, Adam embraces what God has done in Eve's creation; he acknowledges and receives her with his recognition in verse 2:23. "What constitutes this climax is not the fact that man says Yes to woman, but that in this affirmation he says Yes to God in the presence of woman. . . . It makes him what he could not be in his solitariness—a man completed by God."[54] For Barth, that is the fundamental significance of sexual difference for Adam and for men today: it is the occasion for acknowledging what God has made and given, for acknowledging that woman is not indifferent or neutral but a "Thou," for receiving God's creation with recognition and gladness, and, by doing all these things, for taking one's place in the covenant with God. Thus as Adam accepts Eve, Barth claims that "he decides for the decision which has been made concerning him."[55]

But with regard to the command that woman should also encounter man, Barth notes that at this point in the biblical story, Eve does not make a corresponding speech to Adam's; in this scene, she is silent: "The text makes no mention of any corresponding declaration on the part of woman. Woman is as little asked about her attitude to man as was solitary man about his attitude to God when after his formation from the dust of the earth God animated him by his breath. She does not choose; she is chosen."[56] Barth reckons that in this prelapsarian scene, there was no choice because there was no problem for Eve. She did not have to choose between the beasts and the man; unlike the solitary Adam, alone and not good, her humanity was never in question or threatened, needing to be proved or confirmed by confession or recognition of another Thou.[57] She appears only as God has placed her beside man, and in no other state. Thus Barth can say that "she would not be woman if she had even a single possibility apart from being man's helpmeet. She chooses that for which God has chosen her."[58] Unlike Adam, Eve was created in relationship with another human Thou from the first; she did not, like Adam, have to repudiate solitude or imperfect fellowship with animals. Yet, although Eve assumed her place at man's side differently than Adam assumed his place at woman's side, when Eve takes her place at Adam's side she still does reveal a sense in which man and woman are alike: both cannot exist and be what they are without the other, and they are able to be for one another because they assent to God, who has given them to one another. In their assent, they acknowledge themselves as placed under God as creature, and placed in the fellowship of man and woman.

In their assent to God's juxtaposition of their selves, in their assent to their interdependence, Adam and Eve offer a witness for all human relations: "Man does not exist as a male in abstract masculinity, but as the man to whom woman belongs, who has woman at his side as 'his' wife."[59] Similarly, woman is not "neutral, distant and dispensable in relation to him; if she were to him another being, human but only feminine, she would not be woman."[60] Woman is not a merely feminine variation upon the basic human; to be feminine does not make one a woman. To be a woman is to belong to man, although not in the sense that she is "man's property."[61] She is man's by virtue of God's gift, not by virtue of man's right. On man's side, he "is now the follower and adherent of woman."[62]

Man forsakes his parents, "his first and nearest and closest ties . . . and thus becomes an independent man," and then finds woman, "the Thou without which he cannot be I." Finding her, man cleaves to her and relates to this Thou "with the same power with which he is I," and she who was once a stranger becomes "his nearest and dearest."[63] This "unheard of process," this process that can be founded only upon theological knowledge, confirms that it is not good for man to be alone, that woman is his glory, and it is to be realized "only in sacrifice, pain and mortal peril."[64] Man is "the weaker half" in this sense, for the man leaves his roots not in "rebellious self-emancipation" but at cost; he leaves his natural home not for self-aggrandizement; he does not seek "his I but his Thou."[65] Hence the explanation for "the pattern of restlessness and necessity which now drives a man," an arrangement of God's to which man is subordinate, and the precedence man has as the one who chooses (who says Yes when Eve is silent), is only in the light of "the humiliation which he must experience in this event."[66]

## Marriage and Sexual Difference

Barth's discussion of Adam and Eve as prototypically male and female leads him deeper into practical and ethical specification. It also leads him to a discussion of marriage. Barth believes that the question of sexual difference is bigger than marriage but nevertheless that the male-female relation has "its crown and centre in the question of marriage."[67] He says that the male-female encounter is only fully realized "where there is the special connexion of one man loving this woman and one woman loving this man in free choice and with a view to a full life-partnership."[68] For Barth, the matter of the two sexes is certainly not exhausted in discussing such partnerships, that is, marriage, but he claims that whatever happens in the sexual sphere is necessarily related to marriage.[69]

Barth offers many reasons for giving marriage this priority. One such reason is the observation that it is only in marriage where gladness between the sexes and "freedom of heart for the other" can have their "simplest and yet strongest form."[70] Such gladness and freedom of heart Barth believes is on display in the Song of Songs, which he calls, after Genesis 1 and 2, the second "Magna Carta of humanity."[71] Barth writes:

The Song of Songs is one long description of the rapture, the unquenchable yearning and the restless willingness and readiness, with which both partners in this covenant hasten towards an encounter. . . . Gen. 2 speaks of the covenant made and irrevocably sealed. It sets at the beginning that which in the Song of Songs is the goal. It was for the sake of this covenant that God first created man as male and female. And the Song of Songs agrees.[72]

The gladness to which Barth believes men and women are called can only be witnessed in these two parts of Scripture, that is, Genesis and the Song; the gladness "can be ventured only in relation to God's creation, and then again in the eschatological context of the portrayal of Solomon's royal glory."[73]

Barth is fully aware that actual marriages and actual historical relations between the sexes may not be glad, simple, or strong. He is not making an empirical or experience-based claim about marriage with these arguments, and he believes Scripture is amply aware of the fallen nature of much of our actual experience. Amplifying a concern also expressed in passing by Bernard of Clairvaux, who noted how one cannot get to the glories of the Song without passing through Proverbs and Ecclesiastes, Barth notes how subsequent chapters in Genesis and the rest of "Solomonic literature," when they speak of relations between men and women, testify to the fall, to the "disturbance and corruption in the relationship of the sexes," and the "stained and spotted" experience of male and female relationships.[74] The shame of postlapsarian nudity in Genesis 3, the exploitation between men and women so common in subsequent tales within Genesis (e.g., Tamar and Judah in Genesis 38, or Lot's daughters in Genesis 19), or the bitter skepticism of Proverbs and Ecclesiastes (e.g., Proverbs 7, or Ecclesiastes 7:26–28)—these are the sorts of passages with which the Old Testament is rife but of which the Genesis opening and the Song are uniquely innocent.[75] Thus when Barth says that Genesis and the Song must be understood as referring to the nonhistorical eras of creation and eschatology, it is not a theological perspective that is isolated from and ignorant of fallen experience, but neither is it determined by that experience.

Barth also notes that when the Old Testament celebrates sexuality, it tends to be with reference to children and posterity and not the simple delight of husband and wife in each other for their own sake.[76] Only in the Song of Songs do we see the fulfillment of Eden's innocence, "the delight, not of the potential father or head of the family, but simply of man as such, not in the potential bearer of his children but simply in the woman as such; the *eros* for which there is no such thing as shame."[77] Only in the Song of Songs do we also hear woman reply to man and amplify the delight: "For woman is now portrayed in the same rapture. . . . She now answers just as loudly and expressly as she is addressed by him."[78] In this uniqueness, Barth again suggests that the Song is pointing not to an ordinary historical pattern but to an anthropological and eschatological vision. In the Song, Barth believes that we see the covenant for which we were created in its own right, that is, in distinction from the historical significance and biological fecundity our creation also has, but with which it must not be confused. In the Song, we see the married couple as creatures in mutual encounter and not as the parents or dynastic founders they are elsewhere in Scripture.

On what basis, Barth asks, do the Song and the Genesis accounts dare to venture their innocence, to speak so simply of a man and a wife taking delight in one another? Barth wonders where Scripture's authors and redactors found the "courage . . . to treat the matter in this way" when they so clearly knew the possibility of unhappiness between the sexes.[79] Barth concludes that they had no choice but to imagine innocent sexual difference alongside its fallen version. When sexual difference is considered with reference to creation and eschaton, when it is considered in light of God's election, then "in this connection it obviously has to be ventured."[80] The existence of another, more basic covenant than that between man and woman demands that the biblical authors at some point see the covenant between male and female so innocently and seriously. "God the Lord and sexual *eros*, well known in Israel especially as a dangerous dæmon, are brought into close relationship. . . . The authors of Gen. 2 and the Song of Songs speak of man and woman as they do because they know that the broken covenant is still for God the unbroken covenant, intact and fulfilled on both sides."[81] Sexually differentiated gladness and freedom demand Christian testimony because the sexes were created for the purpose of responding to their prototype, Christ and the church, Israel and Yahweh.

That prototype, of course, is a covenant, and hence supplies another reason why Barth believes that marriage, and not some other more provisional relationship, is the center of sexually differentiated relations. Barth explains that we learned in Christ that to love means to commit. With reference to the Sabbath, he explains that God's covenant does not exist provisionally, in the hope or expectation that someone will become someone else; thus, to stay only in nonmarital experimental, conditional relationships means that one has not yet really begun to love on christological grounds.[82] Such particularity and faithfulness is required for cohumanity to be genuinely actualized, because the human prototype is God's faithfulness in his triune self and in his covenant in Christ.

Monogamy is the practice founded on such love, and, once again repudiating natural epistemological support for his position, Barth claims the

Christian practice of monogamy between men and women is not something law or custom can ultimately justify. On their own terms, Barth says these things can not really provide a coherent opposition to practices such as bigamy. He believes that the coherence of Christian life-partnership is based only on the divine command of Jesus Christ.[83] But because God does offer his prototypical faithful covenantal love, because he created male and female in this image, marriage is a human possibility to which a particular man and a particular woman may be called.[84] "Because the election of God is real, there is such a thing as love and marriage."[85] It is impossible for human beings to embody God's love in their creatureliness, but it is also impossible that they ignore it:

> There can be no question of repeating the original of this love of Christ. It is unique and once-for-all. But even less can there be any question of living in the light of this original without accepting the summons to a relative imitation and reflection of this original. This once-for-all and unique light does not shine into the void but into a sphere of men and therefore of males and females, i.e., into the sphere described in Gen. 2, where it is decided that it is not good for man to be alone, where he is to recognise himself in another and another in himself, where humanity relentlessly means fellow-humanity, where the body or existence of woman is the same to man as his own body or existence.[86]

In all of his insistence that men and women must organize themselves in relation to marriage and that they must consider the way in which intra-human relations are brought to fruition in marriage, Barth has not gone so far as to say that marriage is compulsory. He specifically rejects a portrayal of the Reformers (particularly what he calls "the later—though not the earlier—Luther") in which procreative marriage is thought of as a "better state, more pleasing and possibly alone pleasing to God."[87] He appears much more open than Luther or Calvin to the idea that permanent singleness is a viable response to sexual difference. Barth says the decision to marry "is not open to each individual, and there are reasons why it is open to many not to do so."[88] What is compulsory for everyone is some response to the situation of being male and female. Even the unmarried

> are still men and therefore male or female, male and female. . . . Here again we must allow ourselves to be led out into the open by the divine command, not being diverted from the special problem of marriage, but considering it together with the problem of

male and female as it exists and requires to be solved even out-side marriage.[89]

Even those outside marriage "share in the fellow-humanity which is implicit in the dualism of male and female and has its goal in marriage."[90] We might say that in this respect Barth, despite having disavowed Luther's preference for marriage over singleness, reminds us to some extent of Luther's commentary on Genesis. For Barth, as well as for the Luther who offered Noah as an example of someone discerning when to be a virgin and when to marry, it is not that marriage is compulsory but that having been created by God as one sex in a sexually differentiated field of encounter demands a decision and discernment about whether and when one is called to marry.

Nevertheless, Barth is perhaps more sanguine about permanent vir-ginity and theoretically prepared than Luther to accept and explain celi-bacy as a response to sexual difference:

Again it is quite clear that in the Christian community of the final aeon the serious possibility of the unmarried state as a matter of special vocation and gift necessarily has the indirect significance of throwing the problem of marriage into sharper relief, of impart-ing to it, instead of the character of a universal ordinance of nature and self-explanatory custom, that of a special vocation and gift, of a concrete divine authorisation and requirement, and therefore of a free decision and act on the part of the two human beings concerned.[91]

In other words, for Barth, certain aspects of the "final aeon" mean that marriage is not to be entered into automatically, but only on the basis of a divine summons. This possibility of singleness enhances and clarifies the nature of marriage. Barth's position is that one should not automatically assume marriage is the answer, although one must assume marriage as a question.

Barth takes this position because he has a sharp sense, not really dis-cussed since Augustine, of how the birth of Christ and the inauguration of the "final aeon" change the possibilities for faithful sexual life.[92] Barth suggests that Genesis 2 placed marriage at the center of the sexual dual-ism in light of the covenant, launching an Old Testament trajectory in which singleness was not a foreseen possibility. In the Old Testament, the seed of Abraham needed to be carried forward; procreation and the sequence of generations maintaining Israel were theologically significant because of Yahweh's covenant to be faithful to Israel. But, in an argument reminiscent of Augustine, with the birth of Jesus Christ, this history reached its goal, and the significance of a married couple for procreation changed. Being born of the spirit, a child of God through Christ, was revealed as the one ultimately significant relation, and in this light, marriage is a provisional good.[93] *Post Christum natum*, spouses more clearly exist as a penultimate relation and for the sake of their confrontation as cohumanity, as described in the (childless) Genesis accounts and the Song of Songs.

For these reasons, Barth argues that not everyone after Christ will be called to the marital way of being covenantal with the Lord.[94] The man-woman relation has not changed, but marriage now has the dignity of a particular vocation and not a natural necessity.[95] Marriage is now more clearly a matter of witnessing to a created prototype, and it cannot be invested with a false dignity of being itself inevitable or salvific. But marriage's true dignity means that avoiding marriage because of some aversion to or suspicion of the sexual life is a mistake.[96] Barth is clearly not suggesting that the New Testament or the birth of Christ abolished the goods of creation. It is simply that whether to be married or single now revolves around the question of vocation and our response to the commands of God as Father. Barth has faith that the command of God, if we listen, "will find man and woman as what they are in themselves. It will disclose to them the male or female being to which they have to remain faithful." Or, alternatively, "there is a genuine Christian obedience which does not lead a man into marriage but past it. . . . We would only add the warning that they [celibates] should understand their voluntary or involuntary celibacy as a matter of Christian obedience as Paul did."[97] Either way, the point is obedience or the universal obligation to discern one's particular vocation with regard to the other sex.

## Precedence and Subsequence: Further Specification of Sexual Difference

Although marriage is not mandatory in Barth's ethics, it is still, for the reasons explained, the center of the male-female relationship. For that reason, Barth is able to turn to marital imagery in Scripture for further reflection on theological anthropology. Specifically, as we have seen, Barth insists on the noninterchangeability of male and female, to a "precedence" and "subsequence" which means that man and woman cannot exchange their places in the ordering of creation. Ephesians 5, a strongly christological meditation on marriage, allows and compels Barth to say a bit more about what he means about the noninterchangeability of male and female.

Barth says that the whole emergence of woman from man as told in Genesis 2, and thus sexual difference itself, would be "strangely contingent" without Ephesians 5.[98] He does not believe that the innocence of either Genesis or the Song of Songs could be ventured without their christological precedent, and it is in Ephesians 5 that the relationship between male and female and the christological covenant is most explicit:

> It can—and in the Christian Church must—be maintained . . . that the Old Testament as a whole forms a single material context with the New, and that it is in this context, and beyond the confines of the Old Testament, that Genesis 2:18ff. must be seen if it is to be rightly understood. . . . Instead of being arbitrarily ignored, Ephesians 5:25 can and may and must be taken into account as commentary on Genesis 2:18ff., and therefore on the Song of Songs. . . . "This is a great mystery, but I speak concerning Christ and the church." If this is accepted, it cannot be denied that even the obscure language of the creation saga takes on a wholly different form and colour, acquiring a very concrete meaning.[99]

In this passage, Barth is repeating the principle that has guided him from the beginning: that creation is for the sake of the covenant, that what God made in Genesis can only be understood on the basis of what Christ does second in sequence, although not in intention. The two sexes were created for the sake of the covenant, and Ephesians 5 is a passage of great specificity with regard to sexual life and the covenant. For this reason, no account of Barth's version of sexual difference can be complete without addressing Ephesians 5, or what Barth has termed the "precedence" and "subsequence" between the sexes that it describes.

In his exegesis of Ephesians 5:22–33, Barth makes the point that the "reciprocal subordination" Paul calls for between husband and wife precludes any "enthusiasm for equality."[100] This mutual subordination, Barth says, is the sphere described in Genesis 2

> where it is decided that it is not good for man to be alone, where he is to recognise himself in another and another in himself, where humanity relentlessly means fellow-humanity, where the body or existence of woman is the same to man as his own body or existence, where the I is not just unreal but impossible without the Thou, and where all the willing and longing of the I—on the far

side of all egoism or altruism—must be the willing and longing of the Thou.[101]

In Genesis Barth finds a definite ordering of male and female; the duality created is decidedly unequal.[102] We saw this inequality in Barth's observation that Adam offers an exclamation when Eve is brought to him, but Eve is silent. Woman is indispensable, a result of the "divine initiative and attack upon solitary man," but she also "belongs to man, is his helpmeet."[103]

Yet this inequality will not result in the type of male superiority the world might expect. When a man leaves his roots and seeks a wife as per Genesis 2:24, Barth says that it "must not be a rebellious self-emancipation."[104] It is in Ephesians 5 where Barth finds the decisive characterization of this ordering. The Old Testament accounts on their own, Barth says, cannot give more than a riddle pointing to the final answer. Ephesians 5 unlocks this final answer and clarifies the Genesis reading: "When the Old Testament gives dignity to the sexual relationship, it has in view its prototype. . . . It is because Jesus Christ and His church are the internal basis of creation."[105] Ephesians 5 links the self-giving man for other men—Jesus, who is the Father's move to his children gathered in the church—to the paradigmatic human fellowship of man-woman in marriage. It is an unequal fellowship, but the man's precedence is in the style of Jesus' headship of the church, and so calculations about relative power relations are not what they would appear to be based on a natural epistemology:

The normal inequality of man and woman in marriage consists quite simply in the fact that it is primarily the responsibility of the former that their fellowship should always be and become a fellowship in freedom and their freedom a freedom in fellowship. Naturally it is that of the woman too. But the man may not wait. . . . He must seize the initiative. . . . In the last analysis every complaint which arises in marriage is levelled against him.[106]

This type of male headship is one that will lead man into responsibility and service.

For Barth, the fact that woman is welcomed by man under God in the creation sagas should remove "from woman the last pretext for anxiety, self-seeking or rejection."[107] She should not fear man's initiative or whatever "supremacy" this prelapsarian priority may indicate, for whatever position he has as a true man does not in any way come from himself;

it is not what it purports to be if it is abstracted from man's relationship with God, and so any hierarchy in the relationship should not be a cause for alarm or dissembling.[108] Woman was created as the "divine initiative and attack upon solitary man," which means that God is the author of the situation and any "supremacy of man is not a question of value, dignity or honour, but of order. It does not denote a higher humanity of man. This hierarchy is no shame to woman. On the contrary, it is an acknowledgement of her glory, which in a particular and decisive respect is greater even than that of man."[109] Man is simply the one who came first, and who is indeed called upon to say yes in a way woman is not. But woman's creation "signifies the completion" of man. "She is this also because by his Yes to woman, by the recognition of his free thought and the confession of his free word, man participates a second time in her creation and therefore in his own creation, and in this way—honourably enough—in the completion of creation as a whole."[110]

Barth has critics who charge that his emphasis on man's precedence and woman's subordination endorses patriarchy and spoils the "gain" made by his relational anthropology.[111] But defenders of the Barthian position point out that Ephesians 5 is addressed to the husband "not to be an objective doctrine of the sexes, but rather an appeal to the husband not to regard and act upon his position as the head in the sociological sense as being one of simple authority, but rather in the soteriological sense of the imitation of Christ." Thus, according to the defense, cohumanity is determined by christological "love and willingness to serve," which means Barth's argument is a judgment against patriarchal actualization.[112]

In fact, there is no ambiguity in Barth that the woman is her own independent element in the I-Thou ordering, even if her existence is an "appeal to the kindness of man."[113] Because cohumanity really is cohumanity, it is impossible to define the sexes without an account of their responsibility to one another. Because man and woman are not reducible to some more fundamental and androgynous personhood, their responsibilities will look different. Because Barth keeps with the discipline of biblical texts, he perceives husbands in the role of Christ and wives in the role of church. Because these are the prototypes, the male and female roles have the dynamic of servanthood, a difference in which the first shall be last and the last shall be first and greatness is defined in terms of humility. As Barth summarizes:

Man and woman are not an A and a second A whose being and relationship can be described like the two halves of an hour glass, which are obviously two, but absolutely equal and therefore inter-changeable. Man and woman are an A and a B, and cannot, there-fore, be equated. In inner dignity and right, and therefore in human dignity and right, A has not the slightest advantage over B, nor does it suffer the slightest disadvantage.... Yet the fact remains—and in this respect there is no simple equality—that they are claimed and sanctified as man and woman, each for himself, each in relation to the other in his own particular place, and therefore in such a way that A is not B but A, and B is not another A but B.... Every word is dangerous and liable to be misunderstood when we try to characterise this order. But it exists.[114]

As is characteristic of him, Barth refuses to go beyond his theological premises and overprescribe sexual difference, but, on the basis of those premises, he insists that the difference is significant and that it should assume this particular shape and dynamic.

## Why the Meaning of Sexual Difference Excludes Homosexuality and Fornication

Barth's discussion of sexual difference has been disciplined all along by his theme of creation for the covenant. These two interlocking and com-plementary concepts—creation and covenant—work together to give guidance in Christian life. For instance, in contrasting but complemen-tary ways, the two concepts together reveal that Christians will not find freedom and a realization of their status as creatures made for covenant in either the practice of homosexuality or fornication. In the one case, the nature of creation is misunderstood, and in the other case, the nature of covenant is misunderstood. In both cases, Barth's basic point, that cre-ation and covenant must go hand in hand and should not be abstracted from one another, is reinforced.

Barth's discussion of homosexuality is conducted in only one page out of the many hundreds of pages he devotes to sexual difference. In this discussion, Barth acknowledges what he calls the potential of homosexu-ality to be "redolent of sanctity."[115] Presumably Barth is crediting homo-sexual relations for their capacity to be faithful, profound, and rooted in friendship. Superficially, these traits might be taken to resemble the Christian idea of covenant.

However, Barth condemns homosexual relationships, seeing in them at least an implicit refusal of his claim that each man or woman has a vocation with respect to the other sex. It is not, in particular, an attack on homosexuality, for Barth critiques same-sex religious orders, "ladies' circles," and any intention to permanently segregate the sexes on the same grounds.[116] In this critique, we might hear an echo of Augustine's attacking virgins who base their virginity on a disdain for the sexual aspect of creation. In more Barthian terms, any attempt, either as a group or a couple, to live without the other sex is an dehumanizing attempt at self-sovereignty, for such attempts refuse the command of God to fulfill one's cohumanity with the opposite sex.[117] Such neglect of the command of God is, according to what Barth has said elsewhere, impossible, for it is to defy human ontology. God has created humanity with a specific determination, and man "can forget it. He can misconstrue it. He can despise it. He can scorn and dishonour it. But he cannot slough it off or break free from it. Humanity is not an ideal which he can accept or discard, or a virtue which he can practice or not practice."[118]

In other words, in Barth's account, homosexuality must be rejected as an impossible attempt at self-rule. Barth can find no basis in his theological ontology for the possibility that God might command a same-sex marriage, and he finds much to the contrary. Thus, on his logic, homosexual partnerships must be premised on something other than God's command. But such premises—perhaps personal preference or desire— are ruled out if sexual difference itself is a command of God.

To illustrate this point from another perspective, we might recall how Barth insists that the Song of Songs is "not an allegory" without a context in God's covenant.[119] The erotic gladness of the Song of Songs is no allegory or parable about desire as such, a witness to the joy of a covenant in abstraction from creation and detachable from the concreteness of actual maleness and femaleness, testifying to the bliss of sexual pleasure in its own right. As with Bernard of Clairvaux, the Song's celebration of eros cannot be read as an invitation to seek eros over against the revelation of creation. For Barth, when the Song ventures hope in the innocence and grace of human sexuality, it does so only on the basis of God's prior activity in creation, that is, on an account that includes a teleology for male and female.[120] Barth can find no justification for honoring erotic desires based on experience apart from this teleology; his only epistemology can be christological. When it is looked at in this light, the brevity of Barth's treatment of homosexuality is not surprising. Desires that give no account of themselves in terms of "creation for the covenant" do not need interrogating at great length. Any desire for sexual relations would have to be examined in light of creation for the covenant, and in that light, only sexually differentiated relations are oriented toward the covenant.

Barth's critique of coitus and other heterosexual erotic activity with prostitutes makes the same point from another perspective. Here Barth also insists that God's commands in creation, and not individual preference, are authoritative. Barth criticizes sexual relations for the sake of satisfying one's appetite or longing for their failure to live in I-Thou relations with fellow humanity. This kind of sex "personifies human unfaithfulness to God" by engaging in I-It relations in place of genuine encounter.[121] As Helmut Thielicke explains, working from anthropological premises that are very similar to Barth's, when "the ability to perform the (erotic) function becomes the sole criterion of the exchange" and thus the function-bearers become interchangeable, then the personal aspect of the encounter has been lost.[122] As Barth says most succinctly, "Coitus without co-existence is demonic."[123] The two sexes were made for covenant, and if they are not living in covenant, they are not living as God has made them.

We might summarize Barth's general casuistry of sex by saying that in the panoply of sexual possibilities, a possible act is always to be assessed through questions deriving from christological anthropology, for the "command of God is not concerned" with "sexual organs and needs as such but only as they exist in the order and sequence of the rest of" the human being.[124] In Barth's ethic, humanity never belongs to itself and is never seen as itself in isolation; God's creation of the two sexes for mutual participation in the covenant is the inevitable and inexorable background. Promiscuous heterosexual relations and monogamous homosexual relations then, for Barth, point to a similar problem. They may seem different in that homosexual relations fail to honor creation and promiscuous heterosexual relations fail to honor covenant, but creation and covenant are two sides of the same ontological coin. Homosexuality and promiscuous heterosexuality are similar in Barthian terms, for both point to a refusal to ground sexual relations entirely theologically; both are rooted in autonomous human desires; both are refusals to obey the created and eschatological command of God as Barth has exegeted it from Scripture.

In chapter 8 of this book, we will consider two accounts of homosexual relations that attempt to refute Barth's brief treatment of homosexuality by appealing to Barth's larger vision of covenantal I-Thou relations. But as we shall see, both appeals falter in trying to give an adequate account of sexual difference, for they both appear to privilege erotic experience at the expense of an anthropology rooted in the doctrine of creation. For them, covenant hangs abstractly, without much or any account of the significance of male and female in creation. In other words, they do not succeed in moving beyond what Barth anticipated would be the weaknesses of any attempt to justify homosexual relations.

## Conclusion

This chapter has brought to the fore Barth's claim that there is a necessary but easily misunderstood difference between male and female. Recalling Calvin perhaps,[125] we have seen that Barth is reluctant to define this difference, except to speak of a precedence and subsequence and to illustrate that difference with reference to Ephesians 5. Barth is also sure that whatever content this order has, it can only be derived theologically, and so he looks to the Genesis chronology and christological typologies; in other words, he attempts to describe sexual difference with relation to creation and covenant. In this ontology, male and female can only be what they are—that is, they can only belong together—when they are together in a way that is subordinate to God with gladness and gratitude.

This approach gives Barth's account of sexual difference a flexibility and comprehensiveness lacking in earlier accounts. By way of conclusion to this chapter, I would like to suggest that Barth's account of sexual difference is superior to earlier theologies for its capacity to account for virginity and marriage, sexual desire, and the eschatological dimensions of human sexuality.

First, regarding virginity and marriage: every other theologian in this book hitherto can be seen, in some ways, to be wrestling with a hierarchical relation between virginity and marriage. The pre-Reformation theologians, for instance, preferred virginity over marriage, even if they thought that both were good. Luther and Calvin at times appeared to reverse the hierarchy, but in such polemical moments (usually arguing against monasticism), they did not dispute the assumption that there would be a hierarchy. But in Barth, virginity and marriage are now more clearly on a level, with both of them only possible as ways of life on account of a vocation from God. The celibate, just as much as the married, are making a response to the significance of sexual difference. This possibility was present in Luther and was perhaps latent ever since Augustine argued that both virginity and marriage are good, but it is Barth who has made the point most clearly. He reaches this conclusion naturally because his doctrine of sexual difference is related to marriage but is also equally, clearly more fundamental and basic than marriage. The *imago Dei*, seen to reside in the encounter between the sexes, points toward marriage but cannot be reduced to marriage.

Barth's more expansive treatment of sexual desire might also be seen as a result of this ontology of sexual difference. For example, Augustine was wary of concupiscence, defining the threefold goods of marriage either as procreative, or, in a negative sense, as refusing divorce or avoiding adultery. The imagery of rightly ordered desire, so prevalent in the Song of Songs, was not prominent in Augustine's account of marriage. But in Barth's account of sexual difference, there is no need to be similarly wary of the Song's language of rapture, hastening, yearning, and "freedom of heart," all of which Barth himself appears eager to use. Because creation is for the covenant, and because such passion is characteristic of God's activity in establishing the covenant, to celebrate such things is more than compatible with Barth's view of marriage. Because the sexes are created and called to covenants that emulate God's covenant with his creatures, passion within the created form of covenant is to be desired. For Barth, the teleology of the sexes is fulfilled not in an exclusively procreative intercourse, a framework which is bound to see desire as extrinsic to the project, but in the encounter and relationship between the sexes, in which desire housed within the right sort of covenant is seen to be emulating a divine prototype.

Finally, with respect to eschatology, it may be helpful to compare Augustine and Barth. Augustine believed that sexual difference was created for the sake of fulfilling God's covenant in Christ. He described that teleology in terms of procreating and populating the heavenly city. With the advent of Christ, Augustine believed that this teleology had been fulfilled and was no longer a command of God incumbent upon all humans. Procreation was still permitted, for what God had created good remained good, but it was as if this goodness had a retrospective quality, witnessing to the goodness of an earlier dispensation. Augustine was confident in an eschatological presence and significance for sexual difference, but, on his own terms, being more specific about that significance was somewhat awkward, since he also believed that in heaven there would be no more marrying and procreating.

But Barth's beliefs about sexual difference, while also arguing that sexual difference had a created teleology for Christ's birth, do not have similar eschatological awkwardness. Barth's version of the created significance of sexual difference emphasizes the *imago Dei*, which is a dynamic concept that can never be said to have been accomplished once and for all. It is perpetual, in the sense that it relies on emulating the inner dynamics of the triune God's relationality, which is itself inexhaustible. One advantage of Barth's position is that creation itself is more visibly connected with God's final eschatological purposes, and the eschatological significance of sexual difference need not be left as vague and underdetermined as it was in Augustine; procreation might be rendered obsolete in the eschaton, leaving Augustine at a loss for what sexual difference might mean at that time, but Barth need not be similarly reticent. On Barth's terms, men and women will always be beings-in-relation, even when the business of marrying and procreating has been fulfilled. Thus Barth was also able to be explicit about how celibates, whose virginity testifies to eschatological social life, are responding to sexual difference in ways that are related to marriage.

In sum, one is led to conclude that in Barth, several ideas about sexual difference, which have been somewhat at large and unsystematically present in the Christian tradition, have become integrated and interdependent.

In the next chapter, on John Paul II, we will examine a theory of sexual difference that appears to be in sympathetic succession to Barth. Then in chapter 8, we will study some contemporary critiques of Barth's and John Paul II's theories, and I shall make proposals for how their theories might respond to the critique.

## Notes

1. Karl Barth, *The Christian Life* (trans. Geoffrey W. Bromiley; Edinburgh: T&T Clark, 1981), 68.

2. Karl Barth, *Church Dogmatics*, II/2, *The Doctrine of God* (trans. G. W. Bromiley et al.; Edinburgh: T&T Clark, 1957), 509. Hereafter, the abbreviation *CD* will be used after a volume has been cited in full.

3. Karl Barth, *Church Dogmatics*, III/2, *The Doctrine of Creation* (trans. H. Knight et al.; Edinburgh: T&T Clark, 1960), 18.

4. Karl Barth, *Church Dogmatics*, III/1, *The Doctrine of Creation* (trans. J. W. Edwards et al.; Edinburgh: T&T Clark, 1958), 43, 44.

5. *CD* III/2, 3.

6. *CD* III/2, 132.

7. *CD* III/2, 71, 208, 209–10, 211.

8. *CD* III/2, 203.

9. *CD* III/2, 227.

10. *CD* III/2, 160.

11. Karl Barth, *Church Dogmatics*, III/4, *The Doctrine of Creation* (trans. A. T. Mackay et al.; Edinburgh: T&T Clark, 1961), 117.

12. *CD* III/1, 290.

13. *CD* III/2, 324.

14. *CD* III/2, 291.

15. *CD* III/1, 185, 197.

16. CD III/4, 117.

17. *CD* III/1, 198.

18. *CD* III/4, 117.

19. *CD* III/1, 185.
20. Ibid.
21. *CD* III/1, 187.
22. *CD* III/1, 219.
23. *CD* III/1, 224.
24. *CD* III/2, 11.
25. *CD* III/1, 195.
26. *CD* III/2, 287.
27. *CD* III/4, 152.
28. Ibid.
29. *CD* III/4, 153.
30. *CD* III/4, 163.
31. *CD* III/2, 289.
32. *CD* III/1, 214–15.
33. *CD* III/1, 215.
34. *CD* III/2, 296.
35. *CD* III/1, 187.
36. *CD* III/2, 295.
37. Ibid. There is more on this point in *CD* III/4, 164–65.
38. *CD* III/2, 296.
39. *CD* III/2, 295.
40. *CD* III/4, 159.
41. *CD* III/4, 240–85.
42. *CD* III/4, 285–323.
43. *CD* III/4, 117.
44. *CD* III/2, 286; III/4, 302.
45. *CD* III/4, 240, 256, 248.
46. *CD* III/2, 293, 292.
47. *CD* III/1, 324; III/2, 289.
48. *CD* III/1, 187.
49. *CD* III/1, 290.
50. *CD* III/1, 290–91.
51. *CD* III/1, 291.
52. *CD* III/1, 292–93.
53. *CD* III/1, 295.
54. *CD* III/1, 300.
55. *CD* III/1, 293.
56. *CD* III/1, 303.
57. Cf. *CD* III/1, 303.
58. *CD* III/1, 303.
59. *CD* III/1, 208.

60. *CD* III/1, 301.

61. Ibid.

62. *CD* III/1, 304.

63. *CD* III/1, 304–5.

64. *CD* III/1, 305.

65. *CD* III/1, 306.

66. Ibid.

67. *CD* III/4, 118.

68. *CD* III/2, 288.

69. *CD* III/4, 140.

70. *CD* III/2, 289.

71. *CD* III/2, 293–94; cf. III/1, 312ff., and III/4, 216ff.

72. *CD* III/1, 313.

73. *CD* III/1, 314.

74. *CD* III/1, 313, 314.

75. The examples are mine, not Barth's. I offer them to make his point efficiently.

76. *CD* III/1, 312.

77. *CD* III/1, 312–13.

78. *CD* III/1, 313.

79. Ibid.

80. *CD* III/1, 314.

81. *CD* III/1, 314–15.

82. *CD* III/4, 195.

83. *CD* III/4, 195, 200.

84. Cf. *CD* III/4, 142–44.

85. *CD* III/1, 318.

86. *CD* III/2, 315.

87. *CD* III/4, 141.

88. *CD* III/4, 140.

89. *CD* III/4, 140–41.

90. Ibid.

91. *CD* III/4, 217.

92. Paul Ramsey notes that in Christian theological tradition, "only Karl Barth posits as forcefully as Augustine a comparable distinction between the periods *ante Christum natum* and *post Christum natum*." Ramsey, *Human Sexuality in the History of Redemption*, 84n9.

93. *CD* III/4, 142, 143.

94. *CD* III/4, 146.

95. Cf. *CD* III/4, 143, 145.

96. *CD* III/4, 146.

97. *CD* III/4, 151, 148.

98. *CD* III/1, 326.

99. *CD* III/1, 320.

100. *CD* III/2, 313.

101. *CD* III/2, 315.

102. *CD* III/1, 289.

103. *CD* III/1, 301, 302.

104. *CD* III/1, 305.

105. *CD* III/1, 320, 322.

106. *CD* III/4, 193.

107. *CD* III/1, 306.

108. *CD* III/1, 309.

109. *CD* III/1, 301–2.

110. *CD* III/1, 302.

111. See, e.g., Wolf Krötke, "The Humanity of the Person in Karl Barth's Anthropology," in *The Cambridge Companion to Karl Barth* (ed. John Webster; Cambridge: Cambridge University Press, 2000), 169.

112. Helmut Thielicke, *The Ethics of Sex* (trans. John W. Doberstein; Cambridge: John Clarke & Co., 1978), 12, 13.

113. *CD* III/4, 180–81.

114. *CD* III/4, 169.

115. *CD* III/4, 166.

116. *CD* III/4, 165.

117. Cf. *CD* III/4, 166.

118. *CD* III/2, 285.

119. *CD* III/1, 319.

120. *CD* III/1, 320.

121. *CD* III/2, 307–8.

122. Thielicke, *Ethics of Sex*, 23–24.

123. *CD* III/4, 133.

124. *CD* III/4, 132.

125. See p. 132.

# Chapter 7
# JOHN PAUL II

In a series of more or less weekly catechetical teachings beginning in 1979 and lasting until 1984, John Paul II offered a theology of sexual difference that at times is strikingly similar to Barth's. In these addresses, the argument essentially makes a christological reading of the Genesis creation stories, concluding that sexual difference is a divine summons to an I-Thou encounter. On this basis, John Paul II claims that sexual difference should be habituated by Christians in ways that follow from God's initial freedom and graciousness in creating. These are themes an attentive reader cannot help but associate with Barth, and it is easy to take John Paul II, in this instance at least, as Barth's ally and colleague. In this chapter, I will exegete and present this aspect of John Paul II, regarding it as a coherent and comprehensive statement on sexual difference in contemporary Christianity.

However, there are also significant differences between Barth and John Paul II. These differences are apparent when John Paul II departs from the theme of sexual difference in general and attempts to assign specific characteristics to women. Interestingly, John Paul II does not attempt to do this on the familiar grounds of christology or exegesis of the Scriptures concerned with creation or marriage. Instead, Marian meditation leads John Paul II to speak of "women's sensitivity," which he believes can enable women to resist suffering better than men, or to be more attentive to others than men.[1] The nonchristological methodology, as well as the typological conclusion, would, of course, have been anathema to Barth. This chapter will suggest that Christian discussion of sexual difference should refrain from such speculative and unnecessary arguments.

This chapter will also note that current Vatican teaching, in a curial document as recently as 2004, follows John Paul II's catechetical teaching in all important respects. In other words, the 2004 document reiterates both John Paul II's strong arguments about sexual difference as well as his weak arguments about women.

## Prelapsarian Sexual Difference

John Paul II begins his argument with an epistemological premise that might appear to recall Barth but that in all likelihood more directly follows the Second Vatican Council. The premise is that "only in the mystery of the incarnate Word does the mystery of man take on light."[2] John Paul II believes that the New Testament reads and comments upon the Old; for present purposes, that means that on account of Christ, Christians can trust that God's declaration of what is good in Genesis establishes "an unassailable point of reference and a solid basis for a metaphysic and also for an anthropology and an ethic, according to which *ens et bonum convertuntur* (being and the good are convertible)."[3] In Genesis, John Paul II deduces that man's original existential status was one of "original innocence," a created and ontological position to which humanity is still summoned, such as when Christ refers to "the beginning" in Matthew 19.[4] Every historical moment is rooted in the innocence of this prehistory. History is a state of lost grace, but Christ's reference to the beginning as background for understanding historical life means that the grace cannot be entirely lost. Christ's references to Genesis authorize and oblige us to see continuity between the prehistorical beginning and the historical era.[5] Our historical, natural knowledge has a threshold, beyond which it cannot peer into prehistory, and original innocence lives on the other side of that threshold.[6] Following Christ is the only way to peer over the threshold into Genesis at our own original innocence.

John Paul II believes that Genesis 2:25 (naked and not ashamed), reinforced by Matthew 5:27–28 (looking lustfully constitutes adultery), teaches humanity to see a link between personal subjectivity or self-awareness and the visible, sexual body.[7] This link is fundamental to his schema for the original innocence of sexual difference. The lack of shame in Genesis 2:25 is not a lacuna but a "fullness of consciousness and experience" based on what the body really means. John Paul II sees this fullness of consciousness at work when the man and the woman confront one another visibly, externally, and objectively as "bone of my bones and flesh of my flesh," yet also with a particular subjective, interior aspect, "without shame." This unashamed way of seeing the other, as an individual subject who is distinct but also in relationship, suggests to John Paul II that this man and this woman "were united by awareness of the gift."[8] That is, the man and woman gazed upon one another and acknowledged their visible bodily status as sexed creatures—an objective fact—but they did not gaze in such a way that they perceived one another as objects. Their gaze allowed the other to exist as a subject. Thus the sexed body as an "objective reality" includes the subjective experience of sex and the self. Because of their "interior innocence" it was "impossible somehow for one to be reduced by the other to the level of mere object."[9] In their fellowship, they were each permitting the other to exist as a distinct subject, and this fellowship is the original innocence of sexual difference.

That permission for the other to exist as subject is a gift, because when that subjectively generous encounter happens, the divine gift in creation is echoed. The man and woman in Eden are, in both their interior innocence and physical presence to one another, displaying the true "nuptial meaning of their bodies." In this light it may be said that "the body reveals man," or that the masculinity and femininity of the body speak a language the body itself does not author. This Edenic sexual difference, manifested in innocence, constitutes the sacrament of the body, by which the "visible reality of the world" is a sign of the "spiritual and divine" mystery of God's relation to the world. By means of innocent masculinity and femininity, humanity "becomes a visible sign of the economy of truth and love, which has its source in God himself and which was revealed already in the mystery of creation."[10] In these senses, sexual difference in humans might be said to be a manifestation or occasion of the *imago Dei*. Seeing the other without shame is a personal interior state (innocence, seeing the psychosomatic whole as God does) with an external bodily basis (visible nudity before the other). One sex can give itself to the other sex in one flesh while remaining two subjects because of the biological difference, but for that somatic difference to have its original human meaning also requires certain interior spiritual characteristics.[11]

Thus, in sum, to be sexually differentiated is indeed the way of being human, but John Paul II handles sexual difference in such a way that it points back to something deeper than man's "somatic constitution."[12] His description is subtle, placing great importance on the corporeality of sexual difference while all the while finding sexual difference important because it points beyond itself to something nonsomatic and spiritual.

## Postlapsarian Sexual Difference

After the fall, our present historical experience of being a body is alarmingly different from this original innocence. The next section of John

Paul II's reflections on sexual difference explores and explains this departure from paradise.

John Paul II believes that Genesis 3:7 ("the eyes of both were opened") acknowledges and calls attention to the difference between prelapsarian times and now, and so self-consciousness of the body may also be experienced now as shame and alienation from original unity. Furthermore, John Paul II notes many points in the Bible where nakedness is connected with ignominy.[13] The present reality of the body is far from simple and straightforward in history, and so we can only approach the concept of original innocence between the sexes via theological knowledge. Indeed, we cannot passively accept the natural forms of the body as we receive them in history, for discerning the body's objective, ontological meaning is a matter of theological discovery. The human body has a biological drive and apparent biological purpose, but something active in human consciousness and not mere naturalism (biological passiveness or instinctiveness) is necessary for humanity to take possession of that body's ultimate determination and meaning. Natural experience, and biological knowledge on its own, cannot lead to the nuptial meaning of the body.[14]

In fallen life as we now know it, shame has wrenched something in both the interior self and in the relationship with the other, and both the self and the capacity for relationship are damaged. In the individual and between individuals, instead of the original spiritual and somatic unity, now there is a "humiliation mediated by the body." The body becomes a sign of interior contradiction, and humanity experiences a distinction between the "law of my mind" and the way of "my members" as described by Paul in Romans 7. The original simplicity of the relationship between the interior self and the exterior sexual self is gone.[15] The shame induces male and female to hide their sexual difference from each other, and their original capacity to communicate is shattered. The male and female body are no longer "the trustworthy substratum of communion." There is a new threshold that limits their confident giving and their own confident identity. Sexuality is now an obstacle to interpersonal relations.[16]

However, despite these great ruptures, the bodies of man and woman have not changed. It is only the body's interior meaning that has changed and hence the language the body is able to speak. Shame is *not* in the body itself but in the deeper changes in spirit. What the body communicates is now reversed from the ethos of the gift. In Genesis 3:16 (pains for the woman in childbirth and the man ruling over the woman), we see that the body does not cease to stimulate the desires for personal union in masculinity and femininity, but that pain and domination direct desire in a new way, wanting bodily satisfaction and not communion. "From the moment when the man 'dominates' her, the communion of persons—made of the full spiritual union of the two subjects giving themselves to each other—is followed by . . . the relationship of possession of the other as the object of one's own desire."[17]

In other words, sexual difference and what was once the field of gift giving have been turned into a field of "appropriation." The opposite of this gift is to make the other an "object for myself"—a reduction that is the antithesis of gift, representing an "interior collapse."[18] What has changed and collapsed inside each human person is not only the sense of the other as a subject but also the sense of one's self as a free subject in relationship with God. John Paul II summarizes these new internal conditions with words such as "lust" or "concupiscence." Concupiscence "suffocates . . . the sense of responsibility before God." A lustful person questions "the gift and the love from which creation has its origin as donation." A lustful person is detached from God and tries to belong in the world independently. Lust is the fruit of the broken covenant, or life in purely "humanistic autarchy."[19] When lust dominates life between the sexes, when the ontology of coexistence is reduced to feelings of mutual attraction, then the couple who satisfy each other's merely sexual needs are pushed "toward utilitarian dimensions." Instead of interpersonal communion, there is the psychological straining toward the other as an object for the sake of his or her sexual characteristics and the slaking one's own sexual appetite.[20] It is this shift in the significance of sexual difference, from medium of gift to medium of appropriation, which John Paul II sees as a consequence of the fall.

## How Both Celibacy and Marriage Recognize the Significance of Sexual Difference

For John Paul II, to overcome this discord, to live in continuity with the prehistorical innocence of sexual difference, is part of Christ's summons to humanity. Christ commands men and women to live and understand their sexual difference with respect to that which is more ontologically basic than the fall. For John Paul II, to live in that light, to make sexual difference once again evocative of self-gift and not self-seeking, means embracing the asceticism of celibacy or marriage.

John Paul II traces Christ's summons from Matthew 5:27–28, wherein Jesus reckons that looking at a woman lustfully is a type of adultery.[21] Of course the adultery prohibition is older than the Sermon on the Mount, but John Paul II suggests that by drawing our attention to "the look," Jesus is interested in an interior, spiritual purity about which the Decalogue is not so obviously concerned. As read by John Paul II, there is in the Old Testament a great concern for putting order in the social life of men and women. Here, he says, adultery is viewed mainly as a violation of another man's possession. Adultery is understood through a "casuistical" view of the sixth commandment, allowing patriarchal polygamy for the sake of offspring or a remedy for concupiscence.[22] In other words, John Paul II indicates skepticism toward ancient marriage practices, seeing them as all too easily structured to accommodate male desire. He claims that this old view of marriage is inadequate for cultivating the interior freedom to which Christ commands men and women. John Paul II says the Old Testament's view of marriage is concerned with external modesty, the fear of consequences, and "the restlessness of the external man." Even in the prophets who appeal to the imagery of adultery and marriage to represent God's relationship with Israel—especially Isaiah, Hosea, and Ezekiel—John Paul II reads adultery as being reckoned like idolatry, with the emphasis on unfaithfulness to what rightly belongs to a husband.[23] In this view of marriage, the nuptial significance of sexual difference cannot be expressed.

However, according to John Paul II, when Christ speaks in the Sermon on the Mount, a new direction is taken in the theology of marriage, with implications for clarifying our understanding of the significance of sexual difference. Christ knew the old wisdom tradition and its laws, but he redirected attention to the interior person, and he drew attention to "the look" as a threshold between the exterior world and interior truth. Christ is concerned with the freedom of the will, that woman (and man) should not be seen as an object compulsively or possessively grasped.[24] This concern is, for John Paul II, entirely consistent with Christ's reference to Genesis 2 in Matthew 19. In the beginning of Genesis, in John Paul II's account, there was continuity and coherence between the external, visible sex and the interior innocence of the sexual subject. In John Paul II's account of the Sermon on the Mount, Christ is similarly concerned with the question of internal integrity. His words, after all, might apply to a husband looking at his own wife, who technically and externally considered could not commit adultery.[25] Thus John Paul II charts in the Sermon on the Mount an innovation in sexuality, which is that the interior dimension of sexual subjectivity is both restored and held accountable to the conditions of original innocence. Christ appears to be interested in probing the human heart so that the law can be fulfilled and the common life between male and female reordered in the light of freedom and giving of self.[26]

For the sake of this recovery, Christ makes what John Paul II calls the "severe" requirement that a Christian must cultivate an interior consciousness about his or her exterior sex. Christians must cultivate the capacity to give of themselves with respect to the other sex, in light of Christ's reminder of how they were made in the beginning and Christ's foreshadowing of the world to come. According to John Paul II, continence is the name for the project of the retraining of the human heart by listening to its depths. Matthew 5 is read as a call to "the innermost layers of . . . [human] potentiality," layers which must "acquire a voice" and "which the lust of the flesh would not permit."[27] Continent asceticism is the practical, outward form of life that enables this interior voice, and its fruit is the recovery of the original meaning of sexual difference. Asceticism is a call to arrange our external bodily life in ways that reveal our internal freedoms for generosity and gratitude. Such asceticism is "committed to a progressive education in self-control of the will, feelings and emotions" and is "the fundamental condition for the reciprocal language of the body to remain in the truth."[28] Such asceticism is therefore essential for responding to the ontology of sexual difference in a fallen world.

This language of the body, the "mature freedom of the gift," can be expressed in either marriage or abstinence. In these two ways of life, "the same anthropology and the same ethos are found." Both express "the total gift of oneself" that is the nuptial meaning of the body as inscribed in the two sexes at creation: "Continence serves indirectly to highlight what is most lasting and most profoundly personal in the vocation to marriage. It highlights . . . the dignity of the personal gift, bound to the nuptial meaning of the body in its masculinity or femininity."[29] Episodic, conditional erotic liaisons, lacking in the solidarity of a covenant, do not testify to the ontology of the *imago Dei*, and celibates and married people both witness to this point. The being *for* another, which is the call of sexual difference in the beginning and which Christ has reiterated in view of the fall, is a logic that requires either marriage or celibacy:

On the basis of the same disposition of the personal subject and on the basis of the same nuptial meaning of the being as a body, male or female, there can be formed the love that commits man to marriage for the whole duration of his life (cf. Matthew 19:3–10). But there can also be formed the love that commits man to a life of continence for the sake of the kingdom of heaven (cf. Matthew 19:11–12). . . . [The choice] comes about on the basis of full consciousness of that nuptial meaning which masculinity and femininity contain in themselves.[30]

In other words, both the married and the celibate pledge themselves against concupiscence and thus to the same "germ of man's eschatological future."[31] In both forms of life, the human significance of sexual difference is given a form for actual concrete living in the concupiscent historical era.

## How Contemporary Vatican Teaching Summarizes John Paul II

In the summer of 2004, the Vatican's Congregation for the Doctrine of Faith published a *Letter to the Bishops of the Catholic Church on the Collaboration of Men and Women in the Church and in the World*. Here we see a concise summary of John Paul II's argument. He ordered its publication, and he is by far its most frequently cited authority.

In this section of the chapter, we will review the letter to establish its basic congruity with John Paul II's teaching on sexual difference. In the next section, we will use the letter as a concise source for discussing John Paul II's thoughts on women in particular, and, in so doing, we will examine some of the weaker aspects of both John Paul II and the letter.

The letter's opening section notes that "recent years" have seen women wanting redress for "conditions of subordination."[32] However, the letter also says, there are two recurring tendencies in the quest for redress that must be resisted. One is to conceptualize women as "the adversaries of men," as rivals in a contest for power. The other is to minimize or deny the differences between the sexes, to treat the differences of sex "as mere effects of historical and cultural conditioning." Against both tendencies, the letter claims that "faith in Jesus Christ" leads the church to prefer an "*active collaboration* between the sexes precisely in the recognition of the difference between man and woman." In pursuit of this vision of sexual difference, which is not marred by either rivalry or denial of difference, the letter cites John Paul II for authority to look to "the first three chapters of Genesis . . . [as] *the basis of all Christian anthropology*."[33]

Following an exegetical pattern that is by now familiar in this book, the letter says that in Genesis, God creates woman and thus "characterizes humanity as a relational reality." With reference to Genesis 2:25, John Paul II's catechesis is quoted to the effect that "right from the beginning the nuptial attribute, that is, *the capacity of expressing love, that love in which the person becomes a gift* . . . expresses a fundamental aspect of the similarity with the Triune God, whose Persons, with the coming of Christ, are revealed as being in a communion of love, each for the other persons." But original sin has changed the way in which the sexes relate to one another, and love is frequently debased now with self-seeking, and one sex dominates the other. "In this tragic situation, the equality, respect and love that are required in the relationship of man and woman according to God's original plan, are lost."[34]

In this situation, sexual difference "cannot be reduced to a pure and insignificant biological fact" but should be grasped as "a fundamental component" of personhood, one that requires theological interpretation and indicates a "spousal" orientation. Healing the rift between the sexes cannot be done "solely from the standpoint of the situation marked by sin," for that would lead to seeing the sexes as competitors or to denying their difference. Instead, we should look to God's revelation of himself as Bridegroom to Israel's Bride.[35] The letter notes that this language, which it says is "much more than simple metaphors," runs from Genesis, through the prophets and the Song of Songs, through the Gospels, and into the Epistles and Revelation.[36] This exegesis allows the letter to conclude that "male and female are thus revealed as *belonging ontologically to creation* and destined therefore *to outlast the present time*, evidently in transfigured form."[37] Because the difference of sex is ontological, it cannot be escaped and should not be resented, and both marriage and celibacy are given on the basis of this ontology. Again, the point is made that Genesis 2:18–25 shows how marriage is "the fundamental dimension of this call. But it is not the only one." Celibacy must also seek to be a "prophecy . . . of future existence of male and female," in which men and women belong together in ways "no longer . . . subject to the present limitations of the marriage relationship," reminding the married that their way of living sexual difference is only penultimate.[38]

## The Question of Woman and the Question of Theological Method

Thus far the letter has represented concisely a position obviously derived from John Paul II on sexual difference, which itself can be read as a variation on Barthian themes, which, in turn, represent a codification and clarification of ideas at large in Christianity, at least ever since Augustine. In sum, the Vatican letter thus far represents a good summary of the theological significance of sexual difference. This position is internally consistent and coherently integrated with basic Christian professions of faith.

However, after offering this general theology of sexual difference, the letter next proceeds to discuss "the importance of feminine values" in society and in the church. In this progression from one agenda to another, the letter is again following the example of John Paul II. John Paul II has also ventured thoughts specifically on femininity, which he offers in the wake of his more general theory of sexual difference. Four years after the conclusion of his weekly catechesis on sexual difference, John Paul II published an "apostolic letter" entitled *On the Dignity and Vocation of Women on the Occasion of the Marian Year*. In this apostolic letter, John Paul II wrote that the "question of understanding the reason for and the consequences of the Creator's decision that the human being should always and only exist as a woman or a man" precedes and is a basis for subsequent discussion of "the greatness of the dignity and vocation of women . . . in the Church and in society."[39] In other words, having established a general theology of the significance of sexual difference, John Paul II believes he has a basis for proceeding to a specific consideration of women. Thus, while John Paul II regards "the question of woman" as a proper consequence of the question of sexual difference, he is treating the two questions as distinct. To ask why God created two sexes, and what significance the distinction between the two sexes has, is not quite the same exercise as focusing on the specific vocation of one sex or the other.

Both the 2004 Vatican letter and John Paul II, as they move into consideration of women, appeal heavily either to natural epistemologies or the example of Mary, Jesus' mother.[40] For instance, the 2004 Vatican letter asserts that women have a "deep intuition . . . of those actions which elicit life." As justification for this claim, the letter points to "to women's physical capacity to give life." Similarly, the letter claims that women "possess a singular capacity to persevere in adversity, to keep life going even in extreme situations, to hold tenaciously to the future, and finally to remember with tears the value of every human life." John Paul II's phrase "the genius of women," articulated in a 1995 letter to women, is cited for its claim that women should be "significantly and actively present in the family." Every human being, male or female, is supposed to be "for the other," but women are said to be "more immediately attuned to these values." Women "in fact" live these values "with particular intensity and naturalness." These claims are usually asserted either with reference to experience, as if they were self-evident, or with reference to Mary, extrapolating from her example to the effect that the "dispositions of listening, welcoming, humility, faithfulness, praise and waiting" are models of femininity.[41]

This book is about the significance of sexual difference and not the vocation of one sex or the other, so I will not dwell on these arguments at length. However, I will observe that these discussions about women depart from the methodology that has generated the theory of sexual difference, which, so it is claimed, is licensing the conversation about women in the first place. The traditional theory about sexual difference has appealed to creation and Christology, but the Vatican and papal arguments about women appeal to experience and the person of Mary. It would seem that the former methodology generates a theory of sexual difference. The Vatican and John Paul II claim that this theory in turn licenses the discussion of women, but in actual practice, for some reason, the theory's theological methodology is evidently inadequate for sustaining conversation about women. Some departure from theology, and recourse to experience and Mariology, seems to occur. I suggest that this departure helps to corroborate Barth's suspicion that it is extremely difficult to give precise content to sexual difference while adhering strictly to theological premises.

In the history surveyed by this book, arguments based on theological premises have usually led to the conclusion that sexual difference is significant and ought to be observed in Christian life. But subsequent moves, aspiring to be more specific about the actual content of those differences and to define the qualities of one sex or another, have tended to lapse into apparent arbitrariness and been vague about their premises. An early example was Clement of Alexandria, who said, without any apparent theological reasoning, that it was too feminine if men wore their rings on the joint rather than at the root of their little finger, and that women should take their exercise by spinning and weaving rather than by going to the gymnasium.[42] Calvin wrestled with what was and was not necessary for salvation, declaring that some difference of sex must be observed, but concluding that salvation could not be said to depend on whether a woman wore a shawl or had a bare head, as per 1 Corinthians 14.[43] Barth chided other theologians, such as Bovet and Brunner, for lapsing into natural epistemology when they tried to argue about gender roles.[44] In sum, disciplined theological arguments about sexual difference and specific proposals about masculinity and femininity are two different things. For reasons identified by Barth, and confirmed unwittingly by the contemporary Vatican, the important theological premises about sexual difference resist being made into specific claims about the characteristic of each sex. Barth's arguments are logical and internally coherent, but the Vatican does not abide by the same discipline.

Some may say that if Barth's theory of sexual difference cannot give concrete specification to the traits of a particular sex, then it is too vague to make much difference in moral theology. Such suspicions are demonstrably untrue, as our own examination of the ethical implications of Barth's anthropology demonstrated. The sharpness of Barth's theology of sexual difference (and John Paul II's too, prior to his departure from theological method) is potent and efficacious when it comes to constructing a theology of marriage. In the next chapter, we shall study several contemporary attempts to revise the traditional theology of marriage. Each attempt ignores or distorts more traditional theology about sexual difference. As we exegete these revisionist proposals, we will also be examining them from a Barthian perspective. We shall see that Barth's theory of sexual difference reveals major omissions in the revisionist accounts of marriage, and that these revisionist accounts cannot succeed until they can reply to the questions generated by a Barthian perspective.

## Notes

1. John Paul II, *On the Dignity and Vocation of Women on the Occasion of the Marian Year*, 470–71, reprinted in John Paul II, *The Theology of the Body: Human Love in the Divine Plan* (Boston: Pauline Books & Media, 1997), 443–92.

2. John Paul II, *Gaudium et Spes* 22, quoted in the foreword by J. S. Grabowski to John Paul II, *Theology of the Body*, 16.

3. John Paul II, *Theology of the Body*, 29.

4. Cf. ibid., 32–34.

5. Ibid., 33, 53.

6. Ibid., 33–34.

7. See ibid., 55–56, 107.

8. Ibid., 55, 75.

9. Ibid., 218, 75.

10. Ibid., 75, 47, 359, 76.

11. Ibid., 57, 79, 71.

12. Ibid., 48.

13. Ibid., 53, 68.

14. Ibid., 75, 80, 81–82, 215.

15. Ibid., 114, 115, 116.

16. Ibid., 117–18, 119.

17. Ibid., 123.

18. Ibid., 127, 70.

19. Ibid., 145, 110, 111, 109, 191.

20. Ibid., 152, 169.

21. Ibid., 133.

22. Ibid., 137, 135, 134.

23. Ibid., 145, 138ff.

24. Ibid., 146, 151.

25. Ibid., 156.

26. Ibid., 158.

27. Ibid., 176.

28. Ibid., 408.

29. Ibid., 302, 274, 277, 286–87.

30. Ibid., 284.

31. Ibid., 350.

32. Congregation for the Doctrine of the Faith, *Letter to the Bishops of the Catholic Church on the Collaboration of Men and Women in the Church and in the World*, http://www.vatican.va/roman_curia/congregations/cfaith/documents/rc_con_cfaith_doc_20040731_collaboration_en.html, §2.

33. Ibid., §2, 4, 5.

34. Ibid., §6, 7.

35. Ibid., §8, 9.

36. Ibid., §9–12.

37. Ibid., §12.

38. Ibid., §6, 12.

39. John Paul II, *On the Dignity and Vocation of Women*, §1, in John Paul II, *Theology of the Body*, 444.

40. As Agneta Sutton has observed, this mariological move is reminiscent of Hans Urs von Balthasar. See Sutton, "Complementarity of the Two Sexes."

41. Ibid., §13, 14, 16.

42. See p. 36n51.

43. See p. 137n85.

44. See pp. 146–47.

# Chapter 8
# THREE PROPOSALS FOR THE INSIGNIFICANCE OF SEXUAL DIFFERENCE

## Challenges to the Tradition

In the introduction to the fifth and final volume of his history of Christian doctrine, Jaroslav Pelikan observes:

> The modern period in the history of Christian doctrine may be defined as the time when doctrines that had been assumed more than debated for most of Christian history were themselves called into question: the idea of revelation, the uniqueness of Christ, the authority of scripture, the expectation of life after death, even the very transcendence of God.[1]

To that list he could have added claims for the significance of sexual difference. Sexual difference, of course, is more peripheral to classic Christianity than revelation or Christology, but nevertheless, that sexual difference is morally significant is a belief which was once assumed but which is now questioned. In fact, as we have seen, sexual difference is often related to the idea of revelation, Christology, Scripture, our hopes for death, and the difference between a transcendent God and a fleshly, animal creature. If these things are questioned, it should not be surprising that the significance of sexual difference is too.

As with other fundamental beliefs in Christianity, the traditional view on sexual difference came about after an initial period of contest and negotiation. This book has shown how, after an initial patristic period in which Christian beliefs about sexual difference were fluctuating and diverse, a more or less rough consensus on sexual difference existed from the fourth to the twentieth centuries. From chapters 2 through 7, the major theologians of several eras were shown to have either argued or presupposed that sexual difference was a theologically significant part of being human in creation, after the fall, and in the eschaton. Sometimes these beliefs were more presupposed than argued; sometimes beliefs about sexual difference were used to enable theologies of marriage and celibacy but without always being visibly debated. But that these beliefs were presupposed, latent and implicit, did not mean they were insignificant and ineffectual. To the contrary, as we have seen in every chapter, each theology of marriage had some sort of premise about sexual difference at its root.

As we saw in chapters 6 and 7, major Protestant and Catholic theologians have, in the modern period, brought arguments about sexual difference to the fore. In these chapters, the claim is that sexual difference is a theologically significant aspect of anthropology. Appealing to a broad and consistent reading of Scripture, it has been claimed that the encounter between man and woman—each sex being a distinct yet related mode of being human—is a relationship for which every human being must account as he or she responds to God. The claim has been that in the course of relating as a creature to his or her Creator, that is, in the course of keeping our covenant with God in our physical and creaturely aspects, every human being must acknowledge his or her maleness or femaleness with gratitude, praise, thanksgiving, and obedience. Human maleness and femaleness were made to participate in this project. Celibacy and marriage are the gifts or commands from God that enable the human sexual difference to fulfill this obligation and to be seen for what it is, namely, as a dimension of human personhood that is structured for relationship. Celibacy or marriage are forms of encounter with the opposite sex that derive from, and witness to, the covenant that is every human's destiny in Christ, and thus they are modes of life that allow men and women to be what they are created to be.

In this chapter, we shall also see how contemporary theologians dispute this claim. We shall look at three theologians—Graham Ward, Eugene Rogers, and David Matzko McCarthy—who, in effect and in different but allied ways, make proposals for the moral insignificance of sexual difference. These three theologians all profess faith in the covenant structure of Christian life, but they believe that sexual difference is insignificant for this way of life. Thus in theology today, as with the early patristic era, no consensus about sexual difference can be presupposed. In these three contemporary theologies about marriage and celibacy, as with certain ancient theologies, one can see both latent and explicit suspicion or doubt about the theological significance of sexual difference.

There is at least one difference, however, between the contemporary period and the early period. Now, unlike then, arguments for the insignificance of sexual difference can be juxtaposed with traditional arguments and assumptions about the significance of sexual difference. It would have been anachronistic to expect the early theologians to engage with points only raised by subsequent tradition, whereas today's theologians can be expected to take some responsibility for the arguments of their predecessors. The adequacy of arguments today can be at least partially assessed with respect to how well they answer and anticipate objections from the tradition. Making this assessment will also be part of this chapter's agenda.

## Sexual Difference Is Significant Only as a Figure of Speech

Of the three revisionist perspectives on sexual difference we shall discuss in this chapter, the first is represented by Graham Ward, who argues that sexual difference is theologically significant but only in a linguistic sense. I will first exegete and render Ward's case succinctly, then I shall offer criticisms and responses to Ward, explaining why I believe that his argument is unsuccessful and theologically problematic.

### Ward's Argument

Ward proposes that sexual difference matters because it enables discourse about eros between irreducibly distinct and theologically significant subjects. "In the narrative of God's story, male and female are tropes." Ward believes that these tropes are essential because Christian theology needs a way to speak of love and attraction across differences: "*Diastema*, distance, interval, the other cannot be synthesized into a monistic whole," and therefore difference "provides that which is necessary for movement, for economy, for time, for history and therefore is intimately related to soteriology." "God's desire for the salvation of the world" creates a relationship across the *diastema* between Creator and creature. According to Ward, theologically conceived sexual difference captures in human speech both this difference and God's economy of desire: "Sexual difference, in its endorsement of both separation and relation, constitutes we human creatures as the *imago Dei*."[2]

But Ward also believes that when we understand sexual difference from the appropriate theological perspective, "biology *per se*" vanishes, and any stable referent to the bodies of actual men and women is theologically insignificant.[3] In other words, in Christianity Ward wants to claim that the theological language of sexual difference illuminates important spiritual truths but that it has at most only an oblique relationship to biological maleness and femaleness. In one particular essay, Ward attempts to elaborate and explain this argument, presenting it as building upon Barth's account of sexual difference. I shall work with this essay, for it will allow us to ask whether his account of sexual difference is genuinely a development from Barth and, more broadly, whether Ward's position can be sustained in light of the earlier Christian tradition.

Ward aligns himself with Barth's skepticism of natural knowledge in theology: "I do not intend to sketch a natural theology in which human eros and divine pneuma are identified." He also accepts Barth's link between the *imago Dei* and sexual difference, and along with Barth he repudiates the notion that we can work by analogy from human sexual difference and desire into God: "In itself it [sex] remains human, far too human for the development of a *theology*."[4] Ward posits an "ontological difference" between "God's desire for the salvation of the world" and "human eros," as well as a distinction between intra-Trinitarian difference and sexual difference.[5] For Ward and for Barth, all of these various distinctions must be observed in order to discipline the theology of sexual difference.

Of course, it is also axiomatic and basic to both Barth and Ward that there are relations across these differences; that is, for Ward, why sexual difference is a useful trope in the first place. For instance, Ward refers to God's desire for the salvation of the world as an "erotics of redemption," in which "God's desire for me" (which Ward calls "a prerequisite for any doctrine of election") evokes "my desire for God."[6] In keeping with Ward's intent to have a Barthian stance, this relationship of mutual desire always has a bias—"It is an analogy constituted from above—we reflect, we are not the prototype"[7]—but as long as we theologize on the premise of this divine initiative, then we will not risk conflating the divine and human, and the analogy between sexual difference and various other theological differences-in-relation can proceed.

Although Genesis exegesis features prominently in Barth, and although Ward does quote Genesis 1:27 at one point, the creation narratives are not the most basic reason why Ward endorses a connection between the *imago Dei* and sexual difference. Instead, Ward highlights another dimension of Barth's case, the "for other" aspect of intra-Trinitarian life that Christ reveals. For Ward, "separation and relation" is characteristic of the Trinity: "In our attraction-in-difference is reflected the difference-in-relation in our

Trinitarian God."[8] In other words, maleness and femaleness refer to something irreducibly different, and yet these differences are erotically related, and such "attraction-in-difference" is the image of the ontologically basic interior life of the Trinity and in which we find the quintessential life of attraction among irreducibly different persons. Thus we can and should seek insight into human sexual difference not so much through the doctrine of creation (which explains Ward's lightness with regard to Genesis) but through more abstract but nevertheless revealed knowledge of God's own being. In fact, Ward insists, seeming to echo Barth, that there is no other way to proceed if we want to know something about human being, including sexual difference:

> The life breathed into Adam can only be understood in terms of the life that raised Jesus Christ from the dead. . . . The world of nature created by science . . . in which the world is composed of discrete, self-grounding, self-defining objects "out there," is a world-view Barth rejects as false and idolatrous. Corporeality is spiritual by nature and to be understood as such must be understood theologically, not on its own immanent and secular terms.[9]

Whatever bodies mean, whatever sexual difference signifies, for Ward it can only flow from what its Trinitarian precedent allows it to mean.

One might see in Ward's de-emphasis of creation the beginning of his essential criticism of Barth. Ward believes that Barth's account of sexual difference is insufficiently theological, that it is too much obliged to a reification of naturalistic observations based on biology. This accusation is an attempted critique of Barth on Barth's own terms, for Ward thinks certain naturalistic premises are at work in Barth that would, of course, have been anathema to Barth.

To substantiate his critique, Ward claims there are "two quite separate economies of desire" in Barth's portrait of sexual difference. In the first economy, what brings male and female together is a "vocation . . . to be for the other, a vocation that is divine and therefore communicated through the Spirit." This vocation is based in God's love and is "kenotic," corresponding "to the intradivine love of the Trinity," and is "not based on any lack in God but rather the very excess of love in God that pours itself out towards the other."[10] On this point, Ward believes Barth is correct. But Ward also sees in Barth an economy between the sexes that is based in incompleteness, in which male and female make up something for each other without which they would be incomplete, and "the aim is to have one's demand satisfied. Its aim is possession and incorporation of the other, the eclipse and erasure of difference." "It is here that the problems begin," Ward suggests, for he believes that an economy in the image of the Trinity must repudiate notions of scarcity: "Trinitarian difference and sexual difference operate at odds with each other in Barth's thinking."[11]

Ward believes that in describing an economy of necessity for sexual difference, an economy in which one subject completes a lack in the other subject, Barth is describing

> sexual difference from the male perspective. Though he voices a respect for the feminine, she is defined only in relation to what the male lacks—she is the help *meet* for him. His other is not really another at all. It is the other of the same. In Hegelian terms, the woman provides the consciousness with a reflection of itself that it might have a sense of its own identity.[12]

This lack of mutuality cannot be Trinitarian, according to Ward. Put another way, the problem is Barth's hierarchical relation between the sexes. Ward believes that Barth wants a relation "between the I and Thou, the Self and the Other, Israel and Yahweh, the Church and Christ" wherein

> the latter ruptures the autonomy of the former, questioning the authority and privilege of the former. But the hierarchy of the male/female relation means that the female . . . is in no position to question. She does not stand *with* man, or *before* man as other, she stands *for* man. In other words, I suggest, Barth is not able to establish the sexual difference that his theology requires.[13]

Because, at least in Ward's summary of Barth, the female cannot question, because she can only accept her place and fulfill a lack in the man, this economy cannot be a Trinitarian analog.

In sum, Ward accuses Barth of correctly discerning a kenotic eros between different persons in the Trinity and correctly discerning that the human *imago Dei* is based on this eros and difference, but nevertheless failing to apply these insights consistently in his description of sexual difference, which both Barth and Ward believe ought to be the example par excellence of the *imago*.

Ward says that Barth does not see his self-contradiction because Barth believes Christian marriage harmonizes the two economies, bringing eros under agapic control in the church. Ward's Barth believes in a world in which erotic relations—relations between the sexes based on need, lack, and insufficiency—no longer have the last word because the economy of the church gives boundaries and shape to marriage: "Marriage creates the temporal space and the moral field for creative interaction, one with the other—so that alterity is respected and difference maintained within the erotic relation." Ward says that for Barth, marriage places sexual difference "at the crux of a horizontal relation with time and a vertical relation with eternity," for in marriage, the sexes keep a covenant with one another, and in so doing announce humanity's universal ordering for covenant with God.[14] Thus, Ward reckons Barth to be saying, the married couple belong to each other first and foremost in the Lord, in the community of the church's kenosis and economy based on the Trinity, and only secondarily in an erotic complementarity.[15]

Yet Ward thinks that this attempt to balance one type of power with another is a failure. The church cannot transform the sexual economy into a Trinitarian economy. He says that the two rival economies, the one governing and relativizing the other, are mutually contradictory; the complementarity of the sexes, as he believes Barth has described it, is simply antithetical to belonging together in the Lord. Complementarity (the economy of need) cannot be subsumed and governed by the Lord's alternative (the economy of kenosis) because the two are in competition with one another. Barth had left the erotic only as "an economy to restore mutual lack,"[16] when the belonging together in the Lord was itself a form of eros not based in lack, as the Trinitarian relations reveal.

According to Ward, Barth should have described a single erotic economy; he should have omitted notions of complementarity and hierarchy, that is, omitted any hint of scarcity and lack. A properly theological eros, an eros that fully modeled intra-Trinitarian eros among human persons, would not have described relations between men and women as relations based on shortage and insufficiency. Ward calls what Barth has produced a "biologically based metaphysics," too stuck in a naturalistic epistemology of relations between the sexes. Ward alleges that it is "hom[m]osexual," in the sense that it is based on a male perspective. It is rooting eros in what completes and fulfills the male, rather than grounding eros in divine love, and Ward says it "leaves Barth simply peddling the male perspective."[17] It is a biological rather than a fully theological account of sexual difference.

Ward believes a better route could have been taken on Barth's own terms. Ward observes that in Barth's exegesis of Genesis 2 and the Song of Songs, Barth "frequently translates and metaphorizes sexual difference by rephrasing the relationship between the male and female in terms of 'partnership,' 'fellowship,' 'covenantal relationship,' 'helpmeet' or the one appropriate to him or her, 'encountering the stranger,' the recognition of the 'other,' the 'Thou' which is 'immanent to 'I.'"[18] On the basis of this nongendered partnership language, a language of equals that does not reflect hierarchy and scarcity, Ward believes that Barth should have realized where his theological commitments were taking him and that "biological" complementarity was out of place: "Where the true understanding of creation's ontological order comes from a participation in the operation of God's being, the biological—nature as it has been conceived since the seventeenth century as an independent realm of self-grounding, self-defining entities—has no value."[19] When we read sexual difference this way, in pursuit of Trinitarian relations and in flight from the seventeenth century, Ward proposes that "biology *per se*" vanishes, for the world of need and lack is replaced by the world of gratuitous desire and exchange:

> From the point of view of revelation the difference is read in terms of a covenant constituted through reciprocal desire. It is this covenant through desire for the other that forms . . . the economy of relations constituted through reciprocal desire within the Godhead. . . . If you like, God does not see male and female, he sees human being in partnership, in covenantal relationships of I and Thou, One and the Other reflecting His own Triune nature. He sees the couple as human being, not male and female.[20]

Ward believes that read from this perspective, Barth's work can point to "this transfiguration of biological difference. For at the heart of the text the male and the female are also Yahweh and His people as 'one flesh.' Yahweh is Israel's husband and Israel is Yahweh's wife, so erotic love and marriage are transposed as kenotic giving and covenant."[21] Read from a certain angle, Ward is suggesting that Barth points to a significance of sexual difference in keeping with the Trinitarian economy, a significance which obliterates any economy constructed on biological foundations.

Ward contends that his reevaluation of Barth should have implications for the church's practice of marriage, which Ward believes should no longer be premised on biologically based sexual differences. Ward argues that as human "Christian life-partnerships" are narratives of "performance and operation of the divine kenotic," emulating the difference and movement between Creator and creation, then biological differences are no longer the relevant differences for marriage. The relevant difference is the "difference mediated by desire."[22] Whenever there is a desire that can plausibly correlate with kenosis, Ward assumes there is a difference between persons that is significant enough to emulate difference theologically conceived. For Ward, to speak of desire is to speak of "textualities of time, subject to and modifying a particular set of contextual forces."[23]

Within narratives of desire that are capable of theological transformation, Ward calls male and female "condensation points or metaphors for a density of signification above and beyond their anatomical specifications."[24] "Male and female are two differentiated positions within a divinely ordered sociality that signify partnership, covenant, fellowship and helpmates. They are symbolic positions within a divine narrative."[25] This "sociality" is what God orders, creates, and desires; the labels of sexual difference are simply ways of speaking and noting the relational polarities of the subjects who comprise this social ecology. The polar subjectivities in relation are the true theological analog. The differences that matter sexually and theologically are whatever differences create sufficient diastasis for this desire, and biological sexual difference is no longer necessary for this purpose. Other differences can take its place in practice, even if not in rhetoric.

In fact, according to Ward, this point is made particularly clearly by same-sex relations. Given that desire requires difference, "there is nothing surprising about the attraction of opposites" and opposite biological sex attraction "maps too easily onto the logic of those who have and want more and those who lack and are dependent."[26] Attraction between members of the opposite biological sex does not force our attention to the nonbiological nature of theological difference. Yet same-sex relations overthrow fictions such as "Every man wants a woman and every woman wants a man."[27] In same-sex relations, "attraction arises still in difference, in opposition, through alterity. As we have recognized, there is no desire without difference. But exactly what is other in a relationship between two 'women' or two 'men' becomes indefinable."[28] In same-sex relations, Ward believes there are still irreducible distinctions, else there would not be desire.

Ward quotes feminist philosopher Luce Irigaray approvingly: "*Desire* occupies or designates the place of the *interval*. . . . Desire demands a sense of attraction: a change in the interval, the displacement of the subject or the object in their relations of nearness or distance."[29] In Ward's usage, the quote is supposed to suggest that when we see same-sex love, we clearly see that what is loved and desired does not arise from biological complementarity. Instead we see something Ward believes is more theologically helpful: "What is loved in love is difference. Such love of difference, in difference, from difference, to difference" is "the labour of Trinitarian love" and is "the relation of the Godhead to creation and the relation that is possible between two women, two men or a man and a woman."[30]

Ward believes there is still a place for actual human bodies in his system, even if the significance of sexual difference has been transformed into the purely symbolic:

> Male and female are two differentiated positions within a divinely ordered sociality that signify partnership, covenant, fellowship and helpmates. They are symbolic positions within a divine narrative. Their life together constitutes the very fabric of Christian time. As such their performances are corporeal. Symbols *are* corporeal.[31]

But to insist on actual men and women for this performance, as Barth does in rejecting same-sex relations, is, for Ward, "a pity. . . . It is as if he returns to a natural theology his whole theological system is set up to refute."[32]

Apparently, Ward can find no theological warrant for thinking that the substance and corporeal shape of sexually differentiated human beings could have theological significance. "Sexual difference not only *also*, but *primarily*, signifies the cosmic and theological differentiation between I and Thou, Self and Other, Yahweh and Israel, Christ and His Church."[33] Barth and Ward agree that human anatomy exists and takes its meaning from more ontologically fundamental theological prototypes, but Barth and Ward disagree about whether that anatomy retains its significance even as it is transfigured and enabled to signify something theological.

### Criticism of Ward's Argument

Ward's claims are astonishing for only partially reckoning with Barth's argument; when Ward and Barth's arguments are considered side by side, it is apparent that Barth's case succeeds where Ward's fails.

Of course, Ward and Barth agree on the power of sexually differentiated language to testify to distinctions within erotic intimacy and for this intimacy to be transformed christologically through covenants. Ward and Barth would both agree that "a person's physical body, the 'one flesh' of the nuptial body, the church's ecclesial body, the eucharistic body and Christ's eschatological body map one upon another."[34] But Ward would have the significance of the person's physical body disappear under so much symbolism, as if human materiality were indifferent to God's theological purposes, as if Barth had never argued for a connection between creation and covenant.

Ward can say, "Marriage is the narrative of the creative interval between two bodies, maintained by the labour of loving as it moves in hope towards the eschatological coming of the kingdom, which is redemption—personal only in as far as it is also ecclesial."[35] One can imagine Barth agreeing. But Barth would have presupposed that as persons become ecclesial, they do not stop being what they are. On the Sabbath, God enters into relationship with male and female as he has made them, because this animal aspect of humanity is good—and not in expectation that it will become insignificant or in need of some further transformation. Being a creature, being made with a male or female body, was created for being ecclesial, and so when it is ecclesial, the male or female body stays significant—in fact, it becomes more itself, more truly male or female, as it is brought into ecclesial being. Ecclesial being is not built on foundations that are repudiated or redundant; on the contrary, ecclesial forms of life, such as marriage, exist to confirm biological foundations and reveal what they were meant to be all along. The "creative interval between two bodies" does not stop being animal as more figurative meanings are also revealed; the biological differences between the sexes mean something not because they are superseded and given over to symbolic significance but through remaining what they are as they reveal a new teleology. Ward speaks of "transfiguration of biological difference," but what he really means is the annihilation of biological significance. But for Barth, biology was the material presupposition for the covenant, a purpose-built theater made for the covenant, and not the covenant's waste product, not something that can be disposed and overcome once theological perspective is achieved. To suggest that God would enter into covenant with something other than what he actually made would be to break his Sabbath promises as Barth described them.[36]

Moreover, it seems incongruous that Ward is offended by the notion that one sex should be dependent on another. It was axiomatic for orthodoxy's conception of creaturehood that, unlike God, our kenotic potential is limited and that we are dependent and necessarily depend upon one another. When Barth reads one sex as meeting a need or a lack in the other sex, to the extent that there is no *humanum* without both sexes, he is not referring to an erotic appetite or passion that would consume the other for the sake of the satisfaction of male appetite. Barth's point is about ontology. Barth had noted carefully that it is God who presents the sexes to one another; their relation in difference is not governed by their poverty but from God's gift and graciousness to make them what they are through an Other. God is different from a human being because humans are not self-sufficient, and sexual difference is the first sign of human interdependency. Sexual difference is a gift because it is an arena in which human beings can actually be what they are: mutually interdependent and also distinct from one another. Barth says that maleness and femaleness *are* a necessary relation, for it is the theater in which God has placed us, and what *is* cannot be contingent on our desire. Barth has no reason to disagree with Ward that all manner of desires and relations can be transfigured in kenotic ways, but Barth's exegesis of Scripture, which teaches him that the form of our embodiedness is not meaningless, commits him to saying that some differences—notably sexual ones—are more ontologically basic and therefore not contingent on our preferences. This ontological basis for humanity demands thanksgiving, praise, and attention; to deny that, and to premise our relations on our subjective desires and the obsolescence of our bodily forms, as Ward does, is a move tending toward Manichaeism.

Furthermore, contrary to Ward, it does not follow when Ward says, by positing the significance of bodies, or a human sexual economy of lack and mutual fulfillment, that Barth merely peddles the male perspective, or that he is speaking from a naturalistic epistemology. Certainly Barth speaks of a hierarchy, and a degenerate hierarchy between male and female has been a human tragedy ever since Genesis 3:16. Undoubtedly a great deal more could be done to explain how the effects of this tragedy shape Barth's perceptions. But Barth has been clear to speak not of the hierarchy he intends as naturally known, but as created in God's image. If sexual difference really is an image of God's internal movements, or the movement from Creator to creature, then, as Barth puts it, "a movement of precedence and subsequence" can only be expected.[37]

Barth has clearly insisted that man as man is accountable to God and must see woman not as his possession but as his fellow to whom he is bound in Christlike service. Barth rests his case on Genesis read through Ephesians 5, and he is quick to note the demands that these passages place on men; he also notes the mutuality of the Song of Songs as appropriate in its place. Barth has opened the door to a type of theological hierarchy that turns normal, nontheological hierarchies upside down, in which the first are last and the last are first but in which there is still order. Perhaps Barth's rhetoric needs more such radical seasoning— perhaps there are certain suggestions and developments of this basic premise which betray the assumptions of mid-twentieth century Swiss middle class society. But when Ward thinks that in Barth he sees variations on "Romantic erotics which announced the metaphysics of heterosexuality, predicated on medical investigations into the biology of sexual difference," then he is simply not reading Barth according to the internal logic of Barth's own texts.[38] Barth's predicate is no more "medical" than Augustine's. The mature Augustine, and Barth, are both committed to the theological proposition that human sexual difference means whatever it means in and through Scripture and the teleology of salvation history. If Ward wants to dissent from Barth's notion of gender hierarchy, the route must be through a challenge to Barth's exegesis and anthropology, and not by importing "medical" or "biological" categories that are foreign to Barth's argument, and not by leaping to a discussion of the Trinity without sufficient attention to the integrity of creation.

Perhaps one might characterize Ward as being like the early Augustine in *De Genesi contra Manichaeos*: committed to the idea that the Genesis narratives on sexual difference must mean something and cannot simply be discarded, but yet uncomfortable in thinking about how a figurative meaning might also depend upon a material significance and existence. The early Augustine and Ward are not quite Manichaen, for unlike the Manichaens they both assume that the figures of male and female are indeed worthy of spiritual interpretation, but, like that early Augustine, Ward finds the theological connection with actual physical life uncomfortable. A reading of Genesis that takes the flesh seriously is too much for both of them to perform, although perhaps in theory they profess a system that pays homage to the idea of such a reading.

However, even if we draw this connection between Ward and Augustine, there is still a radical difference between the two: at no stage in his career would Augustine have been so complacent about the orderliness and theological significance of sexual desire. Ward simply assumes, rather than argues, that same-sex desire must be congruent with God's desires. He assumes where there is desire there must be theologically significant difference and does not interrogate same-sex desire at any point, asking if it might be postlapsarian in origin and hence, unlike sexual difference, possibly testifying to sin and not to ontologically significant differences. It is as if Augustine's argument against the Pelagians, to the effect that human desires must be subject to theological judgment and cannot simply be trusted for their goodness, had never been made. Augustine wrote persuasively that not all sexually differentiated desires are theologically honorable; desires must be interrogated in relation to the ontology of creation and the love of the heavenly city. Ward seems unprepared to do the same and to inspect same-sex desire from perspectives that might problematize it.

In sum, Ward has misread Barth, and in different ways he is reminiscent of the immature Augustine and of the Pelagians. But one can think of Bernard of Clairvaux as the ultimate counterexample that finally condemns

Ward's position. In Bernard we saw how allegories of sexual difference rooted in Scripture must be read and interpreted by other, more concrete readings of sexual difference. It was clear that an allegory or figure of speech testifying to the love of the Creator undermines itself if it is taken to suggest the meaninglessness or abolition of what the Creator has made. Such self-evisceration is evident when sexual difference is regarded as merely a trope.

## Sexual Difference Is Insignificant for the Ascesis and Sacrament of Marriage

Like Graham Ward, Eugene Rogers proposes a theological epistemology that to a large extent professes to follow Barth. Like Ward, Rogers wants to use that epistemology against Barthian arguments to make a case for same-sex marriages. The difference between Ward and Rogers, however, is the respective strategy for reckoning with the significance of sexual difference. Their two strategies turn out to have many of the same problems, but they begin in different places. For Ward, sexual difference is important as a figure of speech and, at that level, something rhetorically useful. For Rogers, however, the significance of sexual difference is something to minimize theologically. Rogers, like Ward, wants to argue on behalf of same-sex marriage, but Rogers is more urgent about it, spending less time in the linguistic foreground.

Rogers's project is also complex, and, when it is examining marriage in general rather than Barth and sexual difference, it is often beautiful. He rereads Thomas Aquinas on natural law and virtue in interesting ways, and he relies heavily on Orthodox theologies of marriage, suggesting that marriage is similar to *theosis*, as a way of involving the human subject in the interior life of the Trinity. But on the subject of sexual difference, his project seems to have three strands: refuting aspects of Barth, marginalizing procreation, and making sexual desire so significant that the significance of sexual difference is contingent on any individual's preferences. In this section, we shall consider each of these three respective strands.

### Criticisms of Barth

Rogers believes that Barth was mistaken to associate sexual difference and the *imago Dei*. He is blunt: "Jesus did not need a female other half to be fully human."[39] He reasons that if "*God in Christ* determines what reality is,"[40] then his example would hardly lead us to the conclusion that the co-humanity he exemplifies takes man-woman pairs as paradigm cases of I and Thou. If so, then Jesus shows us a deficient case of the image, not its fullness—which is absurd. . . . Then Jesus is a failure, not a saviour.[41]

Rogers thus accepts Barth's premise that Christ indicates cohumanity and being "for others" as an essential determination, an orientation which is the *imago*, but he denies Barth's argument that such Christology requires giving basic theological import to sexual difference. In other words, Rogers raises the question of whether Jesus, as a celibate, is making a response to sexual difference or not. If not, it would seem that the *imago Dei* has no necessary relation to sexual difference. Rogers writes:

That Christ is the image of the Father means that no strict com-plementarity theory will do, according to which no human being represents the image unless he or she is joined with a member of the opposite sex. If Christ is the complete image, then the image need not be a dyad.[42]

Thus not only does Rogers attack Barth for mistakenly proposing a sexu-ally differentiated *imago*, but he also attacks Barth for mistakenly pre-mising the *imago* on a couple. Rogers believes that if we actually look at biblical examples in which Christ exhibits cohumanity, then we also see the Holy Spirit at work in the communities, environments, and third parties that surround Christ and his neighbors. It is the Spirit, Rogers says, who accompanies Christ and deals in the "*messiness* of biblical his-tories, the ways in which God's work *resists* reduction to type."[43] Rogers says that Barth's

I-Thou phenomenology tends to reduce co-humanity to co-individuality and wash out the *ecclesial* nature of the bibli-cal healing stories, which appears signally in the story of the paralytic lowered through the roof. He gets healed and has his sins forgiven *on account of the faith of others*: "And when Jesus saw *their* faith, he said to the paralytic, 'My child, your sins are forgiven.' " Among New Testament illustrations of those relationships Barth might have noticed that I-Thou categories systematically *hide* the presence of third parties and ecclesial mediation: disciples, crowds, friends. The sick are always being brought or even recommended from a distance to Jesus by

*mediating others.* This is the sort of work that Trinitarian thinking appropriates to the Spirit. Christ promises to be with human
beings *not* each individually that we might meet him as I and
Thou, but when *two or three* are *already* gathered in his name.[44]

For Rogers, this ostensibly more Trinitarian concept of cohumanity
means that when one does want to discuss marriage, one should not
theorize a couple as if they were in isolation. Rogers says that biblical weddings always need a third, a witnessing congregation, just as
within the Trinity the Spirit witnesses relations between the Father
and the Son.[45]

> In the Trinity, otherness is a condition for the possibility of love.
> God can be love, because God exists in the relationships among
> Father, Son, and Holy Spirit, not just two others, but also a third,
> a second difference, that their love might not be without celebra-
> tion and blessing and witness. . . . In creation the divine intimacy
> can become physical nearness and temporal duration. God grants
> the creature a body and a history. God enables lovers to make a
> household and a marriage.[46]

For that reason, Rogers believes that the eros of marriage is theologically
"incomplete *à deux*."[47] Thus while Rogers agrees with Barth that "marriage is in microcosm a theatre of God's glory," an image of the covenant
with Israel and the church, he thinks he is correcting Barth by also add-
ing that marriage is "a place where human beings—not just the spouses,
but also their neighbours—are allowed to witness creation as a significant
action of God. So it is that God permits marriage to be a sign of God's will
in creation, of its goodness and reflected glory."[48]

Having made these two observations—which are effectively arguments against the male-female *imago* and against marriages construed
as dyads—Rogers believes that he has neutered Barth's claim that sexually differentiated encounter is at the heart of theological anthropology. Rogers's counterclaim is that when we speak of cohumanity, we
do not need to speak of male and female. When we speak of marriage,
for instance, we need to speak of more triadic models of encounter that
clearly overspill simple maleness and femaleness in encounter.

However, a more careful reading of Barth shows that a sexually differentiated *imago*, having its center in a marriage of one man and woman,
actually respects and anticipates Rogers's concerns. Barth never believed
or professed that his concept of the *imago Dei* made being a part of a

sexually differentiated couple mandatory. Barth never argued or implied that any male-female couple were self-sufficient *à deux*. The point of these clarifications is to show that Rogers's observations about Jesus or the communal nature of marriage do not actually serve his purposes. In other words, Rogers's arguments on these points do not actually marginalize sexual difference and render it insignificant.

On the question of whether couples are self-sufficient, it is clear that Barth explicitly argues the opposite of what Rogers criticizes, that is, it is clear that Barth's concept of marriage opens outward beyond the dyad. An encounter of dyadic sexual difference might be at the core, but it does not follow for Barth that this core is a closed circle. Barth writes:

> When marriage is seen in the light of the divine command . . . marriage cannot and will not be carried through as a purely private undertaking. Even the smallest cottage of the happiest of lovers cannot be habitable inside unless it has at least a door and a few windows opening outwards. At some point it finds itself implicated in affinities and friendships as part of the Christian and civil community. . . . Marriage is not permission to establish an egoistic partnership of two persons.[49]

Thus Rogers's perception that Barth makes the male-female encounter merely an I-Thou encounter, without a triadic openness, is a misplaced criticism. For Barth, the inner logic of marriage requires that it open outward to others; just as Christ and the church form an intimacy with a serving and witnessing dimension, so is the union of male and female. Again, listening to Barth makes the point:

> It is one of the good points in Schleiermacher's doctrine of marriage that he has emphasised this aspect of the matter. . . . He thinks it would be regrettable to involve marriage particularly in the old error that man's best policy is to retire as far as possible from the world. . . . Does the bond between Christ and His Church, which is the prototype of marriage, have as its goal a "pleasantly meditative life?"[50]

Thus when Barth commends marriage as the central form of sexually differentiated social life, he is not recommending a retreat into a sublime dyad but an *imitatio Christi*, an advance forward into the world under God on the basis of our creaturely form, which he takes to be sexually differentiated.

But this point—that our basic creaturely form is sexually differentiated and that this feature of our humanity is ontological and inescapable—does not lead to compulsory membership of a couple. Once again, the real Barth is contrary to Rogers's portrayal of Barth. The real Barth wrote that being a member of a couple is not the only way in which the significance of sexual difference is recognized or enacted. In chapter 6, we saw in Barth a language of vocation, an address from God to men and women arising from the fact of there being sexual difference, in which men and women are called upon to discern whether and when to marry. Here is another such moment when Barth expresses the thought in ways that rebut Rogers particularly clearly:

> The very affirmation of marriage depends upon the serious possibility of its accompanying denial. Forming as it does the focal point and *telos* of the relationship between male and female, from the standpoint of the Gospel it is subject to the command of God who created man as male and female. But it is not a universally obligatory and binding order of creation. The Christian enters into marriage, not on the basis of a natural necessity, but on the special spiritual gift and vocation within his life history and the history of salvation. He does so "in the Lord" (1 Cor 7:39). He does so because he is bidden to represent in this way the relationship between Christ and His community. He does so in the freedom of the Spirit. "To have to marry" is in every sense of the expression a bad thing.[51]

In other words, Barth does not believe that celibates are somehow defective, or that they have withdrawn from the central task of the *imago Dei*. Barth's conception of celibacy is integrated with his concepts of sexual difference and marriage. Barth regards celibates as necessary testimony to the fact that marriage exists as a vocation, as a possibility and not an inevitability. Thus Barth has a framework within which to account for Jesus' celibacy, and Rogers's suggestion—that Jesus' celibacy witnesses against a sexually differentiated *imago*—does not necessarily follow.

On Barth's terms, sexual difference is still theologically significant for those not called to be part of a couple—such as Jesus. On these terms, it is essential to Jesus' humanity that he have a relationship as a man with women, but that is not the same as to say that Jesus required a wife or consort. To be celibate rightly is also to declare a choice in response to sexual difference, and Barth would have us regard that Christ's chastity as a single man is as much a response to sexual difference as marrying.

Barth does demand that one must live in encounter with others in the sexual sphere, but that encounter could take the form of a celibacy that upholds chastity between male and female in the community. By abstaining from temporary liaisons, the chaste and single reinforce the logic of marriage. To be in favor of chaste and ordered relations is not the same as a flight from sexual difference; in fact, for such chastity to be sustainable, one must be honest and familiar with one's desires so that they can be considered with some measure of freedom and detachment. In other words, one must make a full and aware response to the fact of living in a sexually differentiated world even if one intends to be continent. Luther at points, and John Paul II consistently, argued the same thing. In fact, the idea is arguably implicit in Augustine's contention that the goodness of virginity is no mark against marriage.

Reading Barth more faithfully than Rogers, we might summarize our exegesis here and in chapter 6 by saying that in Barthian terms, because human beings are known to be "for others," in light of Christ, and because sexual difference is the paradigmatic instance of difference that establishes otherness between humans, then sexual difference is the first and primary arena of the *imago*. Sexual difference is the first and most basic arena in which a man or a woman must determine specifically how he or she is called to be for others, and the answer to this question may or may not be marriage. Moreover, there is no *imago* if "for others" is not demonstrated in this sphere; as we saw in chapter 6, Barth knew there were many areas of life in which we are called to be "for others," but there is always the sexual one. It never vanishes. Sexual difference is a sine qua non for the *imago* to exist and be known and manifest in our lives, for sexual difference is a *sine qua non* of the shape and form as God made us as creatures. It is therefore impossible to claim that Barth's association of the *imago Dei* and sexual difference implies any sort of compulsory coupling, and Rogers fails in his attempt to displace Barth's *imago* with one that it is sexually generic.

### The Marginalization of Procreation

To understand Rogers's strategy on this front, it helps to bear in mind a passage from "The Body's Grace," an essay by Rowan Williams that features prominently in all of Rogers's writing about sex and marriage. Williams writes:

> In a church that accepts the legitimacy of contraception, the absolute condemnation of same-sex relations of intimacy must rely

> either on an abstract fundamentalist deployment of a number of very ambiguous biblical texts, or on a problematic and non-scriptural theory about natural complementarity, applied narrowly and crudely to physical differentiation without regard to psychological structures.[52]

Chapter 6 of this book—on Barth's discussion of sexual difference, the *imago Dei*, and the reasons for sexually differentiated forms of life—is sufficient to show that Williams's claim is false: Barth is open to the possibility of legitimate contraception,[53] but he is neither fundamentalist, nonscriptural, nor naturalistic about complementarity, and he does not apply his thought narrowly to the physical body without regard to psychology.

However, Williams's claim is interesting for present purposes because it brings to the fore what appears to be in the background for Rogers. Williams's statement suggests that when procreation is no longer necessary in each and every sex act, when procreation becomes optional, such as when Christian arguments that legitimize contraception are accepted, then only fundamentalism and crude naturalism stand in the way of regarding same-sex relations as morally legitimate. By implication, in these situations, it must be incorrect to insist that nonprocreative aspects of sexual difference are so significant as to be necessary for marriage. Rogers certainly wants to draw this inference. In his writing, sexual difference is significant mainly for procreation, and procreation is itself rendered marginal and optional. It is a strategy in service of diminishing the significance of sexual difference in general and for marriage in particular.

This strategy comes into view through an aside Rogers makes about Thomas Aquinas, where he notes that Aquinas "suggests procreation is a good of the species, not of individuals. If Thomas did not make that distinction, he would have more trouble accounting for the celibacy of Jesus and religious."[54] In other words, Rogers notices the same arguments in Aquinas we examined in chapter 4, which I called the "division of labor" approach to procreation: some humans are breeders, but not everyone needs to be, as long as the species is perpetuated.[55] Rogers approves of Aquinas's logic, and, at a later point in his argument, Rogers adapts Aquinas's position as his own, asserting that "procreation is a good of the species, because the species is what procreation exists to promote."[56]

However, Aquinas's argument should not be taken for granted. Augustine offers a rival and more thoroughly theological explanation of procreation.[57] As we explained, Augustine and Aquinas both agree that sexual difference was created for the purpose of procreation, but for Augustine, the perpetuity of the species is not the reason for procreation. In Augustine's discussion, procreation is part of the way that each marriage participates in the telos of creation toward the development of God's covenant with Israel and in Christ. The heavenly city must be populated, and the seed of Israel must bear fruit in a Savior, and married persons fulfill and witness to this task when they procreate. After Christ, celibacy is suddenly possible for the first time. From the point of view of the species' biology on its own terms, absolutely nothing has changed; the inauguration of Christ and the church should change nothing if procreation is about renewing the population and the perpetuity of the species. But in salvation history, within the people of God, as Augustine points out (and as Barth later concurs), everything changes. Celibacy is conceivable as a vocation because the succession of generations is no longer theologically necessary. The "good of the species" was too generic for Barth or Augustine as an account of the purpose of sexual difference, and they took the much more theologically disciplined route: The purpose of sexual difference is that the seed of Israel should bear fruit and the city of God be established, and both of those things have happened now that Christ has come.

For Augustine and Barth, that procreation has become optional in this way does not render sexual difference obsolete. The theological integrity of creation requires that it cannot be. The coming of the covenant does not make creation disposable and superfluous, for it is axiomatic to Augustine's concept of the church and Barth's concept of the covenant that God loves what he has made and wills that his creatures should continue to flourish as they were made. As we saw in relation to Barth's discussion of the Sabbath,[58] God was content to enter into a relationship with this particular human reality distinct from himself. In the Sabbath, God promises that human being does not have to become something else and new in order to be loved. It is loved in the form that it is given, and it can rest in that form and rely on its stability. Human beings have all they need in order to praise, thank, and obey God in the forms given them prior to the Sabbath. In this perspective, that marriage is still a vocation and a gift of God for Christians, even when it is not necessary, is a gift from God. God has made male and female, and God maintains solidarity with what he has made. Marriage recognizes this solidarity and is testimony to the ongoing goodness of creation. Thus sexual difference in marriage, what Augustine called "the seedbed of a city," is significant as part of Christian faithfulness to the graciousness and sufficiency of creation.[59]

For these reasons, it matters how one describes the relationship between procreation and the possibility of celibacy, or the cohabitation in the church of both vocations. Rogers uses his version of Thomism, wherein sexual difference is static and less directly ecclesially significant: sexual difference makes babies and ensures the species survives, and it has this teleology without ecclesial perspective. Of course, as we saw in chapter 4, Aquinas is not baldly naturalistic, and he sees theological purpose and moral obligation interpreting the biological. But Rogers takes procreation as being related to the species *qua* species and omits reckoning with the Augustinian perspective,[60] wherein sexual difference clearly has no extraecclesial origins or purposes; it was always, from the beginning, theologically significant in ways that might change but that cannot repudiate the integrity of the earlier ways. The perspective from an Augustinian concept of history makes it inappropriate to consider procreation from some generic species perspective, and reckoning with an Augustinian perspective would have disciplined Rogers to be more theological, and less naturalistic, about procreation and hence sexual difference.

But as we have seen, Rogers has a motive for making sexual difference a generic species good and something unnecessary in the covenant. He wants to argue for marriage within the church as a sanctifying, moral, ascetical endeavor, and as he uses these concepts, marriage as testimony to the integrity and stability of creation does not feature. As Rogers admits at one point, reckoning procreation as a "good of the *species* leaves room for these considerations."[61] Subordinating sexual difference to a less theologically significant aspect of creation clears the way for neglecting it in a subsequent theology of marriage.

Aquinas's account is also attractive to Rogers because it casts procreation as something one can delegate to others. Delegation of labor, which for Aquinas meant that contemplatives delegated the duty of generation to the married, is a convenient presupposition for a subsequent step in Rogers's argument: that procreation can be delegated to just certain types of marriages. "But procreation is simply not a good that belongs to the couple as such, much less to every sex act. Rather it belongs to the *species*." If procreation is conceptualized as a good of the species, then as long as the species is in no peril, procreation is not mandatory for all. "There need only be enough procreation to keep the species flourishing, and then procreation as the good of the species is fulfilled. And that need, fortunately or unfortunately, is in no danger of going unmet. . . . The earth is now more or less full."[62] Augustine and Barth knew that the time had come to stop procreating because something had happened within salvation history; Rogers reasons that the time has come because the earth appears to have plenty of people. A naturalistic epistemology appears to be at work in Rogers on this point, and the broader theological perspective on marriage and procreation, that children are a good of marriage because of the theological integrity of creation, is simply not considered.

In fairness to Rogers, we should consider his discussion of adoption, which indicates some effort to explain theologically why procreation is less significant. Rogers says, "Christians best imitate God's relation to them as children not when they bear and beget them, but when they *adopt* them." Gentiles "participate in the covenant with Abraham not as Abraham's natural children, but by *adoption*. . . . Because the covenant with Abraham is of *many* nations, there is such a thing as love and marriage raising *adopted* children." "Adoption imitates the adoptive love of God in making human beings God's heirs, and the adoptive love of Joseph in making Jesus his son. Inasmuch as Christians adopt the least of them, they adopt Jesus."[63]

Yet even if these points are true, the only necessary conclusion to Rogers's argument about adoption is that it relativizes procreation. An optional procreation is still a good of marriage, if procreation is seen as testimony to the goodness of creation, alongside adoption's testimony to the graciousness of the covenant. But in Rogers's hands, the adoption motif comes to signify the obsolescence of creation in light of the covenant; he reads the possibility of adoption as deflating the testimony of marriage to the integrity of sexual difference as given in creation. In Rogers's argument, the hospitality of Christian adoption is co-opted to serve the larger thesis that Christian marriage testifies only to covenant, with no ontological and necessary relation to creation. Instead of a creation that enables and is confirmed in the covenant, creation is rendered meaningless in key respects as it is overwritten by the covenant. Rogers writes that "insofar as marriage represents God's creation . . . children are understood as natural to it"—and sexual difference would be natural too—but "insofar as marriage represents God's covenant with Abraham . . . children are understood as in some sense unnecessary and the gift of grace elevating nature."[64] We are meant to conclude that in the covenant, sexual difference is redundant. "Grace elevating nature" becomes, for Rogers, a program in which grace makes nature superfluous, contingent, and, with respect to marriage, sexually indifferent. If procreation is not necessary, and procreation was the purpose of sexual difference, then sexual difference is not necessary.

In Barth's discussion of children in relation to marriage, children are also optional: "Parenthood may be a consequence of marriage which is both joyful and rich in duties, but from a Christian point of view the true meaning and the primary aim of marriage is not to be an institution for the upbringing of children."[65] On this logic, husbands and wives may avail themselves of contraceptive techniques in certain circumstances.

But in Barth, that children are not strictly necessary *post Christum natum* does not dislodge the created goodness of marriage. In fact, it actually clarifies the created goodness of sexually differentiated encounter as good in its own right and not requiring functional products such as children. A married man and woman without children can delight in one another as per the early chapters of Genesis and the Song, as well as being freer to engage with the church and be hospitable to their neighbors. But for Rogers, the superfluity of procreation also means the redundancy of sexual difference and any ontology associated with sexuality in creation. For Rogers, sex is no longer for procreation and the goodness of creation, but "sex before God is for sanctification, for God's catching us up into God's triune life."[66] Sex before God, for Rogers, does not testify to the integrity of creation, to the stability of what God gave and blessed in the beginning: "Creation then is not God's will as such. Creation is grace. God's will is, by creation, graciously and unnecessarily and prodigally to signify God's glory."[67]

One can imagine Augustine, Luther, Barth, or many others agreeing that creation has a telos beyond simply existing. But in the tradition, as distilled in Barth's notion of creation for the covenant, or in Luther's notion that the church exists prior to marriage, the notion that God does not will creation simply as separate and unrelated would not have led to Rogers's conclusion that creation stops being significant in its own natural forms. We recall again Barth's discussion of the Sabbath: for the tradition, although God wills a further meaning for creation—that it have a covenant with him—it does not follow that creation stops being creation, with its own limitations and goodness within those limitations. We recall that for Luther, God established the church in Eden, and then created Eve and brought maleness and femaleness into the project of relating to him in the church. That God makes a covenant with creation in all its distinctness and particularity confirms the significance of creation, for it was *this* creation, and no other, that was made for the covenant. But for Rogers, the forms of creation stop having an integrity of their own, as if the sufficiency of the created order to which the first Sabbath gave witness had stopped being sufficient. Rogers's sexual difference is a prime example of grace rendering created goods not newly significant, but newly insignificant. We shall now see how this problem becomes still clearer and more acute.

## Do Asceticism and Desire Render Sexual Difference Insignificant?

Rogers proposes that there is sufficient and appropriate Christian formation of marriage insofar as there is mediation and emulation of the intra-Trinitarian life of gift and response, which he further claims does not require sexually differentiated terms. If "marriage is no *égoïsme à deux* but a mutual kenosis,"[68] then Rogers proposes that marriage is better understood in these various theologically rich ways, but never in ways that require sexual difference:

> Marriage in Christianity is best understood as an ascetic practice of and for the community by which God takes sexuality up into God's own triune life, graciously transforming it so as to allow the couple partially to model the love between Christ and the Church.[69]

The business of a married couple involves moral, spiritual, and ascetical categories of exchange, desire, and commitment, and these things can be sought and manifested without sexual difference. Ruth and Naomi, for example, are a "typological foreshadowing of the Christ's laying down life for his friends of a covenantal sort," and Jonathan and David exhibit mutuality better than any actual male and female couple in the Bible.[70] These kinds of examples encourage Rogers to conclude that "biblical examples indicate . . . heterosexual marriage does not exhaust covenant. Its whole Trinitarian and salvation-historical basis make it a fluid concept."[71] Rogers's version of the Trinitarian covenant appeals to categories of difference between persons that are more abstract—"fluid"—than sexual difference. If we thought sexual difference meant one thing in creation, it was only an appearance, for grace calls our attention to revised possibilities.

Rogers's account of marriage is poignant in many respects. Criticism of Rogers should not lose sight of the fact that he intends marriage to be evangelical, and this ambition is appropriate. "It is the purpose of Christianity to teach human beings that God loves them," and, as God works in history to establish this relationship of love, "God does not leave my body out of God's desire for me."[72] Marriage, says Rogers, is one of God's ways of bringing our bodies into this project of love. Founded on this outreaching of God, marriage is an initiative that reconfigures what our bodies might mean:

> The love by which God loves human beings is eros, if eros is a love that yearns for union with the other, yearns for the flesh of the

other, is made vulnerable and passionate for the other. . . . It is no part of divinity to need and yearn, but God chooses and takes on need with the flesh, as part of God's humanity, God's body which is in Jesus.[73]

Such choosing, loving, and committing are the substance for which the grace and ascesis of marriage are the shorthand. Rogers quotes repeatedly a line from Barth: "In that the election of God is real, there is such a thing as love and marriage."[74] Rogers describes a logic of justification—"the acceptance of the other as wanted, as desired by God unconditionally"— which drives his account of marriage.[75] Because the Trinity is constituted by this love, this desire, commitment, and kenosis, then our marriages can be as well:

> For eros does not move us up to God, so that because we know eros, we know God, but it moves from God down to us, so that because we read the stories of God's yearning and God's constancy, God's covenant fidelity and God's covenant promise, we learn for the first time what eros is for and what it means. *Eros, therefore, does not reveal God, but God unveils eros.*[76]

Because we have heard of how God loves, we are freed from conceiving marriage as a "fertility cult" or a "private two."[77] Because we know how God loves, our own relations with one another are transfigured.

But the bodies desired by God are apparently not sexually differentiated bodies. This aspect of human creaturehood, shared with animals and linking us to material reality, is not necessary to what God loves and sees as he calls us into marriage. Rogers does not think he is being abstract in his account of marriage; that is, he does not think that by emphasizing "fluid" spiritual functions and affective aspirations for marriage he is abandoning theologically significant creaturely particularities. He believes that he adequately allows for the finitudes of being an embodied creature who participates in grace and marriage:

> Creation permits the possibility of marriage because creation allows the possibility of God's eternal life of grace and gratitude, of God's unconditional response to God's self-giving *also in finitude*—in space and time. Thus it is . . . that marriage can represent the Trinity in space and time.[78]

In other words, Rogers reasons that the theologically significant transformation of marriage is for a human covenant to emulate and participate in the Trinity, and for that, the essential creaturely conditions for marriage are not sexual differences but the more generic creaturely conditions of space and time:

> Indeed, for material creatures, intimacy depends on physical boundaries. You cannot hug someone unless the two bodies have skins to press up against each other. Temporally, finitude means having a beginning and an end. You cannot hug someone unless your bodies adjoin at the same time. . . . This difference is not yet a fault. It is the appropriate condition of creaturely intimacy. It allows for such goods as the spatial intimacy of lovers and the temporal intimacy of generations. It allows for such goods as conversation, which requires both proximity in space and succession in time.[79]

Bodies, then, are essential for Rogers's account of marriage, because they locate us in space and time and make us distinct from one another. That distinction is sufficient for covenants—"any body is taken seriously that extends and deepens the eucharistic entry into God's body"[80]—and Rogers has described the differentiated features of bodies sufficiently that they emulate the eucharistic economy as he has described it. On his own terms, he has accounted for the significance of created bodily differences.

But are these terms adequate? The case being made is that subsidiary bodily features, such as sexual difference, are insignificant compared to simply existing physically in space and time. Rogers's argument is that sexual differences perhaps feature prominently in Christian allegories but that they are not essential to the Christian life, being less significant than simply existing as bodies distinct in space and time. The theologically necessary features of the *humanum* are not sexed:

> The male-female version of the one flesh can be especially apt for representing the union of Christ with his bride, the Church, but not everyone need represent this union in the same way. The analogy is flexible enough already that both celibates and the married represent it. Gay and lesbian couples also need not threaten the aptness of the relation between Christ and the Church, but can be taken up into it.[81]

But is Rogers right? Of course not everyone has to represent Christ and the church through marriage, but traditionally the Christ-church analogy can be embraced by celibates because, as we saw with Bernard of Clairvaux, celibates presume the goodness of created and embodied sexual difference as a concrete reference. Male monks can use sexually differentiated imagery to indicate their relations to Christ because the goodness of marriage is presupposed, distinct, and stable. Underlying their mystical encounters, marriage as an institution is needed to exist as good in order that the currency of discussion can be trustworthy. If they were not able to presuppose this aspect of stability and goodness in the created order, then the power of their imagery would be emptied. They would be using something suspect and unstable to testify to something of supreme importance.

Has Rogers made sexual difference unstable and suspect? Sexual difference, of course, cannot disappear completely for Rogers. It exists. But its significance is now subsidiary, its task of procreation can be delegated, its aptness for representation is not universal, and so, in matters of marriage, it has become elective and contingent. Rogers believes that it matters when somebody is male or female only in particular instances, idiosyncratically, unpredictably, and only to the extent that we discern our true desires correctly:

> Gay and lesbian people care about bodies—otherwise many of them would take the easier route and settle for those of the opposite sex. . . . Only because God gives tabs and slots [penises and vaginas] more to be about—namely God—than insert-tab-A-in-slot-B, it also comes not amiss that God should give it to some to admire others with tabs.[82]

In other words, God gives it to a person to admire "tabs" or not. God gives sexually differentiating features different significance to different persons for the sake of the covenant's larger project of transforming sex into something besides creaturely goodness, that is, for the sake of transforming bodies into being about God. This God, as he transfigures creation, does not respect its order as ontologically significant but as material which is volitionally significant. What sexual difference means for each person is contingent on desire, on gratuitous election. Just as it was gratuitous and free for God to elect the Jews or become incarnate in a certain place and time, it is gratuitous and free whether one is given to prefer the same sex or the opposite sex:

> Bodies . . . are one of the ways in which Christians ought to take particulars seriously: God chose the Jews; the incarnation took place in a particular place and time; the sacraments locate Christ again in space and time; the priest represents Christ still another

way in space and time; particular bodily things—this bread and this wine—do matter. And so, to sum up, it really does matter whether someone has a penis or a vagina.[83]

But this mattering, for Rogers, is conditional, dependent upon an inscrutable will, like God choosing the Jews or becoming incarnate at one particular time and place and not another. This election is still at work today, making a penis matter to one person and a vagina to another. What makes these particularities significant is not any quality that is shared and public, part of the created order, but rather an antinomian contingency, that they are chosen by God, elected, when it could just as easily been otherwise. "The desire for a body of a particular gender—a desire that affects gay and lesbian Christians most of all—does not marginalize but heightens the attention to bodies' 'distinctive attributes.'"[84] The punctiliar surprise of desire, not the trustworthy revelation of the created order, is apportioning significance for sexual difference. Desire brings a body's distinguishing features, its maleness and femaleness, to a significance it would not otherwise have.

This proposal for sexual difference is novel in the Christian history surveyed in this book (perhaps it has affinities with Ockham and the medieval voluntarists, but that would be a different line of investigation). This novelty has profound theological consequences. The significance of sexual difference has never before been contingent upon a creature's preferences, or upon whether or not God gave it episodically to a particular creature to have certain preferences. Sexual difference—even for the pre-Augustinians who were wary about according it significance in the created, reconciling, or redeemed economies—was always a matter of ontology. It meant whatever it meant or did not mean based on its relation to creation and eschatology. As was particularly clear, perhaps for the first time in Luther, the fact of a sexually differentiated creation is reckoned to human beings as a piece of information from God about *who* and *what* it meant to be human. "We are exactly as he created us," wrote Luther, and "it is not a matter of free choice or decision but a natural and necessary thing."[85] On Luther's logic, we are either male or female, and the question posed by Luther and refined by Barth and then by John Paul II is, How are we going to be male and female together? How will we respond to the fact of being either male or female? How will we be and order ourselves in response to what we actually are? Luther's premise—that God will bring Eve to Adam in the church—assumes that God stands by what he has made and is reliable in his use of it. It is as stable as any of God's covenants.

But Rogers is proposing a new thing. Rogers is proposing that our desire or appetite for the body of another may be a revelation from God about the significance sexual difference should have in each individual's particular circumstance. We are sexually differentiated, but in the covenant of grace it might not matter universally. God might do one thing for person A and another thing for person B. That we exist as male or female does not matter until we are struck by a desire for one sex or another. Sexual difference, that unmissable feature of the creation stories and the source of one of Scripture's architectonic images, is significant on an incidental aesthetic basis. Perhaps, on the premise of a desire, we organize our marital lives in response to it, but perhaps not.

Augustine, who so well described sexual appetite as mysterious, unruly, and fickle, would have been amazed to see sexual desire granted so much authority. From at least *Confessionum* onward, Augustine showed that sexual desire was often misleading and liable for misinterpretation, that it was plastic and changeable; one simply could not read one's sexual longings as a vocation from God, because what one desired today might not be what one desired tomorrow. Augustine once believed that were he deprived of the embraces of a woman he would be miserable; he later learned that it was not so. "The single desire that dominated my search for delight was simply to love and to be loved," writes Augustine,[86] and in that sense, he and Rogers might agree that sexual desire is a type of restlessness that ought to point a person toward transfiguration in theological ways. But Augustine also takes the fickleness of his desire seriously, and in his analysis realizes that desire needs to be interrogated by ontology in order to see the direction in which it must ultimately be refashioned for its own satisfaction. What we truly are, what God has made us to be and commands us to be, needs to have sovereignty over our appetite. God has shown us our creaturely nature in a salvation history that is not contingent upon our desire, and, as the course of *Confessionum* shows, part of the Christian project is to remake and reconfigure our desires accordingly. If God has made us as male and female, then that is the relationship we need in order to enjoy a true Sabbath rest. We will be restless until then. Thus the Augustinian line says that ontology reveals our true desires; Rogers says our desires reveal our true ontology.

Why does Rogers invest such authority in desire? His evangelical concern for marriage to teach us that we are loved, and his ascetical concern, that we transfigure our desires in ways that witness to the Trinity, are always evident in his writing. "The grace of justification . . . is a transformation that occurs by being seen a certain way, as wanted, as desired, a grace in which God can cause marriage to participate."[87] To leave someone out of marriage is to leave someone out of a chance to learn that they are desired. It is also to leave that person out of a chance for the sanctification marriage enables. Thus to deny someone marriage is cruel and anti-Christian. "Sexuality, like grace, involves the transformation that comes from seeing oneself as desired by another. . . . For some the desire of God is modelled and mediated through another human being; for others it seems to come directly."[88] Desire is a way of rupturing our self-sufficiency, of making us dependent on closeness with another for respite:

[Christians] experience sharp pangs of attraction to the bodies of others, whether or not that special, desirous appreciation of the beauty God created in their bodies is for anyone's obvious good. It is a way, a particular embodied way, and hopefully a pleasant, promising way, in which human beings cannot escape from the neighbour, and from the neighbour's claim. The bodies of the desired do not leave even the most devoted misanthrope alone.[89]

Rogers hopes that that desire is then brought into a commitment of mutual kenosis and that the desire is transfigured to signify "the love God has for human beings . . . for covenant, holiness, life with God."[90] Of course this transfiguration cannot be taken for granted—it "is compromised, outside of Eden, by the fickleness of sin and the inevitability of death, and it is close enough to justification to offer it falsely, as an alternative to God, and end in idolatry"[91]—but Rogers claims that such transfiguration is God's intention when he gives us such desires. In desire, we learn what we would not otherwise know: such and such a person, in his or her bodily particularity, has a claim upon us, and we are called to transfigure that claim in Trinitarian ways through the commitments of marriage. In that marriage, we learn what it is like to be desired in response, and in that mutuality, we learn to love and be loved in God's image. "Marriage is a sacrament of binding together that proclaims and begins to bring about the truth that a couple belongs primarily to God and the community rather than to themselves alone."[92]

But this claim begs some key questions: Do we need marriage to learn that we are loved, and what effects does demanding this pedagogy from marriage have on marriage's logical connections with the doctrine of creation? Should Christian communities rely on marriage for so much evangelical duty, and is it really an essential arena of sanctification? And can Christian theology sustain the claim that sexual difference is only significant insofar as certain sexual preferences appear to teach us that we are loved?

Rogers says that "for gay and lesbian people, the right sort of otherness is unlikely to be represented by someone of the opposite sex, because only someone of the apposite, not opposite, sex will get deep enough into the relationship. . . . The crucial question is, what sort of created diversity will lead one to holiness?"[93] But an equally crucial question is, How is appositeness revealed—through self-interpreted feelings, or through creation understood in theological perspective? Is appositeness contingent on our feelings, or does it come to us from outside, interrogating and reshaping our feelings? If we find that the same-sex is "apposite" for learning certain lessons about ourselves, how do we know that such a lesson is not analogous to learning about honor among thieves? To learn honor among thieves is to be trained in a certain desirable virtue, certainly, but equally, it is not full and sufficient Christian testimony to the community for which God has made us. To learn that we are loved and lovable in a homosexual relationship, to learn to keep promises and be faithful, is to learn something important, but it is not to learn the fullness of how and why we were created male and female. Such lessons leave an essential feature of human identity inadequately rendered, unintegrated into God's work.

Rogers quotes Rowan Williams approvingly: "The life of the Christian community has as its rationale—if not invariably its practical reality—the task of teaching us to so order our relations that human beings may see themselves as desires, as the occasions of joy."[94] He then adds his own gloss: "Marriage is peculiarly suited to teaching God's desire for human beings, because it mirrors God's choosing of human beings for God's own."[95] But the implication is that when God desires us and sees us as "occasions of joy," as Rogers would have us learn these things, God does not see us as being what the Christian tradition has said that we are. We are not seen as male or female, and thus male and female in relation; we are seen as beings in time and space with certain bodily features, tabs and slots, related to other beings in time and space whose contingent features appeal to our desires. That these features would be male or female is indifferent to Rogers's economy in principle, for they can only happen to matter to certain individuals. Every possible significance Rogers has proposed for sexual difference has been dismissed in order to enable this perspective. But if Christian marriage does not see us as male and female, what has happened to the relationship between marriage and creation? Is the claim that God did not make us male and female, or is Rogers claiming that God no longer regards what he made as significant for our covenants with other humans and with him? With Rogers, we are back among the disputed questions of chapter 1.

Rogers opts for the latter, that God no longer regards what he made as significant for the covenant. There is a "baptismal change"[96] in Christianity that makes created distinctions irrelevant:

> Galatians 3:28 not only describes the community's eschatological polity, but it issues a warning about how to conduct community relations. Its monitory force is this: do not let social or natural distinctions so turn into moral ones that you fail to see the Holy Spirit at work.[97]

In other words, do not let sexual difference have moral significance. Rogers believes that this admonition for insignificance has theological warrant. He reasons that Paul would have regarded "Gentiles, slaves, and women as all suffering from the constitutional inability to observe Torah," but that, over against this natural inability, God has nevertheless included them in the covenant.[98] This is similarly so with same-sex unions. God overcomes nature, rendering natural creaturely distinctions insignificant:

> As God grafts Gentiles, the wild branches, onto the domestic covenant of God's household with Israel, structured by the Torah of the Spirit, so God grafts gay and lesbian couples . . . by a new movement of the Spirit onto the domestic, married covenants of straight women and men.[99]

However, the presumptions necessary to make this analogy work are unacceptable for the Christian theology of creation. When God grafts the Gentiles onto the olive branch, the teleology of creation for the covenant is fulfilled: a new relation between God and his creatures is apparent, but it is one we now see was implicit from the beginning. No parts of creation are abandoned; more is embraced. But were the Spirit to do what Rogers is proposing, when same-sex marriages are grafted onto the symbolism of marriage, the teleology of creation for the covenant is displaced. The created forms of male and female, instead of being fulfilled and enlarged, are rendered incidental. Instead of being an essential theater for human relations, they become volitional.

Reading Galatians 3:28 in this way, of course, is directly against the readings of Augustine, Aquinas, Luther, and Barth.[100] All of them shared Barth's sense for the Sabbath, that when God relates to his creatures he does so on the basis of the sufficiency of certain specified and distinguishing characteristics that individuate and particularize us. Creaturely distinctions retain their moral significance; God simply embraces creatures in their multiple differences as Jew and Gentile, male and female, but he does not make these differences invisible or irrelevant. God's acceptance does not carry the price of homogenizing our diversity. In fact, God's embrace of these differences appears to highlight them as significant, as revealing that these are the differences that shape who we are in meaningful ways.

By contrast, Rogers is proposing that God's inclusiveness renders these creaturely forms insignificant. God does not vindicate and fulfill the ontology of Eden, showing and commanding creatures how to live within it; he supersedes it by suddenly revealing that the significance of its forms was an illusion.[101] The ontology of creation does not have its own integrity on which we can rely and through which God might work to unfold implicit significance; the ontology of creation is revisable. For Rogers, sexual desire can refuse what we might have thought was God's gift in creation. Marriage is no longer a response to an ontology given with male and female; marriage is a response to desire. What the Christian tradition thought was a created order with a teleology is now material with no prior determination; it can be accepted or discarded according to its capacity to inspire certain precious feelings.

In the essay by Rowan Williams to which Rogers so frequently returns, Williams says that the key question for sexual morality is "How much do we want our sexual activity to communicate?"[102] Rogers's answer is theologically informed in many respects. But among the messages communicated by Rogers's version of marriage is the meaninglessness or contingency of sexual difference. In that sense, Rogers's proposals for marriage are not ambitious enough. What Augustine called the seedbed of the heavenly city, what Bernard used as allegorical material, what Luther identified as the form of humanity in which we enter the church, and what Barth and John Paul II called the center of human encounter has all been undercut by making sexual difference a matter of preference—if it's important for you, it's important, but only then.

However, in another sense, Rogers's proposals for marriage are too ambitious. In the pursuit of love and covenant, former creaturely distinctions are drained of their ontological significance and rendered invisible or optional. In the quest to feel loved, the promise of creation, the promise that was sealed on the Sabbath, can be broken. The whole nature of the moral undertaking changes: the promise that patience with creation might yield something worthy of thanksgiving and praise, and that one can rest assured that God will meet us in and through what he has made—this patience may now be seen as a mistake or waste of time. What John

Paul II called "progressive education in self-control of the will, feelings and emotions" may have just been ignorance about one's true destiny in a covenant that overwrites creation.[103] What one thought was a command was instead a delusion; one had thought one was called to respond to the fact of sexual difference, but now one had better discern one's true and essential desires and thus follow wherever that leads, through the other sex or not.

Rogers leaves us with a pastoral problem, but perhaps that is because he was responding to a pastoral problem all along: "The question for both sides then is this: by what sort of sacramental practices can the Church best teach gay and lesbian Christians to see themselves as occasions of joy, that God desires them as if they were God?"[104] This question is profound, but to take it seriously does not imply Rogers's account of marriage as the solution. Perhaps a better theology of baptism, rather than a theology of marriage, is the solution to Rogers's problem. We have seen a variety of theologies of marriage in this book, but none of them has had this pedagogy as its presupposition. Certainly any traditional theologian would argue that Christian discipleship, in whatever form, is ultimately productive of joy, but Rogers appears to want joy at a much more intermediate stage. Perhaps this impatience for joy is the crux of the problem. Rogers asks, "Which liturgical form will better allow Christians to offer their whole selves, their souls and bodies, as communicative signs?"[105] But does a liturgical form that witnesses to the indifference of what God has given in creation communicate the right thing? If sexual difference is present only contingently, if it does not count as being part of the whole self, then our liturgical forms cannot make the intended testimony. We may be in agony with frustration as we wait for an answer, but our impatience for the eschaton is a different matter.

## Sexual Difference Is Insignificant for the Social Function of Marriage

Like Rogers, David Matzko McCarthy asks how the bodies of gays and lesbians can be a sign, or how can they be "given over to be a sacrament of God's creative activity and reconciliation."[106] His answer is to emphasize the social context of marriage more than Rogers. In a sense, he elaborates one dimension of Rogers's case that marriage ought to be analyzed as more than a dyad, with attention to how the couple operate in and are affected by wider social systems. McCarthy sometimes writes specifically about same-sex encounters and sometimes about marriage in general, but the same basic theory of marriage operates in each instance. In this theory, marriage is a Christian countercultural practice, in which the bodies of Christians are brought into social and ecclesial relations not only with each other but with multiple third parties. This project intends to rebel against the construction of desire in contemporary capitalism and construct an alternative Christian environment, and, for this purpose, McCarthy believes sexual difference is relatively insignificant.

McCarthy offers his theory of marriage as an alternative to several anti-Christian aspects of contemporary American culture. Presumably his critique and response is also applicable to Western culture more generally. In this culture, McCarthy believes that sexual desires and domestic patterns are formed in an essentially antisocial habitat.[107] He argues that romantic ideals cultivate the perpetual hope of escape from domestic life, that market economies are structured so that permanently unfulfilled and roaming desire is a normal emotional state, and that liberal political philosophy encourages the privatization of family and kinship, with the consequent diminution of these commitments in public esteem.[108]

According to McCarthy, the cumulative effect is to make it normal to try and structure our "quest for love" in detachment from a practical embrace of our actual circumstances. The dominant culture believes that "sex is a vital source of love, and love is the foundation of a good partnership and a happy home. Yet, ironically, practical matters of home militate against lovemaking."[109] Family home life as it is actually lived is about changing the baby's diapers, fixing the leaky sink, making sure the kids get to soccer practice, dealing with the neighbors, and so forth, all of which indeed mitigates against being a passionate couple à deux. McCarthy's diagnosis is this: "The modern problem of love . . . is a question of its location."[110] The culture teaches that love exists in an isolated context of two, in a dream honeymoon-like encounter, rather than in the place where we live most of the time, which is in the melee of complex and overlapping wider household responsibilities and encounters.

For this reason, McCarthy claims, modern love is often disappointed and modern family life is commonly experienced with bitterness. The reason for our dysfunction is because our culture's capitalist romanticism "takes the joy out of the regular course of things. We must always be looking beyond for moments of self-discovery, liminal experiences, and total abandon."[111] We are not trained to live and love in the context in which we actually dwell, and so we cannot help but be dissatisfied.

Christians can rebel and construct alternative habitats for desire, according to McCarthy, through what he calls the "open" household or home, a place where husband and wife are not the foundation but merely important roles in the middle "of a larger network of preferential loves."[112] Children, neighbors, and fellow church members all feature prominently in McCarthy's descriptions of openness, and they cultivate expectations for marriage that require but relativize the couple at the center. To aspire toward openness means embracing complicated webs of interdependence and presence, where we are mixed together with people who are not like us and who we would not necessarily choose as friends, and where we are held together "by practical ends and intrinsic goods that transcend interpersonal abilities."[113]

The Christian alternative is an attempt to "depose dominant but inferior systems of formation" and to "renarrate the home," in order that love and sexuality can dwell in this more richly social space.[114] In this space, love is about cultivating the sustained habits of dwelling together. A Christian "open" home teaches us the skills of embracing, not escaping, our regular habitat. Sexuality belongs in these wider networks of "social reproduction," where our desires are met by fulfilling our practical roles and "belonging" to our place in the social network. The presumption is that "the household economy actually 're-socializes' and transforms" sexual desire, such that "sheer (adolescent) passion" has no place.[115]

Much of this argument is astute, but the point for our examination of sexual difference is that the practices of marriage have been defined, as with Rogers, in ways that give no account of sexual difference as known in the classic accounts of creation. "Social reproduction" means that the significance of bodies is derivative from their public function. To show what he means, McCarthy proposes a hypothetical lesbian couple with an adopted daughter. According to him, the couple demonstrate that sexual difference is not significant for the important social functions of marriage.

As McCarthy tells it, the hypothetical lesbian couple are appalled by the casual sexuality of popular culture, and they parent in ways to moderate their daughter's exposure to it; they consider their own mutual covenant permanent, and they are faithful to it; and they "delight in their daughter's obvious flirtation with boys," that is, they are not ideological about their own same-sex "orientation." They help with their daughter's schooling, athletics, and music lessons; they serve on committees and share various chores with their neighbors. On Sundays they go to Mass together: "They share Christ's peace with those around them, say the Sanctus, announce that Christ has died, risen, and will come again, and they move forward with the rest of the people toward the altar to break bread." Later on the Sabbath, after a meal, rest, light chores and a bit of play, "the child goes to her room to bed, and the two women go to their room, lay in the same bed, read, talk, embrace, kiss, caress, grow weary, and fall to sleep."[116] The next morning the cycle repeats. McCarthy concedes that this union "obviously lacks elements like male-female complementarity and natural procreative possibilities, but its steadfast fidelity, its nurturing of children, and its contributions to the family-sustaining practices of the community set it within the public network of marriage." This particular same-sex union is an example of an anomaly within predominantly heterosexual communities, but it cannot be excluded from marriage, for it fulfills all the significant public functions.[117] This lesbian couple have given their bodies over to the community and to each other, and they have become signs of covenant, commitment, and hospitality. They are contributing to the Christian social ecology that resists the individualism and displacement of capitalism.

McCarthy briefly considers counterarguments that might undermine the conclusions he draws from this hypothetical. He looks to three recent Catholic documents—a 1986 Vatican letter on pastoral care of homosexuals, and two books by Catholic ethicists from the 1970s and 1980s—that contend for the significance of sexual difference in marriage.[118]

McCarthy does not consider the arguments of the Vatican letter in detail, preferring to simply note that it makes "male-female complementarity, rather than procreation" a "delineation between heterosexual and homosexual acts." He then claims this delineation "at least in its current use, is an innovation in understanding the conjugal union." He says that in *Gaudium et Spes* the companionship between the sexes is "the primary form of interpersonal communion" and an essential relationship for human beings to be what they are, but he also claims that this point is not developed in detail with relation to marriage. The reason, he speculates, is that in these official documents, "The inseparable bond between the marriage union and procreation makes a development of male-female complementarity unnecessary."[119] In other words, because male-female can be presupposed in any account of marriage premised on procreation, other aspects of complementarity have not been developed in detail. Therefore what McCarthy says is the key question—"whether or not a notion of complementarity has a definitive function"—is left hanging by these documents.[120]

In search of this "definitive function" for complementarity—that is, in search of a good argument on behalf of the significance of sexual difference—McCarthy looks to the two Catholic ethicists from the 1970s and 1980s, Philip Keane and James Hanigan, whom he implies are representative of the case for "male-female complementarity" and who represent "the strongest arguments available against the permissibility of gay and lesbian unions."[121]

McCarthy summarizes Keane and Hanigan to the effect that their appeals to the differences between men and women, which do not make recourse to arguments about procreation, are made for the sake of "highlighting the unitive end [of marriage] as autonomous, that is, as a good end in itself."[122] In other words, McCarthy is working with sources that presuppose marriage is constituted by distinct procreative and unitive goods. For the sake of arguing that these two goods are just as important as one another and do not have to be held in relation to one another in each and every marital act—that is, that marital coitus can be legitimately sought for unitive rather than procreative reasons—McCarthy believes these ethicists have pursued new claims about male-female complementarity that did not exist in previous tradition. He concludes that the need for winning arguments in a debate about the interpersonal goods in a couple's internal relations, rather than procreation, has led to the discussion of male-female complementarity.[123]

Examining these arguments for the interpersonal aspects of marriage, which are purposefully made in isolation from the requirement of procreation, McCarthy perceives that the case for unitive goods actually renders "male-female complementarity . . . otiose."[124] As with Rogers, McCarthy says that Thomas Aquinas considers "the social benefit of a relationship between a man and a woman" to be procreation. He continues that having put this aspect of sexual difference aside, his sources do not provide alternative content for whatever male-female complementarity is. Furthermore, when McCarthy reads their actual act-analysis, he sees that the criteria for unitive goods make no appeal to sexually specific features. Instead the criteria are generic, such as, Is the act "consensual? Faithful? In the context of covenant?" Thus, although claims for complementarity accentuate "the physical character of heterosexual intercourse," McCarthy dismisses them because they do not appeal to any actual definitive social function for sexual difference.[125] One can certainly see in these sexually generic criteria—consensual, faithful, and so forth—that despite what advocates of complementarity might claim, the moral intelligibility of the sexual act is not contingent on sexual difference but on the "wider context of marriage" in which gay and lesbian relationships can function just as well.[126]

McCarthy's interpretations of modern secondary sources clearly do not go deep into Christian traditions of sexual difference. His shallowness does not mean, however, that he is wrong to observe that consensus on procreation may serve, in certain ecclesial contexts, as a disincentive for further reflection on complementarity. Theologians today may well be quarreling about contemporary perspectives on procreation, making them myopic as regards the wider tradition. As with Rogers, a certain reading of Aquinas—that sexual difference exists for procreation in a nontheologically interesting sense—can be taken superficially, and the possibility of wider significance is not pursued.

However, McCarthy also brings another point to the fore: the question of functionalism and the role of sexual difference in the social life of the heavenly city. If he had gone deeper into the tradition, what would he have found? McCarthy proposes his hypothetical lesbian couple in order to help his readers imagine a sexually indifferent couple who appear to fit in well with a faithful social community. Everything appears exemplary in the form of its worship, work, and hospitality. Who could not rejoice at a Christendom that actually looked like that, even if it was indifferent about sexual difference? At stake is whether and how a sexually differentiated theological anthropology matters for life in the city of God.

In the tradition, one can find such hypotheticals in actuality. In chapter 1 we looked at Tatian, who believed that the body is like a temple in which God can dwell but who did not feel led by that premise into any conclusions about sexual difference. Instead, eager to repudiate degenerate pagan sexuality, Tatian proposed a Christian polity based on practices to encourage freedom from degenerate passions. McCarthy's proposals share much formal similarity with this program. McCarthy does not propose compulsory celibacy, as Tatian did, but he does try to avert our attention from actual bodies and the significance of particular couplings, and to refocus on the distinctive social life of a countercultural community. The goodness of same-sex unions in McCarthy's case arises not out of an argument for the theological necessity of their erotic encounters, as it did with Rogers, but because same-sex encounters as he has described them are compatible with a Christian social ecology as he has described that. Same-sex couples appear to fit within a wider community of charity, which is his ultimate vision. As with Tatian compiling his *Diatessaron*, redacting Scripture to disassociate Jesus with biological generation, McCarthy seems to imply that Christian life had better not direct its attention to what he implies is minutiae. McCarthy does not invite us to think about what it means and why it is significant that his lesbian couple want to go to bed and cuddle with one another at the end of the Sabbath; he does not follow Augustine and grapple with sexual desire as a psychologically profound force, with the potency to postpone an individual's response to God as well as threaten domestic harmony. Everything is presumed quiet and in order as the lesbians head to bed, and the more important point is their daytime social openness and hospitality. Tatian's followers, the Encratites, lived in villages of group celibacy in Syria and

Asia Minor, and these villages were known for their charity to foundlings. These villages were evidently "not settlements of wild ascetics, but pools of quiet confidence that the Spirit rested on those who had regained, through baptism and continence, the full humanity of Adam and Eve."[127] One imagines that McCarthy's proposed "open households" are similar places, places of quiet confidence and hospitality, where certain questions about sexuality and theological anthropology are simply not engaged. As long as the foundling is welcomed, we need not worry what happens in the hosts' bedroom.

Is such indifference acceptable? No, for many reasons. The road from Tatian to Augustine will simply be recapitulated; Tatian's anthropology left too many questions open, and questions that are ignored will surface again if they are important. The anthropological questions that troubled Augustine are not idiosyncratic but fundamental. For instance, is the human body theologically significant in its sexual features? If it is not, are we the creation of a good God? If it is, how will these features participate in our redemption? What is the relationship between our bodies, our desires, and our true selves? One can be impressed by McCarthy's vision of countercultural Christian hospitality and still think his implicit anthropology is theologically truncated. Appeals to social ecology are helpful for widening the context in which sexual matters are discussed, but they are insufficient for answering many relevant and crucial questions.

McCarthy rejected sexual difference as essential for marriage—he rejected "complementarity"—because his sources could not provide a "definitive function" for it. He looked narrowly at two functions of marriage—procreation and unitive—and decided the former was not necessary for marriage to be marriage and that the latter did not require sexual difference. Sexual difference is rendered insignificant because it is apparently not useful. But here is an anthropology that asks the wrong questions, in which people and institutions are reckoned significant according to their usefulness. It is hard to imagine this premise as a sustainable foundation for hospitality. In McCarthy's perspective, what appears to matter about the body is not what it is, or what God has promised it might become, but that it contribute to a particular version of social life. One's role in life is to serve others and be sanctified by putting up with them when they are awkward. There can be no motive, then, for patiently working within the limitations of a sexually differentiated system of marriage and celibacy to discern one's vocation; such persistence would be a waste of time, accepting a constraint with no purpose. If one finds oneself vexed by sexual desires, the solution is to find a way to integrate them into the social system. Possibly in certain pastoral situations this strategy may be the best and most prudent option available. Presumably one integrates in this way by promise making and promise keeping, by accepting a role and not betraying it. But as a theology of marriage in general, it does not witness to an ontology; this marriage cannot be a gift of God, with boundaries and limitations not of our choosing, a connection to something cosmic and larger than ourselves. Marriage is what we choose and construct, and this marriage fits in well with the world of contracts, which, given that McCarthy's point was to escape the logic of the marketplace, should be a warning sign that marriage is perhaps more than he is offering.

What McCarthy has omitted is the meaningfulness of sexual difference in the salvation history from creation to eschaton. Had he considered it, it would have been open to him to take a broader view of marriage. Augustine, Luther, Barth, and John Paul II are examples of looking first to creation, asking what human beings are as God has made them, and, among other things, learning that there are two sexes. Two sexes become the material precondition that enables marriage. The possibility of marriage or celibacy serves the goodness of the two sexes, revealing possibilities for our social life we would not otherwise know that we have and recognizing that our biological selves are included in the project of redemption. McCarthy reverses this perspective. Having made the case for what he believes reconciled and redemptive community life looks like, he then goes in search of building blocks for that end; having defined the community's teleology as simply to be hospitable, he has no specific account of *to what* and *to whom* we are being hospitable. He has no account of the creature for whom the covenant is prepared.

It seems an awkward silence. About sexual difference—a feature of human biology that has organized cultures from time immemorial, a basic feature of animal biology, a feature McCarthy's own Christian tradition has believed to be ethically significant—he has nothing to say. As with Tatian, McCarthy's theory of marriage would include a faith in which we had no particular hope or testimony for the sexual and bodily aspect of humanity. As with Tatian, one does not need to call him gnostic, or dispute the capacity of his community to be charitable and exemplary in its kindness to the weak or lonely. But in this book, we have encountered arguments that are more ambitious than that. This book has argued that human beings are ontologically (and not merely in appearance) male and female, and so their deepest fulfillment will come through forms of life that welcome this difference and are structured upon it. But McCarthy's account cannot say as much. Perhaps, like Rogers, he is led by pastoral concerns and so is simply unwilling to say to his lesbian couple that their way of life is not ordered to their deepest fulfillment.

If so, why? What shortcomings in the church make a life in which sexual difference has significance seem implausible and lead McCarthy to think one had better not recommend such a course? What has led Christians to believe that the forms of creation are not actually adequate for Sabbath rest? The failure of the visible church to be sufficiently countercultural, such that a social life of lay celibacy is conceivable, is a likely reason. We cannot imagine existing in our culture without the haven of an erotic partnership, because our capacity to belong together in more chaste ways is so limited. In this light, it seems cruel and laughable to suggest that someone would be more fulfilled opting out of the quest for romance and cultivating chastity. A mixed community of virgins as well as married men and women simply does not feature in our imaginations. We cannot see its point. But our own myopia is not an argument for the insignificance of sexual difference. It is not a reason to stop saying that God made us as male and female and that living in ways which testify to that is what shall ultimately make us free.

## Notes

1. Jaroslav Pelikan, *Christian Doctrine and Modern Culture (since 1700)* (Chicago: University of Chicago Press, 1989), viii.

2. Graham Ward, "The Erotics of Redemption—after Karl Barth," *Theology and Sexuality* 8 (1998): 63, 54, 52, 55.

3. Ibid., 62.

4. Ibid., 52, 56.

5. Ibid., 52.

6. Ibid., 55.

7. Ibid.

8. Ibid.

9. Ibid., 57–58.

10. Ibid., 58.

11. Ibid., 59.

12. Ibid., 67.

13. Ibid.

14. Ibid., 60, 61.

15. Ibid., 59, citing Barth at *CD* III/4, 223.

16. Ibid., 68.

17. Ibid., 66, 67, 68.

18. Ibid., 61, referring to *CD* III/2, 245.

19. Ibid., 61–62.

20. Ibid., 62.

21. Ibid.

22. Ibid., 69.

23. Ibid.

24. Ibid.

25. Ibid., 65.

26. Ibid., 70.

27. Ibid.

28. Ibid.

29. Ibid., 71, quoting Irigaray, *Ethics of Sexual Difference*, 15.

30. Ward, "Erotics of Redemption," 71.

31. Ibid., 65.

32. Ibid.

33. Ibid.

34. Ibid., 63.

35. Ibid., 71.

36. See pp. 147–48, and p. 205, for discussion of Barth on the Sabbath.

37. See p. 167n26, and pp. 157–61.

38. Ward, "Erotics of Redemption," 70.

39. Eugene Rogers, "Sanctified Unions: An Argument for Gay Marriage," *Christian Century* 121, no. 12 (2004): 29.

40. Eugene Rogers, *Sexuality and the Christian Body: Their Way into the Triune God* (Oxford: Blackwell, 1999), 159.

41. Ibid., 185.

42. Ibid., 225.

43. Ibid., 168, 189.

44. Ibid., 184.

45. Ibid., 195–96.

46. Ibid., 202–3.

47. Ibid., 196.

48. Ibid., 214.

49. Barth, *CD* III/4, 224–25.

50. *CD* III/4, 225.

51. *CD* III/4, 148.

52. Rowan Williams, "The Body's Grace," in *Theology and Sexuality: Classic and Contemporary Readings* (ed. Eugene Rogers; Oxford: Blackwell, 2002), 320.

53. I have discussed Barth's claim that children are optional in marriage, p. 207.

54. Rogers, *Sexuality and the Christian Body*, 129.

55. See p. 104 and 107.

56. Rogers, *Sexuality and the Christian Body*, 205.

57. See pp. 106–8.

58. See pp. 147–48.

59. See p. 75n104.

60. Without discussion or analysis, Rogers briefly and vaguely acknowledges that Augustine mentions that "in the present time" it is better "not to seek after offspring in the flesh." *De bono conjugali*, §24, quoted in Rogers, *Sexuality and the Christian Body*, 74n18.

61. Rogers, *Sexuality and the Christian Body*, 206.

62. Ibid., 205–6.

63. Ibid., 206, 261, 262.

64. Ibid., 261.

65. Barth, *CD* III/4, 267.

66. Rogers, *Sexuality and the Christian Body*, 206.

67. Ibid., 207.

68. Ibid., 81.

69. Ibid., 75.

70. Ibid., 187, 189.

71. Ibid., 226.

72. Ibid., 83.

73. Ibid., 225.

74. Barth, *CD* III/1, 318, quoted by Rogers in ibid., 27, and in many other places in his book. See also p. 168n85. Rogers appears to be using a slightly different translation, although he cites the same one I have used.

75. Rogers, *Sexuality and the Christian Body*, 235.

76. Ibid., 226.

77. Ibid., 197.

78. Ibid., 200.

79. Ibid., 201.

80. Ibid., 242.

81. Ibid., 242.

82. Ibid., 245–46.

83. Ibid., 238.

84. Eugene Rogers, "The Liturgical Body," *Modern Theology* 16, no. 3 (2000): 371.

85. See p. 135n22.

86. See p. 73n36.

87. Rogers, *Sexuality and the Christian Body*, 236.

88. Eugene Rogers, "Editorial Introduction to 'The Body's Grace' by Rowan Williams," in *Theology and Sexuality: Classic and Contemporary Readings* (ed. Eugene Rogers; Oxford: Blackwell, 2002), 309.

89. Rogers, *Sexuality and the Christian Body*, 227.

90. Ibid., 232.

91. Ibid., 234.

92. Ibid., 34.

93. Rogers, "Sanctified Unions," 28.

94. Rogers, *Sexuality and the Christian Body*, 27.

95. Ibid.

96. Ibid., 66.

97. Ibid.

98. Ibid.

99. Ibid., 65.

100. See pp. 44–45, 103, 121–22, and 148.

101. See Oliver O'Donovan, *Resurrection and Moral Order: An Outline for Evangelical Ethics* (2nd ed.; Leicester, England: Apollos, 1994), 70, for a discussion of creation, historicism, and marriage.

102. Williams, "Body's Grace," 313.

103. See p. 183n28.

104. Rogers, *Sexuality and the Christian Body*, 27.

105. Rogers, "Liturgical Body," 372.

106. David Matzko McCarthy, "The Relationship of Bodies: A Nuptial Hermeneutics of Same-Sex Unions," in *Theology and Sexuality: Classic and Contemporary Readings* (ed. Eugene Rogers; Oxford: Blackwell, 2002), 200–16.

107. This paragraph and the next are adapted from Christopher C. Roberts, "Sex and Love in the Home (Book Review)," *Studies in Christian Ethics* 15, no. 2 (2002), 102–7.

108. See chs. 2, 4, and 5 of David Matzko McCarthy, *Sex and Love in the Home: A Theology of the Household* (London: SCM Press, 2001).

109. Ibid., 20.

110. Ibid., 25.

111. Ibid., 64.

112. Ibid., 216.

113. Ibid., 7.

114. Ibid., 6, 217.

115. Ibid., 209.

116. David McCarthy Matzko, "Homosexuality and the Practices of Marriage," *Modern Theology* 13, no. 3 (1997): 378, 373.

117. Ibid., 379, 372.

118. Ibid., 380–85.

119. Ibid., 382.

120. Ibid.

121. Ibid., 380.

122. Ibid., 383.
123. Ibid.
124. Ibid., 384.
125. Ibid.
126. Ibid., 384–85.
127. Brown, *Body and Society*, 101.

# CONCLUSION

The first chapter of this book showed that early patristic writers did not necessarily have fully formed opinions about sexual difference, and what beliefs they held were often revealed only in asides or short arguments in the service of other themes. Collectively, the variety of their beliefs indicates an overall inchoateness about the significance of sexual difference in early Christianity. The significance of sexual difference varied from one theologian to another, or even within the theology of a single theologian. It was not clear what, if anything, Christian theology ought to say about sexual difference. Sometimes these theologians thought sexual difference was significant, but as a problem to overcome, or a condition of humanity Christians should lament. There were also accounts in which sexual difference had positive significance in God's creation and designs for humanity, although here again, these accounts were often implicit rather than argued directly.

However, this overall inchoateness was eventually succeeded by a more cohesive position. In chapter 2 we saw the foundation of what became a consensus. Augustine argued that God's creation is good and purposeful, and that sexual difference has a theologically significant role in this creation. He concluded, largely on the basis of scriptural exegesis, that sexual difference was created by God. He reasoned that this feature of human embodiment is for the purpose of procreating and enabling a social life (the heavenly city) ordered to the love and worship of God.

Augustine developed a salvation history in which it was axiomatic that God does not repudiate what he has made and called good, even on account of the fall, in light of the achievement of redemption in Christ, or in the eschaton. It follows, then, that on these terms, sexual difference, as a significant feature of God's creation, has some presence or significance with respect to each of these moments in salvation history. Precisely how and why sexual difference matters at these different moments may change, but the point Augustine argued (or, at other moments, implicitly presupposed) is that sexual difference should feature in some way in any comprehensive theological anthropology. What was significant in creation will always be significant in a schema based on the mature views of Augustine; the only question can be how that significance will be adapted in light of God's purposes for humanity in any subsequent theological era.

For example, Augustine insisted that even celibates in the present time could not ignore what God had called good in creation. Their choice for virginity could not be a flight from sex and its teleology but is better construed as a foreshadowing of an eschatological future when men and women are still men and women, yet their life together is no longer premised on marriage and procreation. Augustine did not explore the details of how this eschatological social life integrated maleness and femaleness, but nevertheless, he did claim that sexual difference would exist purposefully in the heavenly city, adapted for some new and appropriate use.

Meanwhile, Augustine also believed that married couples testify to the goodness of the creation of the two sexes by embracing the discipline of marriage and refusing to let unbridled concupiscence be the last word in the way male and female relate to one another. Augustine believed that marriage aims to regard sexual difference as significant not in the way concupiscence would have it—as an occasion for stimulating disobedient sexual desire—but as God would have it, that is, as the material precondition for building the heavenly city.

The most important theologians in Augustine's wake continued to believe similar things about the significance of sexual difference. In chapter 3 we saw how Bernard of Clairvaux affirmed or presupposed all the major arguments of Augustine, and, at least partially on that basis, used marital imagery for allegories of God's love. When he wanted to testify to the relationship between Creator and creature, a relationship of ontological distinction, attraction, and hierarchy, he turned to sexually differentiated marital imagery. Bernard believed that this imagery was appropriate because he also believed that the relationship between the sexes is also one of ontological distinction and hierarchy, and these characteristics can honorably be brought into a relationship of covenant and erotic attraction through marriage. The ways in which God allures and loves his people can be appropriately described with marital imagery, because this imagery is consonant with how the Creator intended men and women to allure and love among themselves.

In succeeding centuries, Aquinas, Luther, and Calvin did not develop Bernard's position, but, as they made their own arguments, they assimilated and modified Augustine's beliefs about sexual difference in several ways.

In chapter 4 we saw that Aquinas did not maintain a theological perspective on sexual difference to the same extent as Augustine, most notably with respect to procreation. To the extent that he perceived sexual difference to be significant for the procreation and perpetuity of species, he had less of a reason for considering the theological significance of sexual difference for celibates.

In chapter 5 we saw how Luther explicitly and directly put the significance of sexual difference on a foundation much more anthropologically basic than procreation. We then saw how Calvin argued and believed things that were consistent with and supportive of Luther's case.

Focusing on Luther, we explored his belief that sexual difference was significant for all men and women. He argued that by creating us with this type of embodiment, God has created a condition to which everyone must respond. In other words, Luther conceptualized sexual difference as an occasion for human response to God, as a situation in which we are called to act with gratitude and obedience. In creation, God has placed us in a sexually differentiated circumstance. A relationship with God through the church is the overall context in which the life of a grateful and obedient creature takes its shape, and responding to God as a sexed creature is also part of the proper human response to God. For Luther, part of the necessary task incumbent on all humans is to consider this physical, somatic aspect of ourselves and to see it in theological perspective. Ordinarily, Luther expected that this perspective would lead to marriage, but not always, as the case of Noah's temporary virginity allowed. The more important theme for Luther was that God has made us as men and women, and it is as men and women that we are called to respond to God.

This point was brought to the fore by Barth, and later by John Paul II as well, as we saw in chapters 6 and 7. Most notably, both of these theologians devoted substantial exegetical attention to Genesis, reading it christologically to argue that the sexual aspect of humanity is a material presupposition and theater for Christian living. The sexual dimorphism of humans is shared with other animals, but humans are also addressed by God and invited to a certain type of freedom on the basis of their animal materiality. Both theologians believed that through Christ, humanity is freed from any cultural or biological compulsion to procreate and instead freed for ways of life that are demonstrably "for others." Both theologians argued that sexual difference is significant as the initial arena for manifesting this "for others," which is the *imago Dei*, or the christological determination of humanity as a creature meant to exist by speaking a "nuptial language" between male and female.

This argument entails moral significance for sexual difference above and beyond procreation. For instance, as with Augustine, continence should not be a choice against the created goodness of sexual difference. Continence and marriage together are, in principle, mutually reinforcing practices that engender a community of men and women. In this community, the men and women premise their social relations on being men and women, that is, they do not organize themselves as if they preferred an androgynous humanity. Yet in this sexually differentiated community, sexual desire and lust are restrained and not permitted to dominate interpersonal relations. Barth and John Paul II point to prelapsarian Eden and the Song of Songs as moments when we can see an integrated, joyful, and uncomplicated harmony between the human body, the interior self, sexual desire, and God. In these moments, sexual difference is visible as it was meant to be prior to the fall, and as it can still be sought through the witness of Christians today.

Thus there is an ancient Christian tradition, from Augustine to John Paul II, which has believed and argued that sexual difference is significant. With varying degrees of explicitness, the greatest theologians in the Christian West have been relatively cohesive on the point that sexual difference, which enables biological procreation and which humans share with animals, has more than physical and animal significance.

To synthesize, based on the material we have examined in this book, I propose the following theological significance for sexual difference: The same God whom we know in Christ has, in his goodness, created us as male and female. To be male or female, then, is to be blessed, for it is to be something that is good. To be this sexually differentiated creature is to be something that will be redeemed, and redeemed as it was made and not as some other creature; in other words, sexual difference itself will be present in our redemption. For that reason, sexual difference is not something human beings should attempt to ignore or deplore. Sexual difference is something humans should embrace and welcome, for to do that is to honor creation and anticipate redemption. Such a way of life, to which Christ calls all human beings, means to love the neighbor and enable the neighbor to be what he or she is meant to be in the sexual sphere.

To restate the point, that we are created as male and female is not incidental to our election in Christ to be God's covenantal people. We are not elected because we are male and female, but it is as male and female that we are elected. God is a being-in-relation, and so are we. We are male and female. There are many types of human relationships, many types of encounters between different human subjectivities, but there is always this one. Sexual difference is the most primordial of the distinctions between different modes of being human, and it is the only distinction that implicates everyone. Humans can resent this distinction, and our life in this sphere can be marred by sin and imperfection, but, in the end, our own humanity depends upon finding ways of life that are premised on gratitude for it. To be what we are, we must find ways of life that thank God for having made us male and female. To be fully human and follow Christ faithfully, there are many things we must do, but among them must be some sort of embrace of sexual difference.

The Christian tradition has believed and argued, at least since Augustine, that it is only on the basis of being sexually differentiated, of being gladly male and female, that we can be ourselves and be obedient to God. The work of the church is to enable all humanity to render praise, thanks, and obedience to God in all aspects of life. To fulfill these tasks, to be glad of being male and female, to be gracious to one another as male and female, is the premise underlying Christian marriage and celibacy. In this tradition, part of the church's project will always and necessarily be to teach and testify that the work of man as man is to be in solidarity with woman, and the work of woman as woman is to be in solidarity with man. Marriage and celibacy are modes of life that God has given and the church has discerned because these practices enable the purpose of being male and female to be fulfilled. Marriage and celibacy are modes of solidarity between the sexes. Marriage and celibacy are gifts from God because they enable each sex to do its work and thus for the whole people of God to make an offering with respect to sexual difference. We are animals, and sexual difference is something we have in common with animals, but we are also humans, called to know ourselves in Christ, and, because God has elected to know us as male and female, for humans, sexual difference has this special significance. Marriage and celibacy are the two practices in which the church recognizes the humanized, theologized significance of sexual difference.

Of course, as I have said many times in this book, even among those who have believed and presupposed this argument, it has not always been made explicitly. Much of what this book has uncovered about sexual difference has been based on inference and close reading of other arguments about marriage and celibacy; sexual difference was not usually a central and sustained topic in its own right until the twentieth century. Certain ideas, although efficacious, were probably so latent that it was perhaps very difficult, prior to the twentieth century's controversies, to articulate them explicitly. That may be one good reason why the church in the late twentieth and early twenty-first century is less than unanimous about sexual difference: to the extent that earlier theologians shared these beliefs but left them implicit, one can fairly say that the attempt to be articulate and explicit about the theological significance of sexual difference is relatively new.

Furthermore, Augustine's influence on the Western tradition—to the effect that theological anthropology must offer some positive account of sexual difference, which is the trajectory that has been traced and emphasized in this book—should not be taken to imply that Christianity as a whole resolved itself along Augustinian lines concerning sexuality, or that the diversity of Augustine's patristic peers and predecessors simply vanished. The conceptual heterogeneity we encountered in the first chapter still stirs debate in contemporary Eastern Orthodoxy, where the patristic sources are not only authoritative but are also ambiguous with regard to the place of sexual difference in creation and anthropology.[1] Furthermore, minority and non-Augustinian beliefs persisted in the Catholic West even during the early Middle Ages, when Augustine's power as a theological authority had relatively fewer rivals and when we might have expected an Augustinian orthodoxy. For instance, John Scottus Eriugena argued that sexual difference would disappear in an eschatological union.[2] It is clear, then, that even where Augustine was and is authoritative, for undoubtedly a variety of reasons he was and is not necessarily read and received homogenously.

Interestingly, however, even the Eastern fathers, or the likes of Eriugena, who might be cited as a countertradition against the one surveyed in this book, are still discussing the subject of sexual difference with reference to creation, salvation history, and anthropology. Were a scholar to write something contrasting these different arguments with the Augustinian tradition, there would at least be these common terms of reference and orthodoxy.[3]

In any case, as theologians and historians today commonly agree,[4] and as this book has demonstrated by studying the most well-known and influential theologians of the West, the mainstream of moral theology about sexuality in Western Christianity proceeded along essentially Augustinian lines until at least, and arguably throughout, the twentieth century. That is why, in order to answer questions about sexual difference, it has been appropriate to prioritize this Augustinian tradition.

However, as we saw in chapter 8, several theologians have attempted to overturn this consensus at the end of the twentieth century and in the early twenty-first. Graham Ward, Eugene Rogers, and David Matzko McCarthy are all trying to minimize the significance of sexual difference. In effect, these theologians have argued that in cases of strong same-sex erotic desire, the hegemony of belief in significant sexual difference should be overthrown. In their perspective, to insist upon the significance of sexual difference for all human beings would be arbitrary.

The revisionist theologians seem willing to allow a modestly privileged place for sexual difference in a general way. For instance, Ward claims that sexual difference retains tropological usefulness. Rogers allows that sexually differentiated marriage might be "especially apt" for capturing the bride-bridegroom imagery of Scripture. McCarthy cannot find a reason, other than procreation, to privilege sexual difference, and so he believes that same-sex couples could fit into Christian social ecology without changing the meaning of marriage. His hypothetical lesbian couple could be assimilated into the wider community, which he seems to assume would be mostly heterosexual.

But for all these apparent concessions, the revisionists insist that sexual difference could not be so significant as to shape all sexual activity and marriages within the church. By their line of reasoning, an individual with strong same-sex proclivities should not live with faith in a created and revealed ontology of significance for corporeal sexual difference, confident that it had some meaning for his or her life in the heavenly city, confident that to be a male or female was a call to either celibacy or marriage to the opposite sex. According to the revisionists, such patience with practices that did not correspond spontaneously to their erotic desires would be a waste of time, and, for Rogers especially, it could be dangerous, for it would be depriving the homosexually inclined of the grace of erotic satisfaction or opportunity. All three revisionists accept in principle the notion of sexual ascesis. All of them insist upon monogamy, for instance, and all of them accept that ecclesial life should reorder social life to be "for others" in ways that could demand self-sacrifice and self-giving. But structuring ecclesial life in general, or marriage in particular, around sexual difference strikes all three revisionists as a spurious constraint. The revisionists profess that monogamy is a worthwhile struggle, ultimately necessary as an imitation of God's covenant and bringing blessing upon those who submit to it, even if one's immediate erotic desires and fantasies might seem to clash with it. But similar forbearance with requirements arising from the place of sexual difference in salvation history is not compelling to them. They cannot accept that limiting marriage to sexually differentiated couples is theologically necessary; they cannot see what blessing can accrue through struggling with this limit.

The revisionists seem able to hold their beliefs because while they are clearly interested in covenant and eros—that is, while they shape their arguments on the dual premises that couples should form covenants and that these covenants should engage the relevant two persons' erotic desires—they are apparently not similarly interested in questions about theological anthropology with respect to creation. This latter perspective on sexuality and salvation history, which has been presupposed since Augustine and brought to the fore in the twentieth century by Barth and John Paul II, remains unacknowledged by the revisionists. The revisionists simply have not engaged all of the arguments and presuppositions that make traditional marriage coherent. Hence their attempts at revising traditional practices of marriage are, at best, incomplete and preliminary.

Ward, for instance, perhaps unwittingly echoing the early Augustine, appears to approach quasi-Manichaeism by dismissing the significance of the actual somatic form of human bodily life. Rogers fails to reckon with any theological account of procreation, except the one indicated to him by a narrow reading of Aquinas, and this superficiality enables him to ignore how the initial teleology of creation might relate to subsequent human life. McCarthy asks no questions about ontology or anthropology, simply referring to some twentieth-century accounts of the companionate aspect to marriage and concluding that this specific type of functionalism does not require sexually differentiated characteristics. Thus, however successful the revisionist argument might appear on its own terms, in comparison with earlier theological tradition, it appears truncated. Too many important questions have not been asked, much less answered. If, hypothetically, one day catholic Christianity were to bless same-sex couples, it could not do so on the basis of the present arguments. It could not do so with integrity and coherence until it could simultaneously account for the theological significance of sexual difference. The revisionists have not yet attempted to probe these depths.

I am not suggesting that the traditional arguments deserve engagement simply because they are traditional. Instead, I am suggesting that the traditional arguments are good arguments, that they establish criteria for overall theological coherence, and that the revisionists have neglected these arguments. Thus the revisionist arguments have not yet been held to the highest possible standard. If revisionists want to create space in Christianity for gay and lesbian marriages, which seems to be one preoccupation of Ward, Rogers, and McCarthy, then more argumentation will be necessary.

Furthermore, accepting the revisionist proposal would mean revising the theology of marriage for heterosexual marriage as well. In the revisionist account, marriage is no longer a response to the ontology and teleology of the two sexes. It is no longer a command of God to respond to the creation of male and female as male and female. In the revisionist account, the opposite sex features in marriage only to the extent that an individual's felt or perceived desires propose to include it. The fact that the human race exists in a sexually dimorphic way is not necessarily personally significant. For the revisionists, the significance of sexual difference becomes aesthetic and private, an incidental feature of human creaturehood, to be valued or not according to an individual's taste. Perhaps sexual difference would still matter with regard to procreation and the perpetuity of the species, but in order to make procreation optional, the revisionists have minimized the theological significance of this task.

If sexual difference were relegated to private taste, if it were not necessary to take it seriously as a theological concept, if it had no mandated significance in Christian social life, then what would that mean? In other words, putting aside the great weight of the theological arguments the revisionists have not yet addressed, what else would follow if the revisionists' implied view of sexual difference were accepted? What would change in Christianity's witness to the world?

We might consider how, after Darwin, it is impossible to write a biology textbook, discuss evolution, or account for the diversity and complexity of plants and animals without some reference to sexual difference. An evolutionary biologist writes:

> The need to find and seduce a mate is among the most powerful forces in evolution. Perhaps nothing in life generates a more ecstatic diversity of tactics and stratagems, a more surprising array of forms and behaviours. In comparison, tricks to avoid predators seem predictable and limited.[5]

Biologists enumerate an array of advantages afforded by sexual difference, including cross-generational adaptations to environmental change, increased capacity to develop a niche, and greater defense capacity against parasites.[6] Biologists have described how significant sexual differences are in shaping a human organism's various characteristics: voice, pelvic shape, hormones, brain organization, height, and strength are just some of the many differences between humans that are, in part or in whole, attributable to sex.[7] Biologists propose that of all the differences among humans, sexual differences are the most significant:

> Sex is easily the biggest physical difference within a species. Men and women, unlike blacks and whites, have different organs and body designs. The inferable difference in genomes between two

people of visibly different races is one-hundredth of 1 percent. The gap between the sexes vastly exceeds that.[8]

Likewise, from the biologist's point of view, sex is at the root of much of what makes human society complex: "There is little question that most primates live in complex social systems and that the dynamics of social relationships within these communities are strongly influenced by the different ways in which males and females pursue their reproductive interests."[9] The biologists propose that sex is at the root of much of what makes life in general interesting and diverse: "If not for sex, much of what is flamboyant and beautiful in nature would not exits. Plants would not bloom. Birds would not sing. Deer would not spout antlers."[10]

In other words, the biologists seem to be saying that if one considers the immanent and material ordering of life from an immanent and material perspective, that is, on the basis of a natural and nontheological epistemology, sexual difference has a way of asserting its significance. Sexual difference is a powerful and basic feature of our identity, shaping psychological and physiological factors not only at the species level but in individuals as well.

Since Augustine, the theological tradition surveyed in this book has been clear, for theological reasons, that the immanent and material world is given by God for good and significant purposes. The created order therefore has an integrity and an identity that is distinct from God and is therefore susceptible to immanent and material study. If, for their own reasons, Darwinian biologists also reach the conclusion that sexual difference is significant, that should not be shocking. Reality is reality, and certain aspects of creation are there to be discovered, even if the theological teleology of that reality cannot be evident in Darwinian terms.

But the biological significance of sexual difference, as deduced and explained by biologists, puts the revisionist theologians of today in a curious situation. They are, of course, free to offer theological reasons for minimizing the theological significance of sexual difference. Such arguments should be interrogated on theological grounds, as they have been in this book. Their success or failure depends upon their theological coherence and not their correlation with evolutionary biology.

Nevertheless, if the revisionist case as it currently stands is to succeed, and if Christianity is to withdraw its claim that an apparently basic feature of human biology is also spiritually significant and necessary for the work of all persons in the church, then does it not seem that we will have taken an implicit step toward disassociating our redemption from the tangible and material world in which we live? Scientists will tell us that strong and compelling forces, arising from the fact of sexual difference, tend to shape human behavior and culture. Meanwhile, theologians will be in the position of saying that these same sexual differences are only personally significant on an idiosyncratic and ad hoc basis. It is perhaps conceivable that such a diastasis between scientific and theological accounts of reality could exist, but to concede that point would require the kind of careful arguing that has not yet been attempted, and it would fly in the face of what the traditional theological argument has led us to expect.

It seems odd that theologians would want to withdraw claims for the universal theological significance of sexual difference, particularly when one considers that the world the biologists present is so often bleak and uninviting. For instance, scientists report that many primates tend to live in violent societies of intense competition between males for mates. The males form coalitions to dominate and co-opt weaker males to serve the possessiveness and territoriality of stronger males, and the females, if they have any influence at all, can only respond with strategies to adapt to this hierarchy.[11] From a purely evolutionary and genetic perspective such societies seem to be successful, and from a Darwinian point of view, one has no grounds for complaint. Here we have a situation in which sexual difference is significant but in which there seems to be little gospel. If one wants to object to such an order for life and declare the gospel with regard to biology, then surely it is helpful to have an account of how real flesh and blood sexual difference somehow features and has a purchase in the Christian account of reality. The Christian tradition has had such an account, which the revisionists appear to want to dismantle.

The Christian tradition, as explained in this book, includes a redemptive vision for sexual difference. It acknowledges the power and force of sexual difference to organize a society and a person. It accounts for that power on its own theological terms, explaining a creation, a fall, and a route toward redemption. But to offer this vision, it does not point to the world of idiosyncratic desire and sexual pleasure. Neither does it point to the world of biological research, selfish genes, and competitive mating strategies. The Christian tradition can account for desire, pleasure, biology, selfishness, competition, and mating, but without relying on any of those things for its premise. Instead, Christianity traditionally proclaims that God offers us a promise about sexual difference, an alternative history in which sexual difference was made for christological purposes. It is this alternative vision—this prophetic announcement that sexual difference can, should, and will mean something other than its fallen versions—that is obscured in the revisionist proposals and that would be lost if they prevail in their current guise.

This potential loss is even more tragic when one considers how deeply ambivalent contemporary Western culture is about sexual difference. On the one hand, books such as John Gray's *Men Are from Mars, Women Are from Venus* reify sexual difference and win millions of eager readers. Dramatizations of Jane Austen's novels are popular in television and film, and offer wry characterizations—"One half of the world cannot understand the pleasures of the other"[12]—that are widely regarded as apt commentary on sexual difference. Pop music and Hollywood show no signs of wearying of basic "boy meets girl" or "war of the sexes" themes; apparently the frisson between the sexes still generates interest and revenue. It would seem that the culture at large has an appetite for comment on the significance of sexual difference, that it perceives the fallen nature of sexual difference and is eager for comment and news that might put the fall in some perspective.

Yet sexual difference appears to be just as often denied any significance in public conversation. Public personalities seem eager to assert that sexual difference is ephemeral and inconsequential. An actress who plays a lesbian on television can explain her enthusiasm for her role by saying, "Gender is of no consequence to me. It's a person's brain that counts."[13] A recent television documentary on reproductive technology speculates that in twenty years "we could face a scenario where the old divisions between masculinity and femininity . . . cease to have any use or need."[14] This novelty is presented as being a problem for men, who would be rendered superfluous, as if, in theory, women could exist satisfactorily as the single sex in some future monosexual world. Academia abounds with theorists eager to reveal the materiality of men and women as indifferent raw material, to see that our sexed bodies are actually available for reinterpretation "as free as mind's play."[15] The theory here is by now familiar: we should hope for a society in which each person is free to accord significance to sexual difference—or not—according to each person's liberated erotic appetite and political agenda.

In sum, in contemporary culture today, we seem to be faced with an ambivalence. Some portraits of sexual difference as fixed and stereotypical—John Gray, Jane Austen, popular music and film—seem to resonate with wide audiences. But various scenarios and theories that invite us to conceive sexual difference voluntaristically—as significant only to the extent that the human will would like it to be—also seem to appeal widely. The time would seem ripe for Christianity to announce that it has good news and alternatives with regard to sexual difference.

However, until the debates created by the revisionist theologies are resolved, it seems unlikely that Christianity will speak with a clear, articulate, and persuasive voice about sexual difference. The churches today seem to share much of the wider culture's ambivalence. Luther claimed in 1522 that God created two sexes, that this fact was not contingent on human will, that God "wills to have his excellent handiwork honoured," and that "whatever is a man must have a woman and whatever is a woman must have a man."[16] But, as the existence of the revisionists suggests, many Christians today are not so sure.

Another obstacle that makes a clear witness difficult for churches today is the pastoral dimension of sexuality. Acceptance of traditional teaching with regard to sexual difference entails a certain asceticism. If sexual difference is so significant that it should be an organizing principle for married life, then, as the revisionists point out, many men and women who want to marry will probably not, for their erotic desires do not appear to respond to the opposite sex. But like the young Augustine, revealed in *Confessionum*, many of these gays and lesbians will equally be unable to imagine a continent life. These people would appear to be trapped. The prospect of life without the embraces of those for whom they long strikes them as miserable and impossible, but a life without marital embraces is what the tradition appears to suggest. Are the churches prepared to insist that such a life is nevertheless necessary and redemptive? Where is the good news here?

It would not be the first time that, for the sake of the gospel, the church has insisted on renunciations that strike the culture as absurd. The rich man in Mark 10 "was shocked and went away grieving" when Jesus told him to sell his many possessions. Are the contemporary romantics and revisionists, the gays and lesbians who want to marry, perhaps a new version of the rich man? The revisionists speak for men and women who, like the young Augustine, are shocked and grieved at the prospect of forgoing certain erotic embraces. Could it be that expectations of erotic fulfillment, an attitude of sexual entitlement, is a variation upon wealth, a new possession modern people grip so tightly that we cannot be wholehearted followers of Christ? If so, then insisting upon a nuptial significance for sexual difference, a significance that would order ecclesial life into the twofold ranks of the continent and the married, would be a difficult thing to do, but it would be prophetic. As with the church's teaching on voluntary poverty, or other types of suffering, a language will have to be recovered, to the effect that there is freedom and joy in a life without those things the world calls necessary.

If the church wants to commend such asceticism as regards sex, it will be credible if the church is a community wherein a life of celibacy and singleness is plausible and attractive. If sexual difference is to be an occasion of freedom, an arena in which men and women together seek a social ecology to mock and rival the ways of concupiscence, then very few aspects of contemporary church life will remain unscathed. The early patristic confidence that ecclesial social life should be visibly different from pagan life, in particular at the sexual level, would need to be reclaimed. How would the church want to respond to youth culture if it genuinely believed that the dynamic of the sexes is grounded in the *imago Dei* and not in romance? How might courtship habits and living arrangements need to be reconfigured if lay celibacy were a bona fide response to sexuality? What new tone of voice would need to be adopted if Christians realized that everyone who has ever lusted selfishly is judged by the tradition's teleology for sexual difference, and not just the homosexually inclined? Reclaiming the theological tradition about sexual difference would entail not only a chastening word to the revisionist theologians but also a thoroughgoing revolution for almost all Christians.

Today's culture is ambivalent about sexual difference, and relations between the sexes are often tense, exploitative, and commercialized. In principle, the Christian faith knows a new, happier way of belonging together as men and women, and both married couples and celibates give of themselves with respect to sex when they help to create and enable this redeemed social life.[17] But this way of life is extremely difficult in our culture, and requires revolutions in everyday expectations and habits for those who would seek to resist the culture. Surely such a venture should not be attempted without prayer, patience, a commitment to self-restraint, a sense of humor, and readiness to forgive and try again. These skills are not always in great evidence, even in the churches.

Just as crucially, reclaiming clarity about sexual difference will depend upon confidence in theological epistemology. From Augustine onward, the key claims of the tradition have relied on theological premises. Luther made it particularly clear that his claims for marriage and the teleology of creation are "extravagant fiction and the silliest kind of nonsense if you set aside the authority of Scripture and follow the judgment of reason."[18] Thus it is consistent with the tradition, as well as pastorally probable, that before one can hear any gospel in the tradition's claims for sexual difference, one has to be already immersed in Christian practice and theological thought.

It follows that if persuading people of the power of theological epistemology is to be a priority—and if one needs to learn the skills of prayer, patience, selflessness, humor, and forgiveness before embarking on asceticism—in pastoral practice there is no reason to assume that sexual issues are the place to begin teaching Christian discipleship. The rich man in Mark 10 was addressed on the point of his wealth only after much more basic issues of religious identity (i.e., his status as a law-abiding Jew) had already been addressed. The tradition's claims about sexual difference make sense only within a larger apparatus of revelation, worship, and a community life grounded in charity. As Augustine insisted, the teleology of sexual life is to include it in the wider social life of the heavenly city, and there are many building blocks to this city. If that is so, then before one can even begin to speak to sinners on the point of their treasures, before the tradition can be heard on the point of costly discipleship at the point of erotic appetite, then one must first establish the trust and expectation that the faith has something to teach. Then, and only then, can the conversation on sexual difference proceed.

Scripture is full of individuals and communities who do not know who they are until God reveals it to them. To insist on a theological premise for understanding sexual difference is to insist that we learn from this pattern and wait in trust that who we are in the sexual sphere is a datum that will come from God and no one else. Israel was once not a people, but now, called together by God, it is "a people" (1 Pet 2:10, alluding to Hos 1:9). Israel cannot know that it is a chosen people, beloved by a faithful God, until it is told and its election is announced to it. At the individual level, biblical patriarchs, prophets, and priests often resist their vocation until their true identity is forced upon them: Abraham, Jacob, Peter, and Paul do not know their true names until God renames them and reorients their lives.

For Christians, especially postmodern Christians bereft of any consensus, sexual difference is a similar category. We will not know what it means until we allow God to tell us what it means. The tradition has claimed that we do not know who we are and what it means to find ourselves differentiated as men and women until we allow the premises and practices of revelation to unfold. In the tradition, stretching from Augustine to John Paul II, sexual difference is not mute, inert, nonexistent, or indifferent. In this tradition, God brings man to woman and tells the two sexes something they would not otherwise know: that their creation is good, that their creation as two sexes is for the sake of enabling a church and a covenant, and that, despite their fallenness, their twoness can in itself become a witness to reconciliation and redemption through marriage. Marriage gives this aspect of our creation the power to testify, and the nonmarried offer supporting testimony through their chastity, which creates the social ecology supporting marriage.

All of this is the far from self-evident significance of sexual difference. But that argument cannot begin to be made without the even more fundamental premise that "your life is hidden with Christ" (Col 3:3).

# Notes

1. See p. 36n64.

2. Bernard McGinn, *The Presence of God: A History of Western Christian Mysticism* (vol. 2 of *The Growth of Mysticism*; London: SCM Press, 1994), 117. See also Allen, *Concept of Woman*, 240.

3. For an example of something like this type of comparison, see Balthasar, *Theo-Drama*, as noted on p. 5n11.

4. See, e.g., surveys such as Michael Banner, "Sexualität," in *Theologische Realenzyklopädie* (vol. 31 [1/2]; Berlin: Walter de Gruyter, 2000), 195–214; or Linda Woodhead, "Woman/Femininity," in *The Oxford Companion to Christian Thought* (ed. Adrian Hastings et al.; Oxford: Oxford University Press, 2000), 755–57.

5. Olivia Judson, *Dr. Tatiana's Sex Advice to All Creation* (London: Chatto & Windus, 2002), 4.

6. David C. Geary, *Male, Female: The Evolution of Human Sex Differences* (Washington, DC: American Psychological Association, 1998), 54.

7. Cf. ibid. and Glenn Wilson, *The Great Sex Divide: A Study of Male-Female Differences* (London: Peter Owen, 1989).

8. William Saletan, "Don't Worry Your Pretty Little Head," *Slate*, January 21, 2005, http://slate.msn.com/id/2112570/.

9. Geary, *Male, Female*, 94.

10. Judson, *Dr. Tatiana's Sex Advice*, 1.

11. Geary, *Male, Female*, 84–95.

12. Jane Austen, *Emma* (London: Adelphi, 1939), 89.

13. Luisita Lopez Torregrosa, "'L Word' Star Basks in an Erotic Mystery," *New York Times*, April 5, 2004, E1.

14. Susan Greenfield, "The Future's Bright, If You're Female . . ." (BBC News Web site, 2004), referring to a program broadcast by BBC2 on March 31, 2004, "If . . . Women Ruled the World."

15. Thomas Walter Laqueur, *Making Sex: Body and Gender from the Greeks to Freud* (Cambridge, MA: Harvard University Press, 1990), 243.

16. See p. 135n22.

17. This sentence and the next two are adapted from Chris Roberts, "The Vatican Combats Today's Manichaeans: A Fourth-Century Heresy Tells Us a Lot about Our Embodied Selves," *National Catholic Reporter*, December 10, 2004, 16–17.

18. See p. 136n58.

# BIBLIOGRAPHY

Aelred of Rievaulx. *Spiritual Friendship*. Translated by Mary Eugenia Laker. Kalamazoo, MI: Cistercian Publications, 1977.

Allchin, A. M., Sandra Figgess, Kallistos Ware, Wendy Robinson, Geoffrey Rowell, Stephen Verney, Rosemary Wickremasinghe, Linda Woodhead, and Graham Woolfenden. *A Fearful Symmetry? The Complementarity of Men and Women in Ministry*. London: SPCK, 1992.

Allen, Prudence. *The Concept of Woman: The Aristotelian Revolution, 750 B.C.–A.D. 1250*. 2nd ed. Grand Rapids: Eerdmans, 1997.

———. *The Concept of Woman*. Vol. 2, *The Early Humanist Reformation, 1250–1500*. Grand Rapids: Eerdmans, 2002.

Aquinas, Thomas. *On the Power of God (Quaestiones Disputatae De Potentia Dei)*. Translated by Fathers of the English Dominican Province. Vol. 3. London: Burns, Oates & Washbourne, 1934.

———. *Summa contra Gentiles: Book III: Providence, Part II*. Translated by Vernon J. Bourke. Notre Dame, IN: University of Notre Dame Press, 1975.

———. *Summa contra Gentiles: Book IV: Salvation*. Translated by Charles J. O'Neil. Notre Dame, IN: University of Notre Dame Press, 1975.

———. *The Summa contra Gentiles: The Fourth Book*. Translated by English Dominican Fathers. Vol. 5. London: Burns, Oates & Washbourne, 1929.

———. *Summa Theologiae: Angels (1a. 50–64)*. Translated by Kenhelm Foster. Vol. 9. London: Blackfriars, 1968.

———. *Summa Theologiae: Man (1a. 75–83)*. Translated by Timothy Suttor. Vol. 11. London: Blackfriars, 1970.

———. *Summa Theologiae: Man Made to God's Image (1a. 90–102)*. Translated by Edmund Hill. Vol. 13. London: Blackfriars, 1964.

———. *Summa Theologiae: Temperance (2a2ae. 141–154)*. Translated by Thomas Gilby. Vol. 43. London: Blackfriars, 1968.

———. *Summa Theologica: Third Part (Supplement): Treatise on the Sacraments (Qq. XXXIV–LXVIII)*. Translated by Fathers of the English Dominican Province. Vol. 19. London: Burns, Oates & Washbourne, 1922.

———. *Summa Theologica: Third Part (Supplement): Treatise of the Resurrection (Qq. LXIX–LXXXVI)*. Translated by Fathers of the English Dominican Province. Vol. 20. London: Burns, Oates & Washbourne, 1922.

Augustine. *Against Julian*. Translated by Matthew A. Schumacher. Vol. 35 of *The Fathers of the Church: A New Translation*. Washington, DC: Catholic University of America Press, 1977.

———. *Answer to the Pelagians, II: Marriage and Desire, Answer to the Two Letters of the Pelagians, Answer to Julian*. Translated by Roland J. Teske. Vol. 1/24 of *The Works of Saint Augustine: A Translation for the 21st Century*. Hyde Park, NY: New City, 1998.

———. *Augustine's Commentary on the Galatians: Introduction, Text, Translation, and Notes*. Translated by Eric Plumer. Oxford: Oxford University Press, 2003.

———. *The City of God against the Pagans*. Translated by R. W. Dyson. Cambridge: Cambridge University Press, 1998.

———. *Confessions*. Translated by Henry Chadwick. Oxford: Oxford University Press, 1998.

———. *De Bono Conjugali and De Sancta Virginitate*. Translated by P. G. Walsh. Oxford: Clarendon, 2001.

———. *Marriage and Virginity: The Excellence of Marriage, Holy Virginity, the Excellence of Widowhood, Adulterous Marriages, Continence*. Translated by Ray Kearney and David G. Hunter. Vol. 1/9 of *The Works of Saint Augustine: A Translation for the 21st Century*. Hyde Park, NY: New City, 1999.

———. *On Genesis: A Refutation of the Manichees; Unfinished Literal Commentary on Genesis; The Literal Meaning of Genesis*. Translated by Edmund Hill. Vol. 1/13 of *The Works of Saint Augustine: A Translation for the 21st Century*. Hyde Park, NY: New City, 2002.

———. *On Genesis: "Two Books on Genesis against the Manichees" and "On the Literal Interpretation of Genesis: An Unfinished Book."* Translated by Roland J. Teske. Vol. 84 of *The Fathers of the Church: A New Translation*. Washington, DC: Catholic University of American Press, 1991.

———. *On the Trinity: Books 8–15*. Translated by Stephen McKenna and Gareth B. Matthews. Cambridge: Cambridge University Press, 2002.

Austen, Jane. *Emma*. London: Adelphi, 1939.

Balthasar, Hans Urs von. *The Dramatis Personae: Man in God*. Vol. 2 of *Theo-Drama: Theological Dramatic Theory*. Translated by Graham Harrison. San Francisco: Ignatius, 1990.

———. *Love Alone Is Credible*. San Francisco: Ignatius, 1963.

———. "Women Priests?" Pages 187–98 in *New Elucidations*. Translated by Mary Theresilde Skerry. San Francisco: Ignatius, 1986.

Banner, Michael. *Christian Ethics and Contemporary Moral Problems*. Cambridge: Cambridge University Press, 1999.

———. "Sexualität." Pages 195–214 in *Theologische Realenzyklopädie*. Vol. 31 (1/2). Berlin: Walter de Gruyter, 2000.

Banner, Michael, Markus Bockmuehl, Timothy Bradshaw, Oliver O'Donovan, Ann Holt, William Persson, and David Wright. "St. Andrew's Day Statement: An Examination of the Theological Principles Affecting the Homosexuality Debate." Pages 5–11 in *The Way Forward? Christian Voices on Homosexuality and the Church*. Edited by Timothy Bradshaw. London: Hodder & Stoughton, 1997.

Barth, Karl. *The Christian Life*. Translated by Geoffrey W. Bromiley. Edinburgh: T&T Clark, 1981.

———. *Church Dogmatics*. II/2, *The Doctrine of God*. Translated by G. W. Bromiley, J. C. Campbell, Iain Wilson, J. Strathearn McNab, Harold Knight, R. A. Stewart. Edited by G. W. Bromiley and T. F. Torrance. Edinburgh: T&T Clark, 1957.

———. *Church Dogmatics*. III/1, *The Doctrine of Creation*. Translated by J. W. Edwards, O. Bussey, H. Knight. Edited by G. W. Bromiley and T. F. Torrance. Edinburgh: T&T Clark, 1958.

———. *Church Dogmatics*. III/2, *The Doctrine of Creation*. Translated by H. Knight, G. W. Bromiley, J. K. S. Reid, and R. H. Fuller. Edited by G. W. Bromiley and T. F. Torrance. Edinburgh: T&T Clark, 1960.

———. *Church Dogmatics*. III/4, *The Doctrine of Creation*. Translated by A. T. Mackay, T. H. L. Parker, H. Knight, H. A. Kennedy, and J. Marks. Edited by G. W. Bromiley and T. F. Torrance. Edinburgh: T&T Clark, 1961.

Behr, John. *Asceticism and Anthropology in Irenaeus and Clement*. Oxford: Oxford University Press, 2000.

———. "A Note on the Ontology of Gender." *St. Vladimir's Theological Quarterly* 42, nos. 3–4 (1998): 363–72.

———. "The Rational Animal: A Re-Reading of Gregory of Nyssa's 'De Hominis Opificio.'" *Journal of Early Christian Studies* 7, no. 2 (1999): 219–47.

————. "Shifting Sands: Foucault, Brown, and the Framework of Christian Asceticism." *Heythrop Journal* 34, no. 1 (1993): 1–21.

Bernard of Clairvaux. *Bernard of Clairvaux: Selected Works.* Translated by Gillian R. Evans. New York: Paulist Press, 1987.

————. *The Letters of Saint Bernard of Clairvaux.* Translated by Bruno Scott James. Stroud, England: Sutton Publishing, 1998.

————. *On the Song of Songs I.* Translated by Kilian Walsh. Shannon, Ireland: Irish University Press, 1971.

————. *On the Song of Songs II.* Translated by Kilian Walsh. Kalamazoo, MI: Cistercian Publications, 1976.

————. *On the Song of Songs III.* Translated by Kilian Walsh and Irene M. Edmonds. Kalamazoo, MI: Cistercian Publications, 1979.

————. *On the Song of Songs IV.* Translated by Irene Edmonds. Kalamazoo, MI: Cistercian Publications, 1980.

Boerresen, Kari Elisabeth. *Subordination and Equivalence: The Nature and Role of Women in Augustine and Thomas Aquinas.* Translated by Charles H. Talbot. Washington, DC: University Press of America, 1981.

Bonner, Gerald. "Augustine's Attitude on Women and *Amicitia*." Pages 259–75 in *Festgabe für Luc Verheijen, Osa zu Seinem 70. Geburtstag.* Edited by Cornelius Mayer and Karl Heinz Chelius. Würzberg: Augustinus-Verlag, 1987.

Brown, Peter. *The Body and Society: Men, Women, and Sexual Renunciation in Early Christianity.* New York: Columbia University Press, 1988.

Calvin, John . *A Commentary on Jeremiah.* Edinburgh: Banner of Truth Trust, 1989.

————. *The Epistles of Paul the Apostle to the Galatians, Ephesians, Philippians, and Colossians.* Translated by John W. Fraser. *Calvin's Commentaries.* Edited David W. Torrance and Thomas F. Torrance. Grand Rapids: Eerdmans, 1996.

————. *The First Epistle of Paul the Apostle to the Corinthians.* Translated by John W. Fraser. *Calvin's Commentaries.* Edited by David W. Torrance and Thomas F. Torrance. Grand Rapids: Eerdmans, 1996.

————. *Genesis.* Crossway Classic Commentaries. Edited by Alister McGrath and J. I. Packer. Nottingham: Crossway Books, 2001.

————. *A Harmony of the Gospels: Mathew, Mark, and Luke.* Vol. 2. Translated by T. H. L. Parker. *Calvin's Commentaries.* Edited by David W. Torrance and Thomas F. Torrance. Grand Rapids: Eerdmans, 1995.

————. *Institutes of the Christian Religion.* 2 vols. Translated by Ford Lewis Battles. Philadelphia: Westminster Press, 1960.

————. *The Second Epistle of Paul the Apostle to the Corinthians and the Epistles to Timothy, Titus and Philemon.* Translated by T. A. Smail.

*Calvin's Commentaries*. Edited by David W. Torrance and Thomas F. Torrance. Grand Rapids, Michigan: Eerdmans, 1996.

———. *Sermons on the Epistles to Timothy and Titus*. Edinburgh: Banner of Truth Trust, 1983.

Cameron, Averil. "Redrawing the Map: Early Christian Territory after Foucault." *Journal of Roman Studies* 76 (1986): 266–71.

———. "Virginity as Metaphor: Women and the Rhetoric of Early Christianity." Pages 181–205 in *History as Text: The Writing of Ancient History*. Edited by Averil Cameron. London: Duckworth, 1989.

Campbell, Douglas A., ed. *Gospel and Gender: A Trinitarian Engagement with Being Male and Female in Christ*. Edinburgh: T&T Clark, 2003.

Chadwick, Henry, and J. E. L. Oulton. "General Introduction." Pages 15–39 in *Alexandrian Christianity*. London: SCM Press, 1954.

Church, F. Forester. "Sex and Salvation in Tertullian." *Harvard Theological Review* 68 (1976): 83–101.

Clement of Alexandria. "The Instructor (Paedagogus)." Pages 209–96 in *Ante-Nicene Fathers*. Vol. 2. Edited by A. Roberts and J. Donaldson. Peabody, MA: Hendrickson, 1995.

———. "The Stromata, or Miscellanies, Book IV." Pages 409–41 in *Ante-Nicene Fathers*. Vol. 2. Edited by A. Roberts and J. Donaldson. Peabody, MA: Hendrickson, 1995.

———. "The Stromata, or Miscellanies, Book VI." Pages 480–520 in *Ante-Nicene Fathers*. Vol. 2. Edited by A. Roberts and J. Donaldson. Peabody, MA: Hendrickson, 1995.

———. "Stromateis III, on Marriage." In *Alexandrian Christianity: Selected Translations of Clement and Origen with Introductions and Notes*. Edited by Henry Chadwick and J. E. L. Oulton. London: SCM Press, 1954.

———. "Stromateis VII, on Spiritual Perfection." In *Alexandrian Christianity: Selected Translations of Clement and Origen with Introductions and Notes*. Edited by Henry Chadwick and J. E. L. Oulton. London: SCM Press, 1954.

———. "Stromateis, Book Two." Translated by John Ferguson. In *Stromateis: Books One to Three*. Vol. 85 of *The Fathers of the Church: A New Translation*. Washington, DC: Catholic University Press of America, 1991.

———. "Stromateis, Book Three." Translated by John Ferguson. In *Stromateis: Books One to Three*. Vol. 85 of *The Fathers of the Church: A New Translation*. Washington, DC: Catholic University Press of America, 1991.

Coakley, Sarah. *Power and Submissions: Spirituality, Philosophy, and Gender*. Oxford: Blackwell, 2002.

Congregation for the Doctrine of the Faith. *Letter to the Bishops of the Catholic Church on the Collaboration of Men and Women in the Church and in the World.* http://www.vatican.va/roman_curia/congregations/cfaith/documents/rc_con_cfaith_doc_20040731_collaboration_en.html.

D'Costa, Gavin. *Sexing the Trinity: Gender, Culture, and the Divine.* London: SCM Press, 2000.

Farrow, Douglas. *Ascension and Ecclesia: On the Significance of the Doctrine of Ascension for Ecclesiology and Christian Cosmology.* Edinburgh: T&T Clark, 1999.

Gaca, Kathy L. "Driving Aphrodite from the World: Tatian's Encratite Principles of Sexual Renunciation." *Journal of Theological Studies* 53, no. 1 (2002): 28–52.

Geary, David C. *Male, Female: The Evolution of Human Sex Differences.* Washington, DC: American Psychological Association, 1998.

Grant, R. "Tatian and the Bible." *Studia Patristica* 1 (1957): 297–306.

Greenfield, Susan. *The Future's Bright, If You're Female . . .* BBC News, 2004, http://news.bbc.co.uk/1/hi/programmes/if/3524338.stm.

Gregory of Nyssa. "On the Making of Man [*De Hominis Opificio*]." In *A Select Library of the Christian Church: Nicene and Post-Nicene Fathers.* 2nd series. Edited by P. Schaff and H. Wace. Vol. 5. Peabody, MA: Hendrickson, 1995.

———. "On Virginity." In *A Select Library of the Christian Church: Nicene and Post-Nicene Fathers.* 2nd series. Edited by P. Schaff and H. Wace. Vol. 5. Peabody, MA: Hendrickson, 1995.

Harrison, V. E. F . "Gender, Generation, and Virginity in Cappadocian Theology." *Journal of Theological Studies* 47 (1996): 38–68.

———. "Male and Female in Cappadocian Theology." *Journal of Theological Studies* 41 (1990): 441–71.

Hunt, Emily J. *Christianity in the Second Century: The Case of Tatian.* London: Routledge, 2003.

Irigaray, Luce. *An Ethics of Sexual Difference.* Translated by Carolyn Burke and Gillian C. Gill. London: Athlone, 1993.

———. *Marine Lover of Friedrich Nietzsche.* Translated by Gillian C. Gill. New York: Columbia University Press, 1991.

Jerome. "Against Helvidius." In *A Select Library of the Christian Church: Nicene and Post-Nicene Fathers.* 2nd series. Edited by P. Schaff and H. Wace, Vol. 6. Peabody, MA: Hendrickson, 1995.

———. "Against Jovinianus." In *A Select Library of the Christian Church: Nicene and Post-Nicene Fathers.* 2nd series. Edited by P. Schaff and H. Wace. Vol. 6. Peabody, MA: Hendrickson, 1995.

———. "Letters." In *A Select Library of the Christian Church: Nicene and Post-Nicene Fathers.* 2nd series. Edited by P. Schaff and H. Wace. Vol. 6. Peabody, MA: Hendrickson, 1995.

――――. "On the Perpetual Virginity of the Blessed Virgin Mary against Helvidius." Translated by John N. Hritzu. In *Jerome: Dogmatic and Polemical Works*. Vol. 53 of *The Fathers of the Church: A New Translation*. Washington, DC: Catholic University Press, 1965.

Jewett, Paul K. *Man as Male and Female: A Study in Sexual Relationships from a Theological Point of View*. Grand Rapids: Eerdmans, 1975.

John Paul II. *The Theology of the Body: Human Love in the Divine Plan*. Boston: Pauline Books & Media, 1997.

Judson, Olivia. *Dr. Tatiana's Sex Advice to All Creation*. London: Chatto & Windus, 2002.

Krötke, Wolf. "The Humanity of the Person in Karl Barth's Anthropology." Pages 159–76 in *The Cambridge Companion to Karl Barth*. Edited by John Webster. Cambridge: Cambridge University Press, 2000.

Lancel, Serge. *Saint Augustine*. Translated by Antonia Nevill. London: SCM Press, 2002.

Laqueur, Thomas Walter. *Making Sex: Body and Gender from the Greeks to Freud*. Cambridge, MA: Harvard University Press, 1990.

Leclercq, Jean. *Monks and Love in Twelfth-Century France: Psycho-Historical Essays*. Oxford: Oxford University Press, 1979.

Luther, Martin. "Commentary on 1 Corinthians 7 (1523)." Translated by Edward Sittler. Pages 3–56 in *Commentaries on 1 Corinthians 7, 1 Corinthians 15, Lectures on 1 Timothy*. Vol. 28 of *Luther's Works*. St. Louis: Concordia Publishing House, 1973.

――――. "The Estate of Marriage (1522)." Translated by Walther I. Brandt. Pages 17–49 in *The Christian in Society II*. Vol. 45 of *Luther's Works*. Philadelphia: Muhlenberg, 1962.

――――. "Judgement of Martin Luther on Monastic Vows (1521/22)." Translated by James Atkinson. Pages 251–400 in *The Christian in Society I*. Vol. 44 of *Luther's Works*. Philadelphia: Fortress, 1966.

――――. *Lectures on Galatians (1535) Chapters 1–4*. Translated by Jaroslav Pelikan. Vol. 26 of *Luther's Works*. St. Louis: Concordia Publishing House, 1963.

――――. *Lectures on Genesis, Chapters 1–5*. Translated by George V. Schick. Vol. 1 of *Luther's Works*. St. Louis: Concordia Publishing House, 1958.

――――. *Lectures on Genesis, Chapters 6–14*. Translated by George V. Schick. Vol. 2 of *Luther's Works*. St. Louis: Concordia Publishing House, 1958.

――――. "A Sermon on the Estate of Marriage (1519)." Translated by James Atkinson. Pages 7–14 in *The Christian in Society I*. Vol. 44 of *Luther's Works*. Philadelphia: Fortress, 1966.

Matter, E. Ann. *The Voice of My Beloved: The Song of Songs in Western Medieval Christianity*. Philadelphia: University of Pennsylvania Press, 1990.

McCarthy, David Matzko. "Homosexuality and the Practices of Marriage." *Modern Theology* 13, no. 3 (1997): 371–97.

———. "The Relationship of Bodies: A Nuptial Hermeneutics of Same-Sex Unions." Pages 200–216 in *Theology and Sexuality: Classic and Contemporary Readings* Edited by Eugene F. Rogers. Oxford: Blackwell, 2002.

———. *Sex and Love in the Home: A Theology of the Household*. London: SCM Press, 2001.

McGinn, Bernard. *The Growth of Mysticism*. London: SCM Press, 1994.

Meilaender, Gilbert. "Sweet Necessities: Food, Sex, and Saint Augustine." *Journal of Religious Ethics* 29, no. 1 (2001): 3–18.

Nellas, Panayiotis. *Deification in Christ: Orthodox Perspectives on the Nature of the Human Person*. Translated by Norman Russell. Crestwood, NY: St. Vladimir's Seminary Press, 1987.

Nolan, Michael. "What Aquinas Never Said about Women." *First Things*, no. 87 (1998): 11–12.

O'Donovan, Oliver. "Homosexuality in the Church: Can There Be a Fruitful Theological Debate?" Pages 20–36 in *The Way Forward? Christian Voices on Homosexuality and the Church*. Edited by Timothy Bradshaw. London: Hodder & Stoughton, 1997.

———. *Resurrection and Moral Order: An Outline for Evangelical Ethics*. 2nd ed. Leicester, England: Apollos, 1994.

———. *Transsexualism and Christian Marriage*. Vol. 48 of *Grove Booklets on Ethics*. Bramcote, England: Grove Books, 1982.

Pelikan, Jaroslav. *Christian Doctrine and Modern Culture (since 1700)*. Chicago: University of Chicago Press, 1989.

Ramsey, Paul. "Human Sexuality in the History of Redemption." *Journal of Religious Ethics* 16 (1988): 56–88.

Reynolds, Lyndon. "Bonaventure on Gender and Godlikeness: Compared to Augustine, Albertus Magnus, and Aquinas." *Downside Review* 106 (1988): 171–94.

Rist, John. *Augustine: Ancient Thought Baptized*. Cambridge: Cambridge University Press, 1994.

Roberts, Christopher C. "Sex and Love in the Home (Book Review)." *Studies in Christian Ethics* 15, no. 2 (2002): 102–7.

———. "The Vatican Combats Today's Manichaeans: A Fourth-Century Heresy Tells Us a Lot about Our Embodied Selves." *National Catholic Reporter*, December 10, 2004, 16–17.

Rogers, Eugene. "Editorial Introduction to 'The Body's Grace' by Rowan Williams." Pages 309–10 in *Theology and Sexuality: Classic and Contemporary Readings*. Edited by Eugene F. Rogers. Oxford: Blackwell, 2002.

————. "The Liturgical Body." *Modern Theology* 16, no. 3 (2000): 365–76.

————. "Sanctified Unions: An Argument for Gay Marriage." *Christian Century* 121, no. 12 (2004): 26–29.

————. *Sexuality and the Christian Body: Their Way into the Triune God.* Oxford: Blackwell, 1999.

Sachs, William. "Anglican Disunion: The Global Response to a Gay Bishop." *Christian Century*, November 16, 2004, 8–9.

Saletan, William. "Don't Worry Your Pretty Little Head." *Slate.* January 21, 2005. http://slate.msn.com/id/2112570/.

Schindler, David L. *Heart of the World, Center of the Church: Communio Ecclesiology, Liberalism, and Liberation.* Grand Rapids: Eerdmans, 1996.

Schlabach, Gerald. *For the Joy Set before Us: Augustine and Self-Denying Love.* Notre Dame, IN: University of Notre Dame Press, 2001.

Stiegman, Emero S. *The Language of Asceticism in St. Bernard of Clairvaux's "Sermones Super Cantica Canticorum."* Ann Arbor, MI: University Microfilms, 1973.

Sutton, Agneta. "The Complementarity of the Two Sexes: Karl Barth, Hans Urs von Balthasar, and John Paul II." *New Blackfriars* 87, no. 1010 (2006): 418–33.

Tatian. "Address to the Greeks." In *Ante-Nicene Fathers.* Edited by A. Roberts and J. Donaldson. Vol. 2. Peabody, MA: Hendrickson, 1995.

Tertullian. "Against the Valentinians." In *Ante-Nicene Fathers*, Edited by A. Roberts and J. Donaldson. Vol. 3. Peabody, MA: Hendrickson, 1995.

————. *Disciplinary, Moral, and Ascetical Works.* Translated by Rudolph Arbesmann, Emily Joseph Daly, and Edwin A. Quain. Vol. 40 of *The Fathers of the Church: A New Translation.* Washington, DC: Catholic University of America Press, 1959.

————. "An Exhortation to Chastity." In *Ante-Nicene Fathers.* Edited by A. Roberts and J. Donaldson. Vol. 4. Peabody, MA: Hendrickson, 1995.

————. "On Monogamy." In *Ante-Nicene Fathers.* Edited by A. Roberts and J. Donaldson. Vol. 4. Peabody, MA: Hendrickson, 1995.

————. "On the Veiling of Virgins." In *Ante-Nicene Fathers*, Edited by A. Roberts and J. Donaldson. Vol. 4. Peabody, MA: Hendrickson, 1995.

————. "To His Wife." In *Ante-Nicene Fathers.* Edited by A. Roberts and J. Donaldson. Vol. 4. Peabody, MA: Hendrickson, 1995.

Thielicke, Helmut. *The Ethics of Sex.* Translated by John W. Doberstein. Cambridge: John Clarke & Co., 1978.

Torrance, Alan. "'Call No Man Father!' The Trinity, Patriarchy, and God-Talk." Pages 179–97 in *Gospel and Gender: A Trinitarian Engagement with Being Male and Female in Christ.* Edited by Douglas A. Campbell. Edinburgh: T&T Clark, 2003.

Torregrosa, Luisita Lopez. "'L Word' Star Basks in an Erotic Mystery." *New York Times*, April 5, 2004.

Volf, Miroslav. *After Our Likeness: The Church as the Image of the Trinity.* Grand Rapids: Eerdmans, 1998.

Vööbus, Arthur. *Celibacy: A Requirement for Admission to Baptism in the Early Syrian Church.* Stockholm: Papers of the Estonian Theological Society in Exile, 1951.

Ward, Graham. "The Erotics of Redemption—after Karl Barth." *Theology and Sexuality* 8 (1998): 52–72.

Watson, Francis. *Agape, Eros, Gender: Towards a Pauline Sexual Ethic.* Cambridge: Cambridge University Press, 2000.

Whittaker, Molly, ed. *Tatian: Oratio Ad Graecos and Fragments.* Oxford: Clarendon, 1982.

Williams, Rowan. "The Body's Grace." Pages 309–21 in *Theology and Sexuality: Classic and Contemporary Readings.* Edited by Eugene F. Rogers. Oxford: Blackwell, 2002.

———. "Macrina's Deathbed Revisited: Gregory of Nyssa on Mind and Passion." Pages 227–46 in *Christian Faith and Greek Philosophy in Late Antiquity.* Edited by Lionel R. Wickham and Caroline P. Bammel. Leiden: E. J. Brill, 1993.

Wilson, Glenn. *The Great Sex Divide: A Study of Male-Female Differences.* London: Peter Owen, 1989.

Woodhead, Linda. "Woman/Femininity." Pages 755–57 in *The Oxford Companion to Christian Thought.* Edited by Adrian Hastings, Alistair Mason, and Hugh Pyper. Oxford: Oxford University Press, 2000.

Zizioulas, John. *Being as Communion: Studies in Personhood and the Church.* New York: St. Vladimir's Seminary Press, 1985.

# INDEX

Lightning Source UK Ltd.
Milton Keynes UK
UKOW06f2357280616

277275UK00002B/83/P